新版托福写作手册

姚钦 丁洁 [加]胡杨 罗健 吴国彬 编著

中国人民大学出版社

·北京·

写作教学一直是英语教育实践的难点，出国考试中写作单项难出高分也一直是写作老师的痛点。2023 年 8 月 25 日，ETS 官方公布了 2022 年全球考生平均分，其中中国内地托福考生平均分首次突破 90 分大关，值得注意的是，写作均分与 2021 年持平（均分 22 分）。整体来看，在听说读写四个单项中，中国内地考生的口语（均分 21）和写作部分仍有提升空间。

我们往往把写作教学难和难出高分归咎于学生的英语基本功不扎实，诸如词句运用能力和逻辑表达能力有待提升等。当然这些问题肯定是客观存在的，但作为写作老师我们也要反思教学方式的科学性和教学的有效性：科学性体现在写作教学的体系化上，即有完整且详实的写作教程；有效性体现在写作教学的结果呈现上，即有基于写作教程的出分率和高分率。在这些方面，广州姚钦老师做了很多有益的探索，也取得了很好的教学效果。姚钦老师专业从事出国考培写作教学十几年，批改过上千篇中国学生的作文，深谙中国学生写作提分的难点，也探索出了适合中国学生写作提分的科学有效的教学体系。

当姚钦老师让我给他新出版的托福写作书写推荐序，我毫不犹豫地答应了，因为我知道，与其说本书是针对 2023 年托福写作改革的教学新书，不如说是他多年写作教学的心得总结和升华，书里的每一个字都凝结着他的心血。我拿到书稿迫不及待地一口气读完，深深为姚钦老师的良苦用心所打动。

首先，我对作者提出的"写作的可迁移论"深有同感。写作教学涉及两个方向的迁移，一是中英语言的迁移，二是教和学的迁移。前者需要突破英汉思维的差异，汉语是我们的母语，是意合语言，而英语是形合语言，这就是学生阅读文本第一反应是读它的意思，而不是分析文本结构的根本原因。后者才是写作教学真正的难点，优秀的写作教师在教学中的角色应该是引领者和规范者，一方面让学生理解写作目标和充分认识写作学习路径，另一方面通过规范严格的训练，逐步让学生掌握写作技巧，从而阶梯性地提升学生的写作能力。

其次，在第一章里，姚钦老师创造性地提出了写作教学的"两个维度和两个层次"：两个维度本质上是"科学教"和"高效学"；两个层次本质上是"逻辑结构"和"语言能力"。这两个维度和两个层次是相互交叉和相互影响的，如何结合教学实践既考验写作教师的基本功，也是检验写作教师是否优秀的黄金标准。

再次，我特别赞赏本书第二章"落笔如有神"中的相关内容。如果说第一章是让同学们理解和掌握写作框架和要求，那么第二章就是手把手地让同学们踏踏实实学会如何表达。当然这些所谓"核心功能句式"远远不够，还需要同学们在学习过程中自己多多积累和总结！

　　总而言之，这本书不仅适合托福写作改革后备考的学生，也值得托福写作教学老师学习和参考。感谢姚钦老师为托福写作教学发展做了有益的尝试和贡献，希望再接再厉，期待后续其他写作教学教研佳作！

　　以上只是拜读这本书后的感悟，权为荐序，希望不辱使命。一本书的好坏，读者的评价才最为真实和真切。

徐清之

中国教育智库联盟留学教育研究中心执行主任
中国逻辑学会逻辑教育专业委员会委员
国际教育教师学术联盟（学盟）创始人

　　改革后新版写作将独立写作换成"学术讨论"，用时从 30 分钟缩短为 10 分钟，新增教授与两个学生对话的模式，并要求考生对讨论"做出贡献"。这种新的考试形式对考生来说，无疑增加了挑战性。针对改革背景下考生对于写作部分的学习需求，本书提供针对性解决方案和大量练习材料，帮助考生在短时间内快速提升写作技能，顺利应对托福写作挑战。

　　我们团队针对托福写作考试中的核心问题进行了深入的研究和探讨，并将这些研究成果汇集在这本书中，解决了以下几个痛点：首先，我们提供了大量满分例文，这些例文结构清晰，可以让考生轻松模仿。通过这些例文，考生可以直观地了解托福写作的技巧和规范。其次，我们努力解决了长期以来困扰考生的一个问题：如何既保证考试文章结构的有用性，又避免陷入单调、冗长的困境。在实践中，我们发现提供 2—3 种不同的范文结构供考生选择，可以有效解决这一问题。此外，我们的写作要点涵盖了综合写作的各个方面，详细到对每一个信息点准确性的讲解。这不仅可以帮助考生深入了解综合写作的评分标准，还可以让考生在备考过程中更加有针对性地进行训练。最后，我们特别强调利用好满分范文中的好词好句。在过去，许多图书只是简单地将范文呈现给考生，而忽略了如何引导考生充分吸收其中的精华。为了解决这一问题，我们在书中设置了丰富的练习，让考生能够通过模仿、改写、复述等，深入体会优秀词句，并将其熟练运用在自己的文章中。

　　编写本书的初衷便是帮助考生应对写作挑战。托福考试不仅要求考生具有扎实的语言基础，还对逻辑思维和写作能力有严格的要求。本书将为考生提供系统实用的写作方法和技巧，帮助考生迅速提升写作水平。此外，本书还可为托福教师提供有价值的备课参考资料，帮助他们更好地指导考生备考托福写作。

　　我们建议考生在备考托福写作时，采用以下方法来充分利用本书：

　　1. 对于学术讨论，考生可以首先快速浏览每一章，了解不同文章结构的特点，然后选择适合自己的结构模式，深入学习。

　　2. 对于综合写作，考生可以先阅读书中的方法论，了解分析题目、整理思路、组织段落等方面的技巧，然后针对每个例题，先写一篇文章，按照文字解读的指导，对核心信息进行梳理和整合，明确自己的观点和论据。通过这种方式，考生可以更好地掌握如何成文成句，提高写作效率。

　　3. 考生在掌握基本的写作技巧和方法之后，还需要注意提升语言质量。可以通过阅读大量的范文和模板，学习如何运用高级词汇和复杂句式来提高语言表达能力和文章质量。

　　4. 最后，考生在备考过程中需要严格按照时间规定完成每一篇文章的写作。可通过模拟真实考试场景，了解自己在有限的时间内能够完成的最佳文章质量。同时通过反复练习，逐渐适应考试节奏，提高写作速度。

我们衷心希望考生能够通过本书的指导，取得满意的托福成绩，为自己的出国留学之路增添信心。同时，也希望同行教师可以借助本书深入交流，共同提高教学水平，为托福写作教学作出更多的贡献。此外，本书也将为写作爱好者提供宝贵的写作思路和灵感，帮助他们开阔视野和提升创作能力。

写作的可迁移论

在语言的学习中，写作向来被认为是一个比较难的科目。从托福教学从业者的角度来看，写作单科比较缺好老师（甚至求职者也是十分少的，另外很多牛人表示不愿意发展写作方向的教学）。这一现象表明，这个科目有它难的地方。

笔者认为一位写作教师如果教学理论与资料整理技能成熟，那对考生都会有所助益，而名师之间 PK 的是所讲内容与所整理材料对考生写作能力迁移质量与速度的影响。基于这一点，教学内容必须要有体系化的结构与逻辑。教学结构是否合理，主要看是否将托福写作出分的关键因素合理地分布在课程内容中，以结果为导向，让课程各部分之间有逻辑性，高效推动考生往能力与成绩双向提升的方向发展。

在教学实践中，要让教学材料的内容——大到篇章框架，小到一词一句——都必须符合与遵守这些教学方法和理论，将方法和例子一一对应，最终呈现的文章就是方法论所讲的样子，考生领会后，通过练习达到熟练，从而运用到新的题目中，渐渐向高分迈进，实现将所学内容应用于自己的作文中的高效迁移。

例如，教学材料与课程设计中讲解的核心句式、范例最终要能运用到真实写作实践中，并通过真实的案例体现出来。不能讲一堆方法，在展示的例文中却没有使用到。

所学必为所用！

//目录//

第二章　落笔如有神　　　　　　　　　　　　　　/65

综合写作例文　/190

1.1 学术讨论

Direction of Academic Discussion

Your professor is teaching a class on Social Studies. Write a post responding to the professor's question. In your response you should:

- express and support your opinion
- make a contribution to the discussion

An effective response will contain at least 100 words. You will have 10 minutes to write it.

Features and Requirements of Academic Discussion

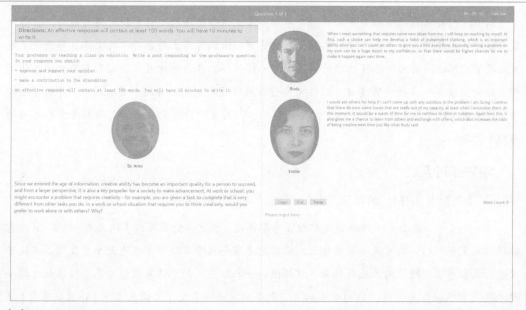

内容:

Academic Discussion

时间:

10 minutes

篇幅:

官方要求:>100 words；实践建议:>170 words【建议 170–210 words】

实战口号:

150 words 以内先求数量，190 words 以上求质量！

Attentions

写作进步的过程:

1. 先会写; 2. 写得多; 3. 写得好; 4. 写得快; 5. 写得又快又好。

写作提升的两个维度和两个层次

写作提升的两个维度

托福写作提升的第一个维度是方法论和案例呈现式的授课与学习。考生可以通过课程讲解与呈现的案例获得方法与明确的写作提升目标,也可以通过自学恰当的材料获得系统的托福写作知识。笔者通过多年的托福写作教学,形成了比较成熟的方法论体系,在此方法论之下生成的案例材料帮助许多考生写好托福作文;笔者也了解写成什么样子会取得优秀的成绩。输出类的写作与输入类的阅读、听力科目有所不同,后者属于被动式的对材料进行理解与反应,在材料引导下学习即可,前者则需要考生心中形成方法论,对写出来的文章所应当达到的标准了然于心,凭空乱写无法写出高分作文。

托福写作提升的另一个维度是反馈式学习。考生通常无法通过自学提升写作能力,自行纠改与提升实属难得。大多数人即便参照标准的范例,依然写不出符合要求的文章,毕竟换了题目就换了内容,写的文章不可能跟范例呈现的一模一样。在这种情况下,需要有经验的老师对作文进行批改并给出提升的建议,让作文质量与风格逐渐向高分靠拢。这也是优秀 [或者后期进入高分层] 的学员在阅读和听力上需要的帮助少,而在输出类的口语和写作部分需要老师的帮助多的原因。

写作的两个层次

从"会写"到"写得好"的过程,涉及写作能力提升的两个层次。

第一个是宏观的结构。这部分是相对容易掌握的,至少学会后写出来的文章"形似"官方青睐的作文是不难的。在宏观框架结构上,根据笔者常年教学实践与学生有效出分反馈,建议考生选择最容易上手的结构来展开作文。这样做,一来容易展开,二来提分率高。将满足这两个要求的文章框架作为首选,方向就明确了,剩下的就是学会它 [上课或自学] 并且熟悉它 [练习]。这个层次的提升较容易,认真上几节名师课就可以解决。但是也有不少人上若干次课后得不到提升。这说明第二层次的问题一直没有得到解决。

第二个层次便是语言。语言方面最基本的是语法问题,接着是用词与表达恰当性问题,然后是句子顺畅与逻辑性问题,最后是句子内部逻辑与简洁性问题、上下文内容逻辑问题。这些问题分为不同的亚层次。语言能力需要在学习过程中不断提升。经常有人误以为作文得分低是作文结构与写作方法出了问题,然后否定老师的方法,又学一个新的思路,而语言与内容细节方面却未精进。不排除老师水平存在问题,但到处换名师成绩都上不去,其实是因为语言层面的问题依旧存在。只有一点点改掉语言细节问题,才能真正提升写作水平。

1.2 学术讨论作文全文框架

TOEFL 文章主流结构

★ 文章主流结构一：并列式展开结构示例

1	Topic Sentence 【回应 Dr./Prof.】	Working and sharing ideas with others is a better choice when people are required to think creatively about solutions to problems in a work or school situation.
2	让步 + 反驳 A 方	Even though working or studying alone may prevent one from being interrupted by others or help develop one's independence, there are limitations and shortcomings in one's ability and performance that should be considered.
3	支撑对 A 方的反驳	In other words, working or studying with others can avoid mistakes or misunderstandings since when flawed ideas are proposed, they are likely to be corrected by the group effort. That's one of the reasons why school educators encourage students to engage in group discussions before they begin their projects.
4	支撑 B 方	What's more, consulting others about what one doesn't know is another benefit that working or studying with classmates or colleagues brings about. No one knows everything, so people working with others may enlarge and deepen their perspective and perception by gaining advice or assistance, which is useful in case they face difficulties.
5	支撑 B 方	In addition, sharing ideas inspires people to think more creatively so that they may come up with new and better ideas for their projects or tasks. It is quite common to see a group of scientists who fight through difficult situations by discussing their ideas and plans with their teammates.

★ 文章主流结构二：对比式展开结构示例

1	Topic Sentence	Personally, I would prefer employment at a company without any family ties.
2	反驳 A	When working for a family member, the chances of being treated differently increase, so many abilities would not be fully developed.
3	扩展支撑反驳 A	For instance, if I make a mistake during a particular task, a superior who is a relative may attempt to assist me by taking over the assignment instead of issuing a warning or punishment,

		thus the mistake I made would not leave a deep impression on me, and I would likely repeat the mistake, which would be detrimental to advancing a skill.
4	认同 B	In contrast, if the same mistake was made at a company with a superior without any close family ties, he would react assertively, which would imprint the mistake on me, reducing the likelihood of repeating the same error.
5	扩展支撑认同 B	A strict workplace environment without any special treatment is more likely to encourage a worker to stride in a direction that would lead to success, since many of his qualities would be tested, such as patience, diligence, or attentiveness.
6	总结	This way, many abilities are refined, and more experience is gained, paving a path for a more prosperous career.

★ 文章主流结构三：提出解决方案模式示例

1	Topic Sentence	I think there are fundamental flaws with Ray and Mary's suggestions.
2	反驳 A	Not many parents can afford the time to supervise their children doing homework since they have many other obligations, such as work and household chores, so this method is impractical for many families.
3	反驳 B	And when it comes to punishment, it is an extremely risky business. If the degree of punishment is not cautiously calculated, punitive measures might inflict adverse effects on the students, like losing confidence, self-doubt, or bullying from others.
4	提出新想法 C	I believe a more practical and less sensitive approach to preventing students from copying each other is to modify their assignments. Teachers can spend time devising homework that encompasses more diversity.
5	展开支撑 C	For example, a math teacher can assign five or six sets of practice to his class and scatter the sets among all the students, thus making it much more inconvenient for students to copy one another. Similar methods can be applied to most academic subjects, and when students discover that copying homework spends more effort than doing it themselves, they are less likely to succumb to its temptation.
6	总结	As long as teachers are willing to spend time and effort composing diversified homework assignments, methods such as the above can effectively alleviate the problem.

★　明确框架的重要性

除了极少数题目适合写成说明文，绝大部分托福写作 Academic Discussion 属于论议文。[为题目所指的问题提供理由并进行论证，或者说明文中事实并对主题句进行支撑。在写作中可不用过于详细区分体裁是议论文还是说明文，因为这类文章的写作均为给出理由或指出相关事实并进行扩展支撑。] Academic Discussion 的出题特征与考试要求决定了它有十分鲜明的主流写作框架。自 2023 年起，笔者团队与其他一线资深托福写作老师就教学方法达成了共识。框架并非只有一种写法，笔者团队结合作文结构的种种可能性和出分倾向性研究，推崇上面所示的三种主流框架。[当然笔者也认可其他的合理可行的框架！我们会在后文继续进行必要的说明。]

在讲解 Academic Discussion 时，我们在最初的课程模块里就让学生明确 TOEFL Academic Discussion 应该写成什么样子。没有进行过托福写作培训的学生应该先详细研究框架，并且按范例文章的框架思路来自主练习写作，直至熟练。若框架正确，成绩还是上不去，则要么是细节语言出了问题，要么就是自己没有意识到框架内部的逻辑问题。可关注后文三大写法的示范。

关于写几段的说明

至笔者写此书之际新版托福已经举办了几场考试并且也出了分（包括家庭版）。关于 Academic Discussion 这个作文应该写成什么样的结构，业内有多种观点，不同老师有各自的考虑。有人认为应和官方提供的例文一样写成一段，也有人认为应写成两段，还有人认为观点和两个支撑论点各占一段，文章共三段。其实，跟以前 Independent Essay Writing 一样，官方并没有表示哪一种结构更受青睐，主流的写法建议都是后来根据考试高分案例总结出来的。考虑到文章的篇幅较短，并且官方给出的例文只有一段，所以本书的例文也都是一段。统一模式有利于学生在学习过程中高效迁移。不过两至三段的处理方式并不无妥，无非就是将一段拆成两至三段，我们在实践教学中是包容这种写法的，若学生习惯于写多段也可以。其实，作文分几段并无本质上的区别。无论是一段、两段还是三段，都有人得高分乃至满分。最终得分取决于作文质量。

Your professor is teaching a class on Educational Science. Write a post responding to the professor's question. In your response, you should:

• express and support your opinion

• make a contribution to the discussion

An effective response will contain at least 100 words. You will have 10 minutes to write it.

Dr. Ferguson:

Over the next few weeks, we are going to look at various methods of improving the quality of education for school children, more specifically, the approaches teachers can take to prevent students from engaging in activities that are detrimental to their education process. So before we dive into the literature, I'd like to know how you would handle this recent phenomenon: More and more students are completing assignments by copying each other's work. What do you think is the most effective way to prevent or reduce this from occurring?

Ray:

Teachers should ask parents to be more involved in their children's education, specifically by asking them to supervise their children when they are doing their homework. After parents have confirmed that their kids have completed their assignments independently, they can sign the work to reassure the teachers.

Mary:

I believe that a degree of punishment can deter a proportion of students from copying others. For example, when teachers discover a student's work to be plagiarism, they can revoke their grades and give them detention after class. When other students see this, they'll think twice about completing assignments using other people's work.

Possible Response I【一段】:

I think there are fundamental flaws with Ray and Mary's suggestions. Not many parents can afford the time to supervise their children doing homework since they have many other obligations, such as work and household chores, so this method is impractical for many families. And when it comes to punishment, it is an extremely risky business. If the degree of punishment is not cautiously calculated, punitive measures might inflict adverse effects on the students, like losing confidence, self-doubt, or bullying from others. I believe a more practical and less sensitive approach to preventing students from copying each other is to modify their assignments. Teachers can spend time devising homework that encompasses more diversity. For example, a math teacher can assign five or six sets of practice to his class and scatter the sets among all the students, thus making it much more inconvenient for students to copy one another. Similar methods can be applied to most academic subjects, and when students discover that copying homework spends more effort than doing it themselves, they are less likely to succumb to its temptation. As long as teachers are willing to spend time and effort composing diversified homework assignments, methods such as the above can effectively alleviate the problem.

Possible Response Ⅱ 【两段】：

I think there are fundamental flaws with Ray and Mary's suggestions. Not many parents can afford the time to supervise their children doing homework since they have many other obligations, such as work and household chores, so this method is impractical for many families. And when it comes to punishment, it is an extremely risky business. If the degree of punishment is not cautiously calculated, punitive measures might inflict adverse effects on the students, like losing confidence, self-doubt, or bullying from others.

I believe a more practical and less sensitive approach to preventing students from copying each other is to modify their assignments. Teachers can spend time devising homework that encompasses more diversity. For example, a math teacher can assign five or six sets of practice to his class and scatter the sets among all the students, thus making it much more inconvenient for students to copy one another. Similar methods can be applied to most academic subjects, and when students discover that copying homework spends more effort than doing it themselves, they are less likely to succumb to its temptation. As long as teachers are willing to spend time and effort composing diversified homework assignments, methods such as the above can effectively alleviate the problem.

Possible Response Ⅲ 【三段】：

I think there are fundamental flaws with Ray and Mary's suggestions.

Not many parents can afford the time to supervise their children doing homework since they have many other obligations, such as work and household chores, so this method is impractical for many families. And when it comes to punishment, it is an extremely risky business. If the degree of punishment is not cautiously calculated, punitive measures might inflict adverse effects on the students, like losing confidence, self-doubt, or bullying from others.

I believe a more practical and less sensitive approach to preventing students from copying each other is to modify their assignments. Teachers can spend time devising homework that encompasses more diversity. For example, a math teacher can assign five or six sets of practice to his class and scatter the sets among all the students, thus making it much more inconvenient for students to copy one another. Similar methods can be applied to most academic subjects, and when students discover that copying homework spends more effort than doing it themselves, they are less likely to succumb to its temptation. As long as teachers are willing to spend time and effort composing diversified homework assignments, methods such as the above can effectively alleviate the problem.

说明:

大家可以从上面三篇例文中看出:

Sample Ⅰ 虽然只安排成一段,结构却很清晰。文章先反驳 Ray 和 Mary,再呈现反驳理由,然后用细节支撑理由,最后表明想法并用细节支撑自己的想法。这是非常可行的模式,不会因为只有一段就显得结构不清晰。

Sample Ⅱ 用了两段式结构,第一段反驳 Ray 和 Mary,第二段表明自己的想法并进行扩展支撑。本质上跟第一个例文没有任何区别。虽然本书主要呈现一段式写法,但这样的写法,包括下面 Sample Ⅲ 的写法,我们都会在实践中包容。

Sample Ⅲ 拆成三段,对 Ray 和 Mary 的反驳作为第一段,表明立场;再安排一段分别展开对 Ray 和 Mary 的反驳;最后一段写自己的想法与支撑观点。这么安排也同样层次分明,没有任何问题。

以上不同段落数的例文在写法上没有本质区别,但为了统一,并让学生学会迁移,我们全书都只用一段式来呈现,喜欢多段的读者也可以适当拆段。

TOEFL Academic Discussion 三大写法

★ 写法一: 单边为重

案例分析与例文 1 TG 36【Education 话题】

◎ 结构展开: 让步指出 A 方的缺点;支撑 B 方;用并列三点支撑 B。

Your professor is teaching a class on **Education**. Write a post responding to the professor's question. In your response you should:

• express and support your opinion

• make a contribution to the discussion

An effective response will contain at least 100 words. You will have 10 minutes to write it.

Dr. Aron:

Since we entered the age of information, creative ability has become an important quality for a person to succeed, and from a larger perspective, it is also a key propeller for a society to make advancement. At work or school, you might encounter a problem that requires creativity. For example, you are given a task to complete that is very different from other tasks you do. In a work or school situation that requires you to think creatively, would you prefer to work alone or with others? Why?

Rudy:

When I meet something that requires some new ideas from me, I will keep on working by myself. At first, such a choice can help me develop a habit of independent thinking, which is an important ability since you can't count on others to give you a hint every time. Secondly, solving a problem on my own can be a huge boost to my confidence, so that there would be higher chances for me to make it happen again next time.

Emilia:

I would ask others for help if I can't come up with any solutions to the problem I am facing. I confess that there do exist some issues that are really out of my capacity, at least when I encounter them. At this moment, it would be a waste of time for me to continue to think in isolation. Apart from this, it also gives me a chance to learn from others and exchange with others, which also increases the odds of being creative next time just like what Rudy said.

◎ 三要点

要点 I：Topic Sentence 一定要回应主题，即 Dr./Prof. 所提出的问题。这有利于避免跑题和偏题。

要点 II：尽可能涵盖 A 和 B 两位学生的讨论观点，这有利于高效写作。写法统一，有利于后期写作速度提升。

要点 III：回应 Dr.，让步 + 反驳 A【或 B】方，支撑 B【或 A】方。这是最常用也最容易掌握的写法。【不是唯一写法，在本书或者笔者团队的课程中我们会补充其他可使用的写法。】按此思路练习，有利于迅速提高熟练度。【练习一种写法有利于提高备考效率，节省时间。】

◎ Construction of Parallel Points

让步 + 反驳A：Avoid mistakes and misunderstandings

支撑B：Consult others for what we don't know

支撑B：Share idea to inspire and enlighten new and good ideas

◎ A Possible Sample 【211 Words】

Working and sharing ideas with others is a better choice when people are required to think creatively about solutions to problems in a work or school situation. Even though working or studying alone may prevent one from being interrupted by others or help develop one's independence, there are limitations and shortcomings in one's ability and performance that should be considered. In other words, working or studying with others can avoid mistakes or misunderstandings since when flawed ideas are proposed, they are likely to be corrected by the group effort. That's one of the reasons why school educators encourage students to engage in group discussions before they begin their projects. What's more, consulting others about what one doesn't know is another benefit that working or studying with classmates or colleagues brings about. No one knows everything, so people working with others may enlarge and deepen their perspective and perception by gaining advice or assistance, which is useful in case they face difficulties. In addition, sharing ideas inspires people to think more creatively so that they may come up with new and better ideas for their projects or tasks. It is quite common to see a group of scientists who fight through difficult situations by discussing their ideas and plans with their teammates.

◎ 结构展开拆解

1	Topic Sentence 【主题句直接回应 Dr./Prof.】	**Working and sharing ideas with others is a better choice when people are required to think creatively about solutions to problems in a work or school situation.**
2	【让步 + 反驳 A 方】	Even though working or studying alone may prevent one from being interrupted by others or help develop one's independence, there are limitations and shortcomings in one's ability and performance that should be considered.
3	【支撑对 A 方的反驳】	In other words, working or studying with others can avoid mistakes or misunderstandings since when flawed ideas are proposed, they are likely to be corrected by the group effort. That's one of the reasons why school educators encourage students to engage in group discussions before they begin their projects.
4	【支撑 B 方】	What's more, consulting others about what one doesn't know is another benefit that working or studying with classmates or colleagues brings about. No one knows everything, so people working with others may enlarge and deepen their perspective and perception by gaining advice or assistance, which is useful in case they face difficulties.
5	【支撑 B 方】	In addition, sharing ideas inspires people to think more creatively so that they may come up with new and better ideas for their projects or tasks. It is quite common to see a group of scientists who fight through difficult situations by discussing their ideas and plans with their teammates.

案例分析与例文 2 TG 19【Psychology 话题】

◎ 结构展开：驳 A 撑 B + 并列三方面展开。

Your professor is teaching a class on **Psychology**. Write a post responding to the professor's question. In your response you should:

• express and support your opinion

• make a contribution to the discussion

An effective response will contain at least 100 words. You will have 10 minutes to write it.

Dr. Green:

Over the next couple of weeks, we're going to look at lots of different materials about the psyche behind the way contemporary people dress. In ancient times, garments were mainly functional, and sometimes they exhibited wealth and status. But with the prolific modern clothing and fashion industries, clothing has evolved to represent many different things. So, first, I'd like you to think about this topic. The question for this discussion board is: Does the way **a person dresses reflect his character**?

Jonothan:

Yes, absolutely. People tend to wear the type or style of clothing they like, which reflects their lifestyle and preferences. Being an athlete myself, I love wearing sneakers, sweats, and jerseys. Anyone who takes a good look at me can see that I'm into sports, and they can assume that I'm an active, outgoing person.

Stacy:

I'm more skeptical about judging people based on their fashion taste. You shouldn't judge a book by its cover, and that works on people as well. Many people can't choose what they wear, they buy whatever they can afford. If we see a person wearing an old worn-out shirt, we can't tell whether he's a good or bad person or any other of his qualities.

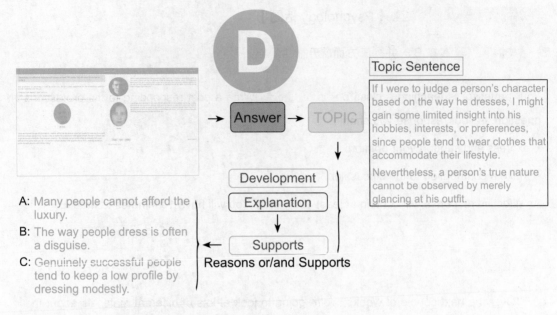

A: Many people cannot afford the luxury.

B: The way people dress is often a disguise.

C: Genuinely successful people tend to keep a low profile by dressing modestly.

◎ 并列细节扩充：根据上方给出的纲要进行扩充

1	Topic Sentence 【Rebut Dr./Prof.】	**If I were to judge a person's character based on the way he dresses, I might gain some limited insight into his hobbies, interests, or preferences, since people tend to wear clothes that accommodate their lifestyle.**
2	Rebut A 【Support B】	Nevertheless, a person's true nature cannot be observed by merely glancing at his outfit.
3	Support Ⅰ	**Many people cannot afford the luxury.** 细节扩充 A：
4	Support Ⅱ	**The way people dress is often a disguise.** 细节扩充 B：
5	Support Ⅲ	**Genuinely successful people tend to keep a low profile by dressing modestly.** 细节扩充 C：
6	Conclusion	To reveal a person's true character, we should look past the surface, and focus on his words and actions.

◎ **Sample Response**

1	Topic Sentence 【Rebut Dr./Prof.】	**If I were to judge a person's character based on the way he dresses, I might gain some limited insight into his hobbies, interests, or preferences, since people tend to wear clothes that accommodate their lifestyle.**
2	Rebut A 【Support B】	Nevertheless, a person's true nature cannot be observed by merely glancing at his outfit.
3	Support Ⅰ	As Stacy has mentioned, many people cannot afford the luxury of wearing the clothes they like or want.
4	Support Ⅱ	In addition, the way people dress is often a disguise that projects an image they wish others to perceive. A con artist, for example, might package himself with an expensive suit and ostentatious accessories, making himself presentable, and creating the illusion of wealth and status. However, if one base his judgment of the conman on his appearance, he would not realize the person underneath the glamorous coating is but a thief and liar.
5	Support Ⅲ	Furthermore, genuinely successful people tend to keep a low profile by dressing modestly. It would be nearly impossible to determine whether a person is smart, industrious, or pragmatic solely by his shirt.
6	Conclusion	To reveal a person's true character, we should look past the surface, and focus on his words and actions.

◎ 结构小结：Typical Structure

1. Topic Sentence—Response to the prompt

2. Development—Concession/Counterargument and rebut

3. Support A [explanation, exemplification and/or details]

4. Support B [explanation, exemplification and/or details]

5. Support C [explanation, exemplification and/or details]

6. Conclusion

> **说明：**
>
> 　　实践中，我们可以看到在 Typical Structure 的基础上，允许有一些小的调整，如果写完 Support C 时已经有 200 词左右，没有时间写 Conclusion 了，并不会影响整个文章质量。综上，我们可以将 Typical Structure 熟记于心，在写作中视情况加以调整。

实战 1 TG 11【Ethics 话题】

◎ 结构展开：支持 B + 并列三方面展开

Your professor is teaching a class on **Ethics**. Write a post responding to the professor's question. In your response you should:

• express and support your opinion

• make a contribution to the discussion

An effective response will contain at least 100 words. You will have 10 minutes to write it.

Dr Waltz:

Nature vs. nurture has been an age-old question that science has yet to answer. Over the next few weeks, we will examine the nurture side of this argument, and closely review the implications of nurture on a human child, specifically, the qualities a child should learn in order to cultivate positive morals and ethics. So, before we officially begin, please consider and discuss the following question: **What is the most important quality** to share with **a child (5–10 years old)**?

Monique:

In my eyes, when **teach** a child between those ages, the **value of honesty** is the most important. At this age stage, children begin to understand the difference between **right and wrong**, so conveying a positive instruction of being **honest** will help them avoid making bad decisions in the future, such as deceiving others to get what they want. Failing to guide them in this direction can lead to many severe consequences in life.

Jesse:

Honesty is an important trait a child should eventually learn, but **before that**, I think it's more important to teach him how to be **considerate of others and to be a kind person**. We live in a society where we are interdependent on each other for a multitude of reasons, and it's an essential factor that led to modern civilization. If we can teach our children to be **compassionate and helpful to others**, they will grow up to be more **responsible** members of society and contribute to the world in their own ways.

◎ **Practice**：根据下面的要求进行翻译和写作练习。

Ⅰ. 中译英

Ⅱ. 针对三个分论点进行细节扩展写作练习

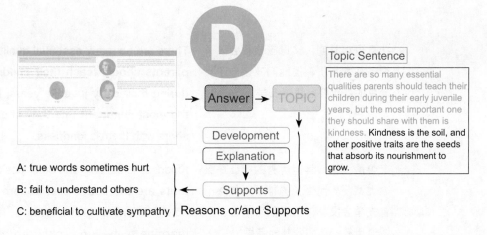

A: true words sometimes hurt

B: fail to understand others

C: beneficial to cultivate sympathy

Reasons or/and Supports

Topic Sentence

There are so many essential qualities parents should teach their children during their early juvenile years, but the most important one they should share with them is kindness. Kindness is the soil, and other positive traits are the seeds that absorb its nourishment to grow.

1	Topic Sentence	在青少年时期，父母应该教会孩子很多基本品质，但他们应该与子女分享的最重要品质是友善。 将句子译为英文：放右边	
2	Explanation	友善是土壤，其他优秀的特征是吸收土壤营养而生长的种子。如果不首先学会友善，孩子们可能会误解或滥用教给他们的其他品质。 将句子译为英文：放右边	
3	Support Ⅰ	**True words sometimes hurt** 细节扩充：写 1–3 句 根据上方提示写 Evidence/Example/Fact/Detail，20–35 词的细节支撑！	
4	Support Ⅱ	**Fail to understand others** 细节扩充：写 1–3 句 根据上方提示写 Evidence/Example/Fact/Detail，20–35 词的细节支撑！	
5	Support Ⅲ	**Beneficial to cultivate sympathy** 细节扩充：写 1–3 句 根据上方提示写 Evidence/Example/Fact/Detail，20–35 词的细节支撑！	
6	Conclusion	因此，考虑到友善是影响孩子成长方向的主要根基，父母应该为他们树立榜样，确保他们成长为心地善良并爱他人的人。 将句子译为英文：放右边	

◎ **Sample Response**

1	Topic Sentence	在青少年时期，父母应该教会孩子很多基本品质，但他们应该与子女分享的最重要品质是友善。	**There are so many essential qualities parents should teach their children during their early juvenile years, but the most important one they should share with them is kindness.**
2	Explanation	友善是土壤，其他优秀的特征是吸收土壤营养而生长的种子。如果不首先学会友善，孩子们可能会误解或滥用教给他们的其他品质。	Kindness is the soil, and other positive traits are the seeds that absorb its nourishment to grow. Without first learning to be kind, children may misinterpret or misuse the other qualities taught to them.
3	Support I	**True words sometimes hurt** 细节扩充：写 1–3 句 根据上方提示写 Evidence/Example/Fact/Detail，20–35 Words 的细节支撑！	For instance, stating an objective observation of someone's physical appearance can be hurtful to the listener, and it could be perceived as inconsiderate or impolite for a child to do so.
4	Support II	**Fail to understand others** 细节扩充：写 1–3 句 根据上方提示写 Evidence/Example/Fact/Detail，20–35 Words 的细节支撑！	Also, it would be challenging to consider the situation and sentiments of others without having a kind heart.
5	Support III	**Beneficial to cultivate sympathy** 细节扩充：写 1–3 句 根据上方提示写 Evidence/Example/Fact/Detail，20–35 Words 的细节支撑！	With kindness, children can cultivate a stronger sense of sympathy and empathy, which helps them assess the consequences of their actions.
6	Conclusion	因此，考虑到友善是影响孩子成长方向的主要根基，父母应该为他们树立榜样，确保他们成长为心地善良并爱他人的人。	So given the fact that kindness is the foundation that influences the general direction of a child's development, parents should set an example for them to ensure that they flourish into loving people with kindness in their hearts.

注意:

　　中文的主要作用是在写作练习过程中提示需要表述的内容, 引导想不到关键点的学生, 使其有内容可以写, 让学生学习写作初期有方向: 先从翻译开始, 再到能自主输出恰当的内容。本书并非翻译教材, 因此弱化了翻译时的忠实度, 译文主要偏重两点: 一是符合题目的内容支撑与逻辑展开的要求, 二是语言流畅、恰当。在满足这两点的基础上, 学生可进行一定的自主发挥。

实战 2 TG 48【Education 话题】

◎ 结构展开: 提出新想法 + 并列三个点扩展支撑

Your professor is teaching a class on **Education**. Write a post responding to the professor's question. In your response you should:

• express and support your opinion

• make a contribution to the discussion

An effective response will contain at least 100 words. You will have 10 minutes to write it.

Dr. Fay:

In class last week, we concluded that it is helpful for a university to provide its newly enrolled students with a planned summer vacation. The school believes this will help students better exploit their free time. This week, we are going to emulate such a plan, so I would like to ask you to provide your views on what kind of summer vacation programs would be most helpful for students.

Gloria:

If I were a counselor, I would organize my students to visit history museums or historical sites because I believe they chose my university not only for the university itself but also for the city where the school is situated. If I help them get to know the city where they will spend the next few years before they embark on their learning journey, they will develop a stronger sense of belonging here and thus enjoy their college life better.

Stephen:

I prefer my target university to host functions where new students get a chance to know each other. My brother, who is already a university student, tells me that the relationship between students at university is more distant than in high school because they don't spend much time having classes together like in high school. Therefore, I believe parties can be helpful in making new friends.

◎ **Practice Ⅰ：** 根据下面的要求进行翻译和写作练习

Ⅰ. 中译英

Ⅱ. 针对三个分论点进行细节扩展写作练习

1	Topic Sentence	对学生最有帮助的暑假项目之一是暑季学校项目，由各种课程或活动组成，有助于学生以后融入大学生活。 将句子译为英文：放右边	
2	Explanation	这些项目可以为学生提供探索新科目和发展新技能的机会，同时也为即将到来的新学年做好准备。 将句子译为英文：放右边	
3	Support Ⅰ	Courses like science, technology and engineering benefit student. 细节扩充：写 1–3 句 根据上方提示写 Evidence/Example/Fact/Detail，20–35 词的细节支撑！	
4	Support Ⅱ	Clubs and programs benefit leadership development, teamwork and communicative ability. 细节扩充：写 1–3 句 根据上方提示写 Evidence/Example/Fact/Detail，20–35 词的细节支撑！	
5	Support Ⅲ	Projects offer opportunities for community service and volunteer work. 细节扩充：写 1–3 句 根据上方提示写 Evidence/Example/Fact/Detail，20–35 词的细节支撑！	
6	Conclusion	一个由各种课程和项目组成的综合性暑季学校项目可以满足几乎所有专业学生的兴趣，让他们为即将到来的高等教育挑战做好准备。 将句子译为英文：放右边	

◎ **Practice** Ⅱ：根据下面的要求进行中译英

1	Topic Sentence	对学生最有帮助的暑假项目之一是暑季学校项目，由各种课程或活动组成，有助于学生以后融入大学生活。	**One of the most helpful types of summer vacation programs for students is a summer school program comprised of various courses or activities conducive to their later integration into college life.**
2	Explanation	这些项目可以为学生提供探索新科目和发展新技能的机会，同时也为即将到来的新学年做好准备。	These programs can provide students with opportunities to explore new subjects and develop new skills, while also preparing them for the upcoming school year.
3	Support Ⅰ	一些课程可能侧重于提高学术能力，从专注于科学、技术、工程和数学的夏令营到沉浸式语言课程和创造性写作研讨会，应有尽有。 将句子译为英文：放右边	
4	Support Ⅱ	除了学术提升项目，关于个人成长和促进社会发展的暑期课程也会让学生受益。专注领导力发展、团队合作和沟通的课程可以帮助学生培养基本的生活技能，这些技能将在教育阶段和未来走向社会时让他们受益匪浅。 将句子译为英文：放右边	
5	Support Ⅲ	对于那些有意愿成为公职人员的人，学校可以提供社区服务和志愿工作的机会。这些项目可以帮助学生培养社会责任感和公民参与感，同时也提供了寻找新的兴趣和结识新朋友的机会。 将句子译为英文：放右边	
6	Conclusion	一个由各种课程和项目组成的综合性暑季学校项目可以满足几乎所有专业学生的兴趣，让他们为即将到来的高等教育挑战做好准备。	A comprehensive summer school program consisting of various courses and projects can accommodate the interest of students of almost all majors, which prepares them for the upcoming challenges of tertiary education.

◎ Sample Response

1	Topic Sentence	对学生最有帮助的暑假项目之一是暑季学校项目，由各种课程或活动组成，有助于学生以后融入大学生活。	**One of the most helpful types of summer vacation programs for students is a summer school program comprised of various courses or activities conducive to their later integration into college life.**
2	Explanation	这些项目可以为学生提供探索新科目和发展新技能的机会，同时也为即将到来的新学年做好准备。	These programs can provide students with opportunities to explore new subjects and develop new skills, while also preparing them for the upcoming school year.
3	Support I	一些课程可能侧重于提高学术能力，从专注于科学、技术、工程和数学的夏令营到沉浸式语言课程和创造性写作研讨会，应有尽有。	Some courses may focus on academic enrichment, from summer camps focusing on science, technology, engineering, and math to language immersion programs and creative writing workshops.
4	Support II	除了学术提升项目，关于个人成长和促进社会发展的暑期课程也会让学生受益。专注于领导力发展、团队合作和沟通的课程可以帮助学生培养基本的生活技能，这些技能将在教育阶段和未来走向社会时让他们受益匪浅。	In addition to academic enrichment programs, summer classes on personal and social development can also benefit students. Programs that focus on leadership development, teamwork and communication can help students build fundamental life skills that will serve them well in school and beyond.
5	Support III	对于那些有意愿成为公职人员的人，学校可以提供社区服务和志愿工作的机会。这些项目可以帮助学生培养社会责任感和公民参与感，同时也提供了探索新兴趣和结识新朋友的机会。	And for those aspiring to become public servants, the school can offer opportunities for community service and volunteer work. These programs can help students develop a sense of social responsibility and civic engagement, while also providing opportunities to explore new interests and meet new people.
6	Conclusion	一个由各种课程和项目组成的综合性暑季学校项目可以满足几乎所有专业学生的兴趣，让他们为即将到来的高等教育挑战做好准备。	A comprehensive summer school program consisting of various courses and projects can accommodate the interest of students of almost all majors, which prepares them for the upcoming challenges of tertiary education.

实战 3 TG 41【Education 话题】

◎ 结构展开：支持 A，让步 B，并列三方面展开。

> Your professor is teaching a class on **Education**. Write a post responding to the professor's question. In your response you should:
>
> • express and support your opinion
>
> • make a contribution to the discussion
>
> An effective response will contain at least 100 words. You will have 10 minutes to write it.

Dr. Chalmers:

Tremendous changes have been witnessed by us all over the past decades, and these changes not only happen in how we produce but also in the way we see the world. So it makes sense to say that people of older generations probably have a different worldview from younger people. So here comes the question for the class discussion board: Do you believe that grandparents cannot give useful advice to their grandchildren because the world of today and the world of 50 years ago are too different? Why or why not?

Terrance:

The world has indeed been changing, but it doesn't change fast enough so that experience from the past remain relevant throughout the times. Grandparents, despite their lack of knowledge of current affairs, can still pass on their experience to their grandchildren. Numerous creeds of life remain constant through time: planning, execution, or prioritizing, all of which are timeless advice that can be passed on.

Alice:

Even though the world doesn't change that fast, according to Terrance, the aspects to which every individual is confined hinder their experience from being passed on. As far as I can see, no matter how successful a person can be, there will always be something he has little knowledge of, which along with the forward march of time, cannot produce advice that can advance with the times.

◎ **Practice** Ⅰ：根据下面的要求进行翻译和写作练习

Ⅰ.中译英

Ⅱ.针对三个分论点进行写作扩展练习

1	Topic Sentence	祖父母一生积累了丰富的关于人生起伏的生活经验，可以为孙辈提供建设性的建议和适当的指导。 将句子译为英文：放右边	
2	Explanation	尽管世界随着时间的推移而逐渐变化，但正如特伦斯所说，一些核心价值观并没有改变。 将句子译为英文：放右边	
3	Support Ⅰ	Knowledge, perception, and experience can be taught to the grandchildren. 细节扩充：写 1–3 句。 根据上方提示写 Evidence/Example/Fact/Detail，20–35 词的细节支撑！	
4	Support Ⅱ	Improve their studies and behave properly/Available for them to consult/Broaden their perspectives and deepen their understanding. 细节扩充：写 1–3 句。 根据上方提示写 Evidence/Example/Fact/Detail，20–35 词的细节支撑！	
5	Support Ⅲ	Be enlightened/Develop into well-rounded adults/Successful businessmen share experience with younger generations. 细节扩充：写 1–3 句 根据上方提示写 Evidence/Example/Fact/Detail，20–35 词的细节支撑！	

◎ **Practice Ⅱ**：根据下面的要求进行中译英

1	Topic Sentence	祖父母一生积累了丰富的关于人生起伏的生活经验，可以为孙辈提供建设性的建议和适当的指导。	**With their enriched living experience of life's ups and downs accumulated throughout their lives, grandparents can give constructive advice and appropriate guidance to their grandchildren.**
2	Explanation	尽管世界随着时间的推移而逐渐变化，但正如特伦斯所说，一些核心价值观并没有改变。	Even though the world changes gradually over time, some core values do not shift, as Terrance suggests.
3	Support Ⅰ	由于祖父母经历了很多，他们的知识和感悟不断积累，这对年轻一代来说是实用的。由于年龄小，缺乏经验和智慧，青少年很容易犯错误，他们的祖父母可以帮助他们避免在日常生活或学校学习中犯错误。 将句子译为英文：放右边	
4	Support Ⅱ	他们可以教孙辈提高学业水平或在社交生活中表现得体，从而提高学习成绩或在社交中被接受。年轻一代在很小的时候很难无所不知，所以他们需要学习，他们可以向祖父母咨询。在祖父母的建议下，他们可以拓宽视野，加深理解，以防遇到困难或有任务需要处理。 将句子译为英文：放右边	
5	Support Ⅲ	有了对过去的认识和理解，年轻一代可以得到启迪，从而成长为全面发展的成年人，过上更加平衡的生活。一个成功的老商人在吃饭时和他的孙辈分享他的生活经验是很常见的。 将句子译为英文：放右边	

◎ **Sample Response**

		中文	English
1	Topic Sentence	祖父母一生积累了丰富的关于人生起伏的生活经验，可以为孙辈提供建设性的建议和适当的指导。	**With their enriched living experience of life's ups and downs accumulated throughout their lives, grandparents can give constructive advice and appropriate guidance to their grandchildren.**
2	Explanation	尽管世界随着时间推移逐渐变化，但正如 Terrance 所说，一些核心价值观并没有改变。	Even though the world changes gradually over time, some core values do not shift, as Terrance suggests.
3	Support I	由于祖父母经历了很多，他们的知识和感悟不断积累，这对年轻一代来说是实用的。由于年龄小，缺乏经验和智慧，青少年很容易犯错误，他们的祖父母可以帮助他们避免在日常生活或学校学习中犯错误。	Since grandparents have gone through a lot, their knowledge and perception accumulate, which is practical for the younger generation. Because of their young age and lack of experience and wisdom, juveniles may easily make mistakes, so their grandparents can help them avoid making mistakes in their daily lives or their studies at school.
4	Support II	他们可以教孙辈提高学业水平或在社交生活中表现得体，从而提高学习成绩或在社交中被接受。年轻一代在很小的时候很难无所不知，所以他们需要学习，他们可以向祖父母咨询。在祖父母的建议下，他们可以拓宽视野，加深理解，以防遇到困难或有任务需要处理。	They can teach their grandchildren how to improve their studies or behave properly in social life so that they can improve their academic performance or be accepted in their social interactions. The young generations can hardly know everything at a young age so they need to learn, and their grandparents are available for them to consult with. With advice from their grandparents, they may broaden their perspectives and deepen their understanding in case they face difficulties or have tasks to tackle with.
5	Support III	有了对过去的认识和理解，年轻一代可以得到启迪，从而成长为全面发展的成年人，过上更加平衡的生活。一个成功的老商人在吃饭时和他的孙辈分享他的生活经验是很常见的。	With the knowledge and understanding of the past, younger generations can be enlightened so they can develop into well-rounded adults that can lead to more balanced lives. It is common to see a successful old businessman sharing his life experience with his grandchild while having dinner.

实战 4 TG 32【Public Administration 话题】

◎ 结构展开：让步并转折反驳 A，支撑 B，并列四个事例展开。

> Your professor is teaching a class on **Public Administration**. Write a post responding to the professor's question. In your response you should:
>
> • express and support your opinion
>
> • make a contribution to the discussion
>
> An effective response will contain at least 100 words. You will have 10 minutes to write it.

Dr. Roger:

As the conclusion that we have reached over the last several lessons, it is necessary to impose some additional rules above the basic laws on certain occasions, such as wearing a helmet when riding a motorcycle or not smoking inside a public place, which has obvious benefits. But there are some other rules whose effects are not so attractive at first sight, such as the one about people's clothes. If you were a policymaker, do you think it is essential to implement rules about the types of clothes that people wear at work and at school?

Janet:

I believe what people wear should be mainly based on personal will rather than rules and restrictions. How people decide to dress falls well within the range of basic civil liberties as long as they stay within moral boundaries and tacit social etiquette. Therefore, policymakers shouldn't overreach their powers and attempts to control what people should wear.

Bandy:

I don't agree with Janet that it is entirely personal freedom or will that determines what kind of clothes people wear, although it is that way at home, not in the society. People are social creatures so it is possible for some of their dressing styles to influence others as well as themselves. For example, wearing a suit and tie is a conventional rule for interviews, whose significance I think is so considerable that no one thinks about breaking it.

◎ **Practice Ⅰ**：根据下面的要求进行翻译和写作练习

Ⅰ. 中译英

Ⅱ. 针对三个分论点进行写作扩展练习

1	Topic Sentence	如果我是一名政策制定者，我认为制定人们在某些场所着装的相关规则是很重要的。 将句子译为英文：放右边	
2	Explanation	社会逐渐形成一些规则，约束人们对他人有害的行为。尽管一个人的着装对他人的影响不像在公共场合吸烟、乱扔垃圾或闯红灯那么明显，但穿着不当的人也会对周围人产生负面影响。 将句子译为英文：放右边	
3	Support Ⅰ	Eccentric or offensive dress results in bad impression. 细节扩充：写 1–3 句。 根据上方提示写 Evidence/Example/Fact/Detail，20–35 词的细节支撑！	
4	Support Ⅱ	A financier who dresses as a street thug cannot persuade his client to invest a lot. 细节扩充：写 1–3 句。 根据上方提示写 Evidence/Example/Fact/Detail，20–35 词的细节支撑！	
5	Support Ⅲ	Unwise clothing choice is harmful to one's career, such as an elementary school teacher wearing revealing clothes. 细节扩充：写 1–3 句 根据上方提示写 Evidence/Example/Fact/Detail，20–35 词的细节支撑！	
6	Support Ⅳ	Being presentable is a sign of respect. Negligence of religious dress codes may result in punishment. 细节扩充：写 1–3 句 根据上方提示写 Evidence/Example/Fact/Detail，20–35 词的细节支撑！	

◎ **Practice Ⅱ**：根据下面的要求进行中译英

		中文	英文
1	Topic Sentence	如果我是一名政策制定者，我认为制定人们在某些场所着装的相关规则是很重要的。	**Having rules about the types of clothes that people wear in certain areas, in my opinion, if I were a policymaker, is important.**
2	Explanation	社会逐渐形成一些规则，约束人们对他人有害的行为。尽管一个人的着装对他人的影响不像在公共场合吸烟、乱扔垃圾或闯红灯那么明显，但穿着不当的人也会对周围人产生负面影响。	Some rules have gradually been constituted to restrain people's behavior that is harmful to others. Even though a person's outfit has an impact on people less conspicuously than smoking and littering in public or running a red light, people who dress inappropriately impose a negative influence on the people around them.
3	Support Ⅰ	例如，如果着装过度自我或有冒犯性着装偏好的人不把自己的品味局限于家里或指定场所这样的私人空间，他们可能会给周围的人留下不好的印象，这可能会导致严重的后果，比如丢掉工作或失去晋升的机会。 *将句子译为英文：放右边*	
4	Support Ⅱ	一个打扮成街头暴徒的金融专员可能无法说服他的客户在一个商业项目上进行大规模投资。投资者会对这位金融专员的性格持怀疑态度。 *将句子译为英文：放右边*	
5	Support Ⅲ	同时，不明智的服装选择对职业生涯可能具有破坏性的影响。如果小学老师给孩子上课时穿暴露的衣服会怎么样？她可能会引发家长甚至公众的不满，从而危及她的工作。 *将句子译为英文：放右边*	
6	Support Ⅳ	此外，在进入特定环境（如宗教场所）时，穿着得体有时被视为一种尊重的表现。忽视宗教着装规范可能会使人面临风险甚至危难，因为在世界一些角落，这种行为被视为亵渎神明，甚至可能会导致死刑。 *将句子译为英文：放右边*	

◎ Possible Response

1	Topic Sentence	如果我是一名政策制定者，我认为制定人们在某些场所着装的相关规则是很重要的。	**Having rules about the types of clothes that people wear in certain areas, in my opinion, if I were a policy maker, is important.**
2	Explanation	社会逐渐形成一些规则，约束人们对他人有害的行为。尽管一个人的着装对他人的影响不像在公共场合吸烟、乱扔垃圾或闯红灯那么明显，但穿着不当的人也会对周围人产生负面影响。	Some rules have gradually been constituted to restrain people's behavior that is harmful to others. Even though a person's outfit has an impact on people less conspicuously than smoking and littering in public or running a red light, people who dress inappropriately impose a negative influence on the people around them.
3	Support I	例如，如果着装过度自我或有冒犯性着装偏好的人不把自己的品味局限于家里或指定场所这样的私人空间，他们可能会给周围的人留下不好的印象，这可能会导致严重的后果，比如丢掉工作或失去晋升的机会。	For example, if people with eccentric or offensive dress preferences do not confine their taste to the privacy of their homes or designated venues, they may leave a bad impression on the people around them, which could lead to consequences, such as losing their occupation or an opportunity for promotion.
4	Support II	一个打扮成街头暴徒的金融专员可能无法说服他的客户在一个商业项目上进行大规模投资。投资者会对这位金融专员的性格持怀疑态度。	A financier who dresses as a street thug probably cannot persuade his client to make a sizable investment in a business project. The investor would be skeptical about the character of the financier.
5	Support III	同时，不明智的服装选择对职业生涯可能具有破坏性的影响。如果小学老师给孩子上课时穿暴露的衣服会怎么样？她可能会引发家长甚至公众的不满，从而危及她的工作。	In the same breath, unwise clothing choices can be destructive to a professional's career. What if a teacher in an elementary school wears revealing clothes when she gives lessons to kids? She may draw complaints from parents and even the public, putting her job on the line.
6	Support IV	此外，在进入特定环境(如宗教场所)时，穿着得体有时被视为一种尊重的表现。忽视宗教着装规范可能会使人面临风险甚至危险，因为在世界的一些角落，这种行为被认为是亵渎神明，甚至可能会导致死刑。	In addition, being presentable is sometimes viewed as a sign of respect when entering particular settings, such as houses of religion. Negligence of religious dress codes can put one at risk and in harm's way, as in some corners of the world, this behavior is considered sacrilegious, which could even result in capital punishment.

并列式思维的重要性

前面我们主要是用并列式思维进行写作练习,通过列举不同方面的事实或例子来证明主题。并列式不一定非得三点并列,也可以两点或者四点并列(正反对比属于两点并列)。在扩充文章时,要善于将思路进行并列或者对比,只要做到这两点,基本上就能解决学术讨论作文的文内细节支撑问题。写作过程中我们可以并列名词、短语、从句、句子、例子等。并列式思维一旦形成,我们扩展文章会更加得心应手,文章的信息量也会更大。

并列式框架(首推)之外的其他补充

我们前面解释过为什么只练习一种主流写法:它能运用于绝大多数文章;反复使用同一种写法进行训练也非常有利于熟悉文章展开模式,从而在短时间内提升写作速度;熟练度提升后,我们可以拿出一部分精力来检查语法,从而大大减少语法上的失误,保障高分。

下面我们会呈现一些其他的写作框架作为补充,例如对比、驳论并提出新想法来展开文章等。在实践中,首推的并列式写作框架可以应用于大部分试题,但是偶尔也会想不到展开的点,这时就需要有其他的写法作为补充:一来防止遇到难题时想不出点,无法完成写作;二来让自己的写作能力更强,写出来的文章更丰富多样,而不是简单重复一种模式。毕竟除高效备考外,多数考生也希望通过学习托福写作来提升自己的写作能力。综上,考生要掌握一种主流的写作框架,但同时在写作实践中也要会针对具体题目灵活变通。

★ 写法二:均衡双边

案例分析与例文 1 TG 21【Business 话题】

◎ 结构展开:均匀反驳 A;支撑 B

Your professor is teaching a class on **Business**. Write a post responding to the professor's question. In your response, you should:

• express and support your opinion

• make a contribution to the discussion

An effective response will contain at least 100 words. You will have 10 minutes to write it.

Professor Johnson:

When the world has more requirements for university students, they need to have more practical skills for their future careers. Internship seems to be important for the current graduates since more and more greenhorns are unable to adapt to the professional environment. What do you think is the most significant effect that an internship has on university students? Why do you think this affect you?

Christopher:

One way internships influence graduates is that if they don't have any experience in the occupation, they could not have appropriate expectations for their future work. Internships shed light on what they would do, and whether they would like the job. If they're uninterested in the job, they can change their mind and try another one in case of wasting time.

Leo:

Even though taking a part-time internship helps to spot an appropriate career, it is time-consuming. As students in university, they need to spend their time on studies and learning more. Getting into a job too early prevents a student from learning. That is a significant drawback since it harms their education.

◎ Outlining of a Contrast Structure for the Prompt

驳B ： Internship would not be a distraction to student's academic affairs.

立A ： Internship helps graduates discover themselves better besides helping them know the jobs they are taking.

◎ Sample Response

Internship compensates the shortage of school education that lacks practical skill cultivation and offers a chance for student to anticipate what a successful career needs. Unlike what Leo said, I don't think internship would be a distraction to students' academic affairs. As we all know, the conventional time when students gain work experience is during vacation or near graduation, during which they don't have many burdens from school, so there wouldn't be a contradiction between work and study. Moreover, internship can also help graduates discover themselves better besides helping them know the jobs they are taking as Christopher has mentioned. However open and diverse the universities today have become, they are, compared with the all-inclusive society, still ivory towers inside which the beings cannot obtain a bird's-eye view of themselves, so they might hold Utopian thoughts about the roles they would play in society. It is simply natural for an academic all-rounder to find it hard to earn a penny after graduating. Internship, though, can provide a transitional phase where students can learn their strengths and weaknesses so that they can confront frustrations, and accept them with the appropriate composure.

◎ 结构展开详解

1	Topic Sentence	**Internship compensates the shortage of school education that lacks practical skill cultivation and offers a chance for students to anticipate what a successful career needs.**
2	Rebut B	Unlike what Leo said, I don't think internship would be a distraction to students' academic affairs.
3	Supports	As we all know, the conventional time when students gain work experience is during vacation or near graduation, during which they don't have many burdens from school, so there wouldn't be a contradiction between work and study.
4	Agree with A	Moreover, internship can also help graduates discover themselves better besides helping them know the jobs they are taking as Christopher has mentioned.
5	Supports	However open and diverse the universities today have become, they are, compared with the all-inclusive society, still ivory towers inside which the beings cannot obtain a bird's-eye view of themselves, so they might hold Utopian thoughts about the roles they would play in society. It is simply natural for an academic all-rounder to find it hard to earn a penny after graduating.
6	Conclusion	Internship, though, can provide a transitional phase where students can learn their strengths and weaknesses so that they can confront frustrations, and accept them with the appropriate composure.

◎ Construction of a Contrast Formation

1. Topic Sentence—Response to the prompt

2. Rebut Person B—Point out the shortcoming of the opinion

3. Supports [explanation, exemplification and /or details]

4. Agree with Person A—Point out the advantage of the opinion

5. Supports [explanation, exemplification and /or details]

6. Conclusion

案例分析与例文 2 TG 16【Career Planning 话题】

◎ 结构展开：均匀反驳 A；支撑 B

> Your professor is teaching a class on **Career Planning**. Write a post responding to the professor's question. In your response, you should:
> • express and support your opinion
> • make a contribution to the discussion
> An effective response will contain at least 100 words. You will have 10 minutes to write it.

Dr. Mutombo:

I'm sure many of you have entrepreneurs in the family. I bring this up because we spoke of nepotism, the favoritism you obtain due to a relationship, and its implications on a person's career. Some view it as an advantage for people to get ahead quicker, but others view it as taboo, and people should not let it influence their future. Eventually, you will pursue a career, make a living, and provide for yourself. So most of you will enter the job market to seek a suitable job. Concerning this topic, I'd like you to answer this question: Is it better to work for a business owned by someone in your family or to work for a company owned by someone you don't know?

Janice:

I'm in favor of working for a business owned by a family member, at least in the beginning stages of one's career. People can gain more knowledge and experience from superiors who are close to them because of their intrinsic familial bond. If my uncle were my boss, for instance, he would teach me everything he knows about his business unreservedly, and that would give me a competitive edge over my peers.

Omar:

Unlike Janice, I wouldn't prefer to work for a company owned by my family. I come from a very traditional family, so they always expect me to behave in a certain manner, and it can feel very restrictive and stressful at times. I just can't imagine being closely monitored by an elder all the time, even if he's well-intended. I would lose my sense of freedom.

◎ **Outlining of a Contrast Structure for the Prompt:**

主题 : I would prefer employment at a company without any family ties.

驳A : When working for a family member, the chances of being treated differently increase, so many abilities would not be fully developed.

立B : If the same mistake was made at a company with a superior without any close family ties, he would react assertively, which would imprint the mistake on me, reducing the likelihood of repeating the same error.

◎ 对比细节扩充：根据上方给出的纲要进行全文扩充

1	Topic Sentence	Personally, **I would prefer employment at a company without any family ties.**
2	Rebut A	When working for a family member, the chances of being treated differently increase, so many abilities would not be fully developed.
3	Supports	Mistakes will be solved by a relative and help will be offered so that improvement stops. 细节扩充
4	Agree with B	In contrast, if the same mistake was made at a company with a superior without any close family ties, he would react assertively, which would imprint the mistake on me, reducing the likelihood of repeating the same error.
5	Supports	A strict workplace environment forces a worker to improve his abilities. 细节扩充
6	Conclusion	In this way, many abilities are refined, and more experience is gained, paving a path for a more prosperous career.

◎ **Possible Sample**

1	Topic Sentence	Personally, **I would prefer employment at a company without any family ties.**
2	Rebut A	When working for a family member, the chances of being treated differently increase, so many abilities would not be fully developed.
3	Supports	For instance, if I make a mistake during a particular task, a superior who is a relative may attempt to assist me by taking over the assignment instead of issuing a warning or punishment, thus the mistake I made would not leave a deep impression on me, and I would likely repeat the mistake, which would be detrimental to advancing a skill.
4	Agree with B	In contrast, if the same mistake was made at a company with a superior without any close family ties, he would react assertively, which would imprint the mistake on me, reducing the likelihood of repeating the same error.
5	Supports	A strict workplace environment without any special treatment is more likely to encourage a worker to stride in a direction that would lead to success, since many of his qualities would be tested, such as patience, diligence, or attentiveness.
6	Conclusion	In this way, many abilities are refined, and more experience is gained, paving a path for a more prosperous career.

实战 1 TG 35【Social Studies 话题】

◎ 结构展开：均匀支撑 A；反驳 B

> Your professor is teaching a class on **Social Studies**. Write a post responding to the professor's question. In your response you should:
>
> • express and support your opinion
>
> • make a contribution to the discussion
>
> An effective response will contain at least 100 words. You will have 10 minutes to write it.

Dr. Mallards:

In today's class, we are going to talk about how the government should spend its budget on building facilities. Before our class, I want you to think about two types of facilities proposed: an art museum and concert hall that can improve people's artistic and cultural appreciation; a swimming pool and playground that can serve as recreational functions. If you had to choose, which type do you think should be constructed and why?

Alex:

If we had to build public facilities to improve people's lives, I believe the purpose of entertainment should be considered the top priority. Since people are so engaged in their daily routines, they need something that can provide amusement, relaxation, or physical exercise. In addition, compared with art and culture, recreational venues can accommodate a larger population, which determines that building swimming pools or playgrounds can cater to the mass market better than museums or concerts.

Taylor:

I would choose the former that we should build museums or concert halls to improve people's appreciation for art. Just like Alex has said, people are so engaged in their daily routines, but it means, I think, they are living in a world filled with interests and vanities, which transforms them into machines. Therefore, they gradually forget about sympathy, aesthetic, and perception, all of which they used to have but now is numbed by hectic lifestyles.

◎ **Practice：** 根据下面的要求进行翻译

1	Topic Sentence	政府应该优先将预算用于建设游泳池和游乐场等基础设施，以提高大多数公民的基本福利和生活水平。 将句子译为英文：放右边	
2	Support A	在预算紧张和有限的情况下，政府首先应该考虑哪一种投入会让更多的人受益。 将句子译为英文：放右边	
3	Supports	几乎每天都有更多的人光顾游泳池和游乐场，以改善他们的健康或丰富他们的日常生活，政府优先推动这些设施的建设是值得且合理的。 将句子译为英文：放右边	
4	Rebut B	相反，在完成基础设施之前，建造美术馆和音乐厅实属浪费，因为在这种情况下普通公民的基本生活需求无法得到保障，更不用说欣赏艺术了，这是富人和上层社会满足基础需求后的第二选择。 将句子译为英文：放右边	
5	Supports	事实上，富有和受过教育的人也需要首先保障基本日常生活需求，然后才能追求他们的艺术和文化体验。 将句子译为英文：放右边	
6	Conclusion	除非基本的设施已经配备好了，不然政府在一个落后的城市建造美术馆、音乐厅这样的艺术设施是荒谬的。 将句子译为英文：放右边	

© Sample Response

1	Topic Sentence	政府应该优先将预算用于建设游泳池和游乐场等基础设施，以提高大多数公民的基本福利和生活水平。	**The government should prioritize spending its budget on building infrastructure like swimming pools and playgrounds in order to elevate the basic welfare and living standards of most citizens.**
2	Support A	在预算紧张和有限的情况下，政府首先应该考虑哪一种投入会让更多的人受益。	With a tight and limited budget, the government should, firstly, consider which installment would benefit more people.
3	Supports	几乎每天都有更多的人光顾游泳池和游乐场，以改善他们的健康或丰富他们的日常生活，政府优先推动这些设施的建设是值得且合理的。	Since swimming pools and playgrounds are commonly patronized by a larger population almost every day to improve their health or enrich their daily life, it would be worthwhile and rational for the government to promote their construction first.
4	Rebut B	相反，在完成基础设施之前，建造美术馆和音乐厅实属浪费，因为在这种情况下普通公民的基本生活需求无法得到保障，更不用说欣赏艺术了，这是富人和上层社会满足基础需求后的第二选择。	On the contrary, it will be wasteful to build art museums and concert halls before completing fundamental infrastructure because, under such conditions, the basic living demands of the average citizen cannot be guaranteed, let alone appreciate art, which is a secondary option for the affluent and privileged.
5	Supports	事实上，富有和受过教育的人也需要首先保障基本日常生活需求，然后才能追求他们的艺术和文化体验。	In fact, wealthy and educated people also need to secure their basic daily living requirements first and then pursue their artistic and cultural experiences.
6	Conclusion	除非基本的设施已经配备好了，不然政府在一个落后的城市建造美术馆、音乐厅这样的艺术设施是荒谬的。	It is ridiculous for the government to build arts facilities like art museums and concert halls in a less-developed city unless the basic infrastructure has been already equipped.

实战 2 TG 54【Social Studies 话题】

◎ 结构展开：无

> Your professor is teaching a class on Social Studies. Write a post responding to the professor's question. In your response you should:
>
> • express and support your opinion
>
> • make a contribution to the discussion
>
> An effective response will contain at least 100 words. You will have 10 minutes to write it.

Dr. Martin:

Last week, we discussed the advancements that scientific progress has brought us and concluded that new science and technology continue to evolve, addressing current challenges and paving the way for further improvements in the future. So here comes the question for the discussion board: Do you think that although new technology and science will continue to advance and improve people's life, the most significant improvement has been made?

Shelly:

The most game-changing improvements resulting from technology and science have already happened, such as historical breakthroughs like antibiotics and electricity that revolutionized our lives. These advancements tackled major problems and made a huge positive impact. While future advancements will undoubtedly occur, they are unlikely to match the magnitude and impact of these groundbreaking achievements.

Elvis:

We haven't seen the most significant improvement yet. Technology and science keep evolving, and we're on the brink of even more amazing discoveries. With emerging fields like artificial intelligence, space exploration, and renewable energy, there's enormous potential to reshape our lives in unimaginable ways. I believe that the future holds even greater transformations as we continue to push boundaries and tackle global challenges.

◎ **Practice** Ⅰ：根据下面的要求进行翻译和写作练习

Ⅰ. 中译英

Ⅱ. 针对三个分论点进行细节扩展写作练习

1	Topic Sentence	必须承认创新是一个持续的过程，每一步都建立在先前成就的基础上。因此，认为人类社会已经取得了最为实质性的突破还为时过早。 将句子译为英文：放右边	
2	Rebut A	乍一看，似乎 Shelly 的看法并没有什么问题，但深思之下发现，它既有逻辑谬误，也与事实相悖。 将句子译为英文：放右边	
3	Supports	Antibiotics have revolutionized healthcare and saved people, but they need to be developed. Electricity has transformed our life, and new energy sources that meet human needs should be developed. 细节扩充：写 2–4 句。 根据上方提示写 Evidence/Example/Fact/Detail，30–50 词的细节支撑！	
4	Support B	相反，我同意 Elvis 的观点，最显著的进步尚未到来。 将句子译为英文：放右边	
5	Supports	Technological and scientific advancements do not slow down. New development continues such as AI, renewable energy, genetic engineering. 细节扩充：写 2–4 句 根据上方提示写 Evidence/Example/Fact/Detail，30–50 词的细节支撑！	
6	Conclusion	这些新兴领域表明尽管已经取得非凡的进步，但它们并不是进步的顶峰。 将句子译为英文：放右边	

◎ **Practice Ⅱ：** 根据下面的要求进行中译英

1	Topic Sentence	必须承认创新是一个持续的过程，每一步都建立在先前成就的基础上。因此，认为人类社会已经取得了最为实质性的突破还为时过早。	**It is essential to acknowledge that innovation is a continuous process, and each step forward builds upon previous achievements. Therefore, it would be premature to assert that the most substantial improvement has been made.**
2	Rebut A	乍一看，似乎 Shelly 的看法并没有什么问题，但深思之下发现，它既有逻辑谬误，也与事实相悖。	It seems no shortage in Shelly's view at first sight, but it suffers from both logical and factual fallacies.
3	Supports	抗生素确实通过拯救无数生命和治疗曾经致命的传染病而彻底改变了医疗保健，然而抗生素耐药性的增加带来了重大挑战，随着时间的推移，一些抗生素的疗效会降低。电无疑改变了我们的生活方式，为我们的家庭、工业生产和技术设备供电。然而，太阳能和风能等可再生能源的发展正在重塑能源格局。 将句子译为英文：放右边	
4	Support B	相反，我同意 Elvis 的观点，最显著的进步尚未到来。	On the contrary, I agree with Elvis that the most significant improvement is yet to come.
5	Supports	科技进步的步伐没有减缓的迹象。研究人员不断突破界限，为紧迫的问题找到新的解决方案，并发现新的可能性。人工智能、可再生能源和基因工程的出现只是持续进步有望彻底改变人类生存领域的几个例子而已。 将句子译为英文：放右边	
6	Conclusion	这些新兴领域表明尽管已经取得非凡的进步，但它们并不是进步的顶峰。	These emerging fields suggest that even though substantial advancements have been achieved, they are not the definitive pinnacle of progress.

© **Sample Response**

1	Topic Sentence	必须承认创新是一个持续的过程，每一步都建立在先前成就的基础上。因此，认为人类社会已经取得了最为实质性的突破还为时过早。	**It is essential to acknowledge that innovation is a continuous process, and each step forward builds upon previous achievements. Therefore, it would be premature to assert that the most substantial improvement has been made.**
2	Rebut A	乍一看，似乎 Shelly 的看法并没有什么问题，但深思之下发现，它既有逻辑谬误，也与事实相悖。	It seems no shortage in Shelly's view at first sight, but it suffers from both logical and factual fallacies.
3	Supports	抗生素确实通过拯救无数生命和治疗曾经致命的传染病而彻底改变了医疗保健，然而抗生素耐药性的增加带来了重大挑战，随着时间的推移，一些抗生素的疗效会降低。电无疑改变了我们的生活方式，为我们的家庭、工业生产和技术设备供电。然而，太阳能和风能等可再生能源的发展正在重塑能源格局。	Antibiotics have indeed revolutionized healthcare by saving countless lives and treating once-deadly infections. However, the rise of antibiotic resistance poses a significant challenge, rendering some antibiotics less effective over time. Electricity has undoubtedly transformed the way we live, powering our homes, industries, and technological devices. However, the development of renewable energy sources, such as solar and wind power, is reshaping the energy landscape.
4	Support B	相反，我同意 Elvis 的观点，最显著的进步尚未到来。	On the contrary, I agree with Elvis that the most significant improvement is yet to come.
5	Supports	科技进步的步伐没有减缓的迹象。研究人员不断突破界限，为紧迫的问题找到新的解决方案，并发现新的可能性。人工智能、可再生能源和基因工程的出现只是持续进步有望彻底改变人类生存领域的几个例子而已。	The pace of technological and scientific advancements shows no signs of slowing down. Researchers are constantly pushing boundaries, finding new solutions to pressing problems, and uncovering novel possibilities. The advent of artificial intelligence, renewable energy, and genetic engineering are just a few examples of areas where ongoing progress promises to revolutionize human existence.
6	Conclusion	这些新兴领域表明尽管已经取得非凡的进步，但它们并不是进步的顶峰。	These emerging fields suggest that even though substantial advancements have been achieved, they are not the definitive pinnacle of progress.

实战 3 TG 55【Sociology 话题】

◎ 结构展开：无

> Your professor is teaching a class on Sociology. Write a post responding to the professor's question. In your response you should:
>
> • express and support your opinion
>
> • make a contribution to the discussion
>
> An effective response will contain at least 100 words. You will have 10 minutes to write it.

Dr. Charles:

Career choices made by younger individuals are a critical issue that deserves careful consideration, with some of them thinking about it from an early age. This process would be influenced by their passions, interests, and the guidance they receive from mentors, parents, and educational institutions, so before our next class, I want you to consider such a question: Is it better for children to choose jobs that are similar to their parents' jobs or to choose jobs that are very different from their parents' jobs?

Mia:

I believe that growing up in an environment where parents are engaged in a particular profession provides unique advantages. Children may have early exposure to the industry, gain insights from their parents' experiences, and benefit from the knowledge and connections that their parents have built. Following their parents' footsteps can provide a sense of familiarity and potential career opportunities, leading to a smoother transition and higher chances of success.

Daniel:

Individuality and personal exploration should be encouraged. Choosing a different career path allows children to pursue their own passions, interests, and talents, rather than feeling constrained or obligated to follow a predetermined path. It encourages them to think independently, explore diverse opportunities, and discover their own unique strengths.

◎ **Practice** Ⅰ：根据文章框架进行全文写作

注意用对比式结构展开

1	Topic Sentence	
2	Rebut A	
3	Supports	
4	Support B	
5	Supports	
6	Conclusion	

◎ **Practice** Ⅱ：根据文章框架写支撑细节

1	Topic Sentence		**Embracing diverse career choices not only fosters personal growth but also enriches the fabric of our collective endeavors.**
2	Rebut A		It is true that children choosing jobs similar to their parents' jobs often possess the advantages of what Mia has said. However, this viewpoint overlooks the potential drawbacks of limiting one's development opportunities and inhibiting individual growth.
3	Supports	细节扩充：写 2–4 句。 根据前文观点写 Evidence/Example/ Fact/Detail，30–50 词的细节支撑！	
4	Support B		Conversely, I would say a different job from their old ones not only allows children to pursue their own passions or interests like Daniel mentioned, but it can also promote a diverse society.
5	Supports	细节扩充：写 2–4 句。 根据前文观点写 Evidence/Example/ Fact/Detail，30–50 词的细节支撑！	
6	Conclusion		Ultimately, by following their own unique paths, individuals can lead more fulfilling lives and make meaningful contributions to the world around them.

◎ **Practice Ⅲ**：根据下面要求进行翻译

1	Topic Sentence	接受多样的职业选择不仅有助于个人成长，还丰富了社会结构。	**Embracing diverse career choices not only fosters personal growth but also enriches the fabric of our society.**
2	Rebut A	确实孩子们选择与父母相似的工作往往具有 Mia 所说的优势。然而这种观点忽略了一些潜在的缺点，它限制个人发展的机会，并且还抑制个人成长。	It is true that children choosing jobs similar to their parents' jobs often possess the advantages of what Mia has said. However, this viewpoint overlooks the potential drawbacks of limiting one's development opportunities and inhibiting individual growth.
3	Supports	完全严格跟随父母职业步伐，孩子们可能会在不经意间扼杀自己的创造力，并限制他们接触其他更符合他们激情和天赋的领域。选择类似父母职业的工作也会导致缺乏多样的经历，阻碍个人发展，并可能使个人的抱负无法实现。 *将句子译为英文：放右边*	
4	Support B	相反，我认为不同于父母职业的工作，不仅可以让孩子们像 Denial 所提到的那样追求自己的激情或兴趣，还可以促进一个多元的社会。	Conversely, I would say a different job from their old ones not only allows children to pursue their own passions or interests like Daniel mentioned, but it can also promote a diverse society.
5	Supports	通过追求不同的职业，个人将各种经验、想法和观点带到各自的领域。这有利于丰富合作方式，培养创造力，并带来更大的社会进步。以这种方式产生的新观点挑战传统的思维，打破障碍，开辟新的创新可能性。 *将句子译为英文：放右边*	
6	Conclusion	最终，通过走自己独特的道路，个体的人生会更加充实，并为周围的世界做出有意义的贡献。	Ultimately, by following their own unique paths, individuals can lead more fulfilling lives and make meaningful contributions to the world around them.

◎ **Sample Response**

1	Topic Sentence	接受多样的职业选择不仅有助于个人成长，还丰富了社会结构。	**Embracing diverse career choices not only fosters personal growth but also enriches the fabric of our society.**
2	Rebut A	确实孩子们选择与父母相似的工作往往具有 Mia 所说的优势。然而这种观点忽略了一些潜在的缺点，它限制个人发展的机会，并且还抑制个人成长。	It is true that children choosing jobs similar to their parents' jobs often possess the advantages of what Mia has said. However, this viewpoint overlooks the potential drawbacks of limiting one's development opportunities and inhibiting individual growth.
3	Supports	完全严格跟随父母职业步伐，孩子们可能会在不经意间扼杀自己的创造力，并限制他们接触其他更符合他们激情和天赋的领域。选择类似父母职业的工作也会导致缺乏多样的经历，阻碍个人发展，并可能使个人的抱负无法实现。	By strictly adhering to parental footsteps, children may inadvertently stifle their own creativity and limit their exposure to alternative fields that could better align with their passions and talents. Choosing similar jobs can also lead to a lack of diverse experiences, hindering personal development and potentially leaving individuals unfulfilled.
4	Support B	相反，我认为不同于父母职业的工作，不仅可以让孩子们像 Denial 所提到的那样追求自己的激情或兴趣，还可以促进一个多元的社会。	Conversely, I would say a different job from their old ones not only allows children to pursue their own passions or interests like Daniel mentioned, but it can also promote a diverse society.
5	Supports	通过追求不同的职业，个人将各种经验、想法和观点带到各自的领域。这有利于丰富合作方式，培养创造力，并带来更大的社会进步。以这种方式产生的新观点挑战传统的思维,打破障碍,开辟新的创新可能性。	By pursuing different professions, individuals bring a variety of experiences, ideas, and perspectives to their respective fields. This enriches collaboration, fosters creativity, and leads to greater societal progress. The new born viewpoints in this way challenge conventional thinking, break down barriers, and open up new possibilities for innovation.
6	Conclusion	最终，通过走自己独特的道路，个体的人生会更加充实，并为周围的世界做出有意义的贡献。	Ultimately, by following their own unique paths, individuals can lead more fulfilling lives and make meaningful contributions to the world around them.

实战 4 TG 56 【Education 话题】

◎ 结构展开：无

> Your professor is teaching a class on Education. Write a post responding to the professor's question. In your response you should:
>
> • express and support your opinion
>
> • make a contribution to the discussion
>
> An effective response will contain at least 100 words. You will have 10 minutes to write it.

Dr. Matthew:

Teachers serve as facilitators who guide and support students in their learning journey. They design and deliver lessons, create engaging learning environments, and provide the necessary resources to foster student growth and development. Before the class next week, I would want you to think about such a question: Do teachers now have more influence on their students than they did in the past?

Ava:

Teachers today have a greater influence on their students compared to the past. Advancements in teaching methodologies and technologies provide teachers with innovative tools and techniques to engage students and make learning more influential. Additionally, increased access to information and resources allows teachers to deliver a more comprehensive and dynamic education.

Andrew:

I believe that several factors have decreased the influence of teachers today. One factor is the increasing influence of external sources of information and media, which compete with teachers for students' attention and shape their perspectives. Moreover, social changes, such as the increased prevalence of dual-income households, reduced time for parent-teacher involvement, and the growing emphasis on standardized testing, have shifted some of the responsibility for students' education away from teachers.

◎ **Practice Ⅰ**：根据文章框架进行全文写作

注意用对比式结构展开

1	Topic Sentence	
2	Support A	
3	Supports	
4	Rebut B	
5	Supports	
6	Conclusion	

◎ **Practice Ⅱ**：根据文章框架写支撑细节

1	Topic Sentence		**While it remains a controversial issue, I do believe that the influence of teachers on students is undergoing an evolutionary process.**
2	Support A		Just like what Ava said, teachers today are better equipped to understand and address the diverse needs of their students.
3	Supports	细节扩充：写2–4句。 根据前文观点写 Evidence/Example/ Fact/Detail，30–50 词的细节支撑！	
4	Rebut B		Regarding Andrew's statement, I hold a divergent perspective.
5	Supports	细节扩充：写2–4句。 根据前文观点写 Evidence/Example/ Fact/Detail，30–50 词的细节支撑！	
6	Conclusion		In conclusion, teachers did hold significant influence in the past, and the evolving nature of education has provided new opportunities for teachers to have an even greater impact on their students.

◎ **Practice Ⅲ**：根据下面要求进行翻译

中译英

1	Topic Sentence	虽然这依然是一个有争议的问题，但我相信教师对学生的影响正在发生变化。	**While it remains a controversial issue, I do believe that the influence of teachers on students is undergoing an evolutionary process.**
2	Support A	正如 Ava 所说，如今的教师能够更好地理解和满足学生的各种需求。	Just like what Ava said, teachers today are better equipped to understand and address the diverse needs of their students.
3	Supports	除此之外，现在教师们采用了综合的方法，解决学生社交和情绪状态方面的问题，提升其价值，并培养他们的基本生活技能。通过创造积极和兼容并包的课堂环境，教师可以塑造学生的性格，灌输对学习的热爱，并激励他们成为对社会有积极贡献的人。 将句子译为英文：放右边	
4	Rebut B	关于 Andrew 的说法，我持有不同的见解。	Regarding Andrew's statement, I hold a divergent perspective.
5	Supports	越来越容易获得信息，这不应被视为对教师影响力的一种稀释，而应被视为老师指导和帮助学生巡览这一广阔知识版图的一个机会。教师拥有专业知识和批判性思维技巧，可以帮助学生从海量的信息内容中辨别可靠、准确的信息。他们教学生如何评估信息来源、分析信息和使用批判性思维，从而使其能够作出明智的决定并形成全面的观点。 将句子译为英文：放右边	
6	Conclusion	总之，教师在过去确实具有重大影响力，而教育的不断演变为教师提供了新的机会，使其能够对学生产生更大的影响。	In conclusion, teachers did hold significant influence in the past, and the evolving nature of education has provided new opportunities for teachers to have an even greater impact on their students.

◎ **Possible Sample**

1	Topic Sentence	虽然这依然是一个有争议的问题，但我相信教师对学生的影响正在发生变化。	While it remains a controversial issue, I do believe that the influence of teachers on students is undergoing an evolutionary process.
2	Support A	正如 Ava 所说，如今的教师能够更好地理解和满足学生的各种需求。	Just like what Ava said, teachers today are better equipped to understand and address the diverse needs of their students.
3	Supports	除此之外，现在教师们采用了综合的方法，解决学生社交和情绪状态方面的问题，提升其价值，并培养他们的基本生活技能。通过创造积极和兼容并包的课堂环境，教师可以塑造学生的性格，灌输对学习的热爱，并激励他们成为对社会有积极贡献的人。	More than that, teachers now embrace a holistic approach, addressing students' social and emotional well-being, promoting values, and developing essential life skills. By cultivating a positive and inclusive classroom environment, teachers can shape students' character, instill a love for learning, and inspire them to become active contributors to society.
4	Rebut B	关于 Andrew 的说法，我持有不同的见解。	Regarding Andrew's statement, I hold a divergent perspective.
5	Supports	越来越容易获得信息，这不应被视为对教师影响力的一种稀释，而应被视为老师指导和帮助学生巡览这一广阔知识版图的一个机会。教师拥有专业知识和批判性思维技巧，可以帮助学生从海量的信息内容中辨别可靠、准确的信息。他们教学生如何评估信息来源、分析信息和使用批判性思维，从而使其能够作出明智的决定并形成全面的观点。	The increasing availability of information sources should not be seen as a dilution of teachers' influence but rather an opportunity for them to guide and help students navigate this vast landscape of knowledge. Teachers possess the expertise and critical thinking skills to help students discern reliable and accurate information from the overwhelming sea of content available. They teach students how to evaluate sources, analyze information, and think critically, enabling them to make informed decisions and form well-rounded perspectives.
6	Conclusion	总之，教师在过去确实具有重大影响力，而教育的不断演变为教师提供了新的机会，使其能够对学生产生更大的影响。	In conclusion, teachers did hold significant influence in the past, and the evolving nature of education has provided new opportunities for teachers to have an even greater impact on their students.

★ 写法三：提出新想法

案例分析与例文 1 TG 03【Educational Science 话题】

◎ 结构展开：反驳 A 和 B，提出新想法 C，并进行支撑

> Your professor is teaching a class on Educational Science. Write a post responding to the professor's question. In your response, you should:
>
> • express and support your opinion
>
> • make a contribution to the discussion
>
> An effective response will contain at least 100 words. You will have 10 minutes to write it.

Dr. Ferguson:

Over the next few weeks, we are going to look at various methods of improving the quality of education for school children, more specifically, the approaches teachers can take to prevent students from engaging in activities that are detrimental to their education process. So before we dive into the literature, I'd like to know how you would handle this recent phenomenon: More and more students are completing assignments by copying each other's work. What do you think is the most effective way to prevent or reduce this from occurring?

Ray:

Teachers should ask parents to be more involved in their children's education, specifically by asking them to supervise their children when they are doing their homework. After parents have confirmed that their kids have completed their assignments independently, they can sign the work to reassure the teachers.

Mary:

I believe that a degree of punishment can deter a proportion of students from copying others. For example, when teachers discover a student's work to be plagiarism, they can revoke their grades and give them detention after class. When other students see this, they'll think twice about completing assignments using other people's work.

◎ Outlining of giving new idea with rebut to both ideas

Topic : There are fundamental flaws with Ray and Mary's suggestions.

New idea : A more practical and less sensitive approach to preventing students from copying each other is to modify their assignments.

◎ **Sample Response of Full Score**

　　I think there are fundamental flaws with Ray and Mary's suggestions. Not many parents can afford the time to supervise their children doing homework since they have many other obligations, such as work and household chores, so this method is impractical for many families. And when it comes to punishment, it is an extremely risky business. If the degree of punishment is not cautiously calculated, punitive measures might inflict adverse effects on the students, like losing confidence, self-doubt, or bullying from others. I believe a more practical and less sensitive approach to preventing students from copying each other is to modify their assignments. Teachers can spend time devising homework that encompasses more diversity. For example, a math teacher can assign five or six sets of practice to his class and scatter the sets among all the students, thus making it much more inconvenient for students to copy one another. Similar methods can be applied to most academic subjects, and when students discover that copying homework spends more effort than doing it themselves, they are less likely to succumb to its temptation. As long as teachers are willing to spend time and effort composing diversified homework assignments, methods such as the above can effectively alleviate the problem.

◎ 结构展开拆解

1	Topic Sentence	**I think there are fundamental flaws with Ray and Mary's suggestions.**
2	Rebut A	Not many parents can afford the time to supervise their children doing homework since they have many other obligations, such as work and household chores, so this method is impractical for many families.
3	Rebut B	And when it comes to punishment, it is an extremely risky business. If the degree of punishment is not cautiously calculated, punitive measures might inflict adverse effects on the students, like losing confidence, self-doubt, or bullying from others.
4	New Idea C	I believe a more practical and less sensitive approach to preventing students from copying each other is to modify their assignments. Teachers can spend time devising homework that encompasses more diversity.
5	Support	For example, a math teacher can assign five or six sets of practice to his class and scatter the sets among all the students, thus making it much more inconvenient for students to copy one another. Similar methods can be applied to most academic subjects, and when students discover that copying homework spends more effort than doing it themselves, they are less likely to succumb to its temptation.
6	Conclusion	As long as teachers are willing to spend time and effort composing diversified homework assignments, methods such as the above can effectively alleviate the problem.

◎ **Construction of giving new ideas or solutions.**

1. Topic Sentence—Response to the prompt

2. Rebut person A—point out the shortcoming of the opinion

3. Rebut person B—point out the shortcoming of the opinion

4. Put forth an opinion—give new ideas

5. Supports—Explanation, exemplification and /or details

6. Conclusion

案例分析与例文 2 TG 46【Social Studies 话题】

◎ 结构展开：反驳 A + 反驳 B + 提出 C 并进行支撑

Your professor is teaching a class on Social Studies. Write a post responding to the professor's question. In your response you should:

• express and support your opinion

• make a contribution to the discussion

An effective response will contain at least 100 words. You will have 10 minutes to write it.

Dr. Selma:

In the last class, we concluded how the level of motivation and initiative of employees determine the overall productivity of a company. Today we're going to make an extension to this topic and talk about what can give birth to such motivations and initiatives, so before class begins, I want you to think about this question: What is the most important factor that help an employee work productively?

Sonia:

As far as I'm concerned, I like an environment that subjects me to no noise and no distractions, which, I think, would be a preference for most people. When people are dealing with work that requires creativity or rigorous thinking, a disturbance would ruin all previous efforts. On the contrary, a quiet environment free of noises enables a smooth process of such work and thus saves time.

Wade:

I believe most workers work for money, and that is a fact we always ignore. So if you ask me what makes a worker work faster, I would say the answer is money. Knowing what you will get for what you are doing can be the most basic stimulus that expedites the overall working process since an economic reward is a quantitative measurement of a person's value and a direct change to his situation.

◎ **Outlining of giving new idea with rebut to both ideas**

> Topic : Creating a distraction-free environment is not easy while monetary stimulus may lead to exhausted career.

> New idea : Incentives such as extra vacation days, gift packages, or reduced healthcare rates rather than money stimulate one's motivation.

◎ **全文扩充**：根据上方给出的纲要进行全文扩充

1	Topic Sentence Rebut A	
2	Supports	
3	Rebut B	
4	Supports	
5	New idea C Supports	
6	Conclusion	

◎ **Sample Response of Full Score**

1	Topic Sentence Rebut A	**Minimizing distractions and disruptions in the workplace can promote higher-quality work and increase productivity. However, creating a distraction-free environment is not always easy.**
2	Supports	In many workplaces, a variety of factors can contribute to distractions and interruptions, including loud noises, interruptions from coworkers, and frequent meetings and deadlines. Employers need to take steps to minimize these distractions, such as providing noise-canceling headphones, creating designated quiet areas, and establishing clear guidelines for interruptions and meetings.
3	Rebut B	In addition to create a distraction-free environment, employers can offer incentives, not just monetary ones, to workers to stimulate their motivation.
4	Supports	While financial gains are favorable, if it's the only reward for employees, it may lead to exhaustion, thus workers may lose sight of other valuable meanings of their jobs, such as the sense of accomplishment and self-worth.
5	New Idea C Support	Other incentives such as extra vacation days, gift packages, or reduced healthcare rates not only give workers satisfaction from doing their jobs but also help them balance their personal lives, which puts them in a better mental and physical state to tackle with future challenges.
6	Conclusion	Therefore, company administrators should consider both the professional environment and the private lives of their employees when devising policies to improve productivity.

实战 1 TG 51【Sociology 话题】

◎ 结构展开：无

> Your professor is teaching a class on Sociology. Write a post responding to the professor's question. In your response, you should:
>
> • express and support your opinion
>
> • make a contribution to the discussion
>
> An effective response will contain at least 100 words. You will have 10 minutes to write it.

Dr. Bertrand:

As discussed in our previous class, most of us live in interconnected communities with many social ties that form the fundamental composition of our social lives. Community groups provide a sense of belonging and companionship, and within them, we find security, love, friendship, and so on. Before we further examine the effects of social interactions, I'd like you to respond to this question: Which activity would you prefer to do with a group of people the most? Why?

Peter:

For me, the most suitable group activity would be doing homework. Having others who are engaged in the same task as you makes the assignment more interesting because you can share ideas or give each other suggestions. Last weekend, I had a group study session with a few of my classmates, and it was very insightful!

Florence:

My choice would be to listen to music with friends. I think it's a fun way to strengthen the bond between people since we can all dance and sing to the same tunes. Many of my fondest memories include singing with friends in a car during a road trip and bobbing our heads at a rock concert.

◎ **Practice** Ⅰ：根据下面要求进行翻译

中译英

1	Topic Sentence	写作业和听音乐可能符合 Peter 和 Florence 社交活动的偏好，但我认为这些活动还是单独做更好。 将句子译为英文：放右边	
2	Rebut A	当年轻人聚在一起完成作业时，可能会失去对主要任务的关注，因为他们可能会谈论他们觉得有趣的话题，比如游戏、电影或体育。 将句子译为英文：放右边	
3	Rebut B	此外，听音乐应该是一个私人化的过程，因为人们可能有不同的音乐品味。当人们独自欣赏音乐时，他们不必担心他人的偏好。 将句子译为英文：放右边	
4	New Idea C	餐桌是我喜欢他人陪伴的理想地方。 将句子译为英文：放右边	
5	Supports	用餐时的氛围提供了绝佳的机会去进行有趣的对话、与老朋友叙旧，或者增进人际关系，尤其是在一个优雅的场所。此外，人们不必担心彼此的食物偏好，因为每个人都可以只点自己的菜，从而会更加关注面前的人。而且，大多数用餐聚会的目的是玩得开心，与他人互动，因此不用担心没有关注到特定的事情。 将句子译为英文：放右边	
6	Conclusion	考虑到这些优势，与他人共享一顿饭是我可以与他人一起做的最优先的事情。 将句子译为英文：放右边	

◎ Possible Sample

1	Topic Sentence	写作业和听音乐可能符合 Peter 和 Florence 社交活动的偏好，但我认为这些活动还是单独做更好。	**Doing homework and listening to music may suit the preference of Peter and Florence as social activities, but I find them more appropriate when done independently.**
2	Rebut A	当年轻人聚在一起完成作业时，可能会失去对主要任务的关注，因为他们可能会谈论他们觉得有趣的话题，比如游戏、电影或体育。	When young people gather to complete homework together, they might lose focus on the primary task as they are likely to talk about topics that they find interesting, like gaming, movies, or sports.
3	Rebut B	此外，听音乐应该是一个私人化的过程，因为人们可能有不同的音乐品味。当人们独自欣赏音乐时，他们不必担心他人的偏好。	Also, listening to music should be a private process since people are likely to have diverse musical tastes. When people enjoy music alone, they need not be concerned about the preference of others.
4	New Idea C	餐桌是我喜欢他人陪伴的理想地方。	An ideal setting for me to fully appreciate the company of others is the dinner table.
5	Supports	用餐时的氛围提供了绝佳的机会去进行有趣的对话、与老朋友叙旧，或者增进人际关系，尤其是在一个优雅的场所。此外，人们不必担心彼此的食物偏好，因为每个人都可以只点自己的菜，从而会更加关注面前的人。而且，大多数用餐聚会的目的是玩得开心，与他人互动，因此不用担心没有关注到特定的事情。	The atmosphere of mealtimes provides, especially at a classy venue, the perfect opportunity to have intriguing conversations, catch up with old friends, or improve relationships. In addition, people would not have to worry about each other's food preferences since they can simply order their own dishes, hence, giving more attention to the people in front of them. Furthermore, the purpose of most meal gatherings is to have a good time and interact with others, so the concern for the loss of focus on a particular task would be absent.
6	Conclusion	考虑到这些优势，与他人共享一顿饭是我可以与他人一起做的最优先的事情。	Given these advantages, sharing a meal with others makes the top of my list of things I could do with other people.

实战 2 TG 52【College Prep Class 话题】

◎ 结构展开：无

> Your professor is teaching a **College Prep Class**. Write a post responding to the professor's question. In your response, you should:
>
> • express and support your opinion
>
> • make a contribution to the discussion
>
> An effective response will contain at least 100 words. You will have 10 minutes to write it.

Dr. Wang:

Most of you enrolled in university or college to maximize your potential so you can further pursue your passions and endeavors. In other words, the success of your university education will play a crucial role in your future. With such importance, it's essential to help new students recognize the factors that can aid their educational success. The question I'd like you to answer for this discussion board is this: What do you think is the most important factor for a student to succeed in university or college?

Celeste:

I imagine that university life would present many new challenges to students who first enter. It involves facing not only more difficult academic work but also a relatively independent lifestyle. In this case, the support and encouragement from friends and family can alleviate the anxiety or stress of a student, reinforcing their determination and motivation to succeed.

Sheldon:

I think finding a tutor, a senior at the same university, to help you face various problems during university life is the best way to ensure success. They have already experienced many issues that might be fresh to you, which enables them to give you the most practical advice to overcome potential challenges.

◎ **Practice** Ⅰ: 根据下面的要求进行翻译和写作练习

Ⅰ. 中译英

Ⅱ. 针对三个分论点进行细节扩展写作练习

1	Topic Sentence	依靠他人、朋友、家人或高年级学生帮助并不是高等教育成功的最重要因素。 将句子译为英文：放右边	
2	Rebut A	Prevent students from being self-sufficient and independent. 内容扩充：写 1–2 句。 根据上方提示写 15–30 词的内容！	
3	Rebut B	Campus tutors are busy/unlikely to meet students' need. 内容扩充：写 1–2 句。 根据上方提示写 15–30 词的内容！	
4	New Idea C	我相信高中教育打下的扎实的基础是在大学取得优异成绩的最关键因素。 将句子译为英文：放右边	
5	Supports	Receive fundamental knowledge/prepare for college. Build positive habits/useful for future education and career. 细节扩充：写 2–4 句。 根据上方提示写 Evidence/Example/Fact/Detail，30–50 词的细节支撑！	
6	Conclusion	因此，总的来说，依靠自己取得成功是更可行和合理的，这始于一个人进入大学之前，而不是之后。 将句子译为英文：放右边	

◎ **Practice** Ⅱ：根据下面的要求进行翻译

中译英

1	Topic Sentence	依靠他人、朋友、家人或高年级学生帮助并不是高等教育成功的最重要因素。	**Relying on the help of others, friends, family, or senior students, is not the most important factor to the success of tertiary education.**
2	Rebut A	朋友和家人可能会提供安慰，帮助学生缓解情绪压力，但也会剥夺学生变得更加自力更生和独立的机会。 将句子译为英文：放右边	
3	Rebut B	此外，学校的导师很可能专注于自己的学术兴趣，因此他们不太可能在你需要的时候帮助你。 将句子译为英文：放右边	
4	New Idea C	我相信高中教育打下的扎实的基础是在大学取得优异成绩的最关键因素。	I believe a solid foundation of high school education acts as the most critical factor in achieving excellence in university.
5	Supports	首先，当学生对高中期间教给他们的基础知识有了充分的理解时，他们理解和吸收大学课程中的新信息就不会很费力了。其次，积极的学习习惯通常在高中教育期间养成，例如记笔记、学习日程表和专注力，这些使得大学的学习更加得心应手。 将句子译为英文：放右边	
6	Conclusion	因此，总的来说，依靠自己取得成功是更可行和合理的，这始于一个人进入大学之前，而不是之后。	So, generally speaking, it is more feasible and rational to depend on oneself for one's own success, and that begins before one enters college, not after.

© Sample Response

1	Topic Sentence	依靠他人、朋友、家人或高年级学生帮助并不是高等教育成功的最重要因素。	**Relying on the help of others, friends, family, or senior students, is not the most important factor to the success of tertiary education.**
2	Rebut A	朋友和家人可能会提供安慰，帮助学生缓解情绪压力，但也会剥夺学生变得更加自力更生和独立的机会。	Friends and family members may provide the comfort that helps students mitigate their emotional stress, but it also takes away the chance for a student to be more self-sufficient and independent.
3	Rebut B	此外，学校的导师很可能专注于自己的学术兴趣，因此他们不太可能在你需要的时候帮助你。	Also, campus tutors are most likely occupied by their own academic interests, thus, they are unlikely to be at your service whenever you need them.
4	New Idea C	我相信高中教育打下的扎实的基础是在大学取得优异成绩的最关键因素。	I believe a solid foundation of high school education acts as the most critical factor in achieving excellence in university.
5	Supports	首先，当学生对高中期间教给他们的基础知识有了充分的理解时，他们理解和吸收大学课程中的新信息就不会很费力了。其次，积极的学习习惯通常在高中教育期间养成，例如记笔记、学习日程表和专注力，这些使得大学的学习更加得心应手。	Firstly, when a student has a firm understanding of the fundamental knowledge taught to them during high school, they will have less trouble comprehending and absorbing new information from college lectures. Secondly, positive learning habits are usually cultivated during high school education, such as note-taking, study schedules, and attentiveness, which makes the later learning process in college much more proficient.
6	Conclusion	因此，总的来说，依靠自己取得成功是更可行和合理的，这始于一个人进入大学之前，而不是之后。	So, generally speaking, it is more feasible and rational to depend on oneself for one's own success, and that begins before one enters college, not after.

实战 3 TG 53【Education 话题】

◎ 结构展开：无

> Your professor is teaching a class on **Education**. Write a post responding to the professor's question. In your response, you should:
> • express and support your opinion
> • make a contribution to the discussion
> An effective response will contain at least 100 words. You will have 10 minutes to write it.

Dr. Greenwell:

Last week, we looked at lots of different materials on teaching. We read various methods of improving teaching abilities, especially for high school teachers, and their effects on the students and the teachers. We all know that the outcome of education largely depends on the capability of teachers, so I want you to answer this question for the class discussion board: Which ability do you think would be the most important for a high school teacher? Why?

Jordan:

Most high school students are confused and uncertain about their future, so I think teachers should have the ability to help them make choices and plan for their life after high school. I was very fortunate to have had wonderful counseling from my high school teacher who encouraged me to choose the major I'm currently studying.

Erica:

One of the most important things we take from our education should be the ability to learn on our own under any given circumstance. That's why I think a high school teacher has to know how to teach their students to learn outside of the classroom. When they graduate from high school, whether they choose to enter the workforce or pursue higher education, this ability will be critical to their success.

◎ **Practice Ⅰ**：根据文章框架进行全文写作

注意用对比式结构展开。

1	Topic Sentence	
2	Rebut A	
3	Rebut B	
4	New Idea C	
5	Supports	
6	Conclusion	

◎ **Practice Ⅱ**：根据文章框架写支撑细节

1	Topic Sentence		**Although Jordan and Erica both present good ideas, their proposals have certain limitations.**
2	Rebut A	内容扩充：写 1–2 句。 根据上方提示写 15–30 词的内容！	
3	Rebut B	内容扩充：写 1–2 句。 根据上方提示写 15–30 词的内容！	
4	New Idea C		In my opinion, the most important skill for a high school teacher is versatility, specifically, the ability to identify each student's distinct problem and provide help accordingly.
5	Supports	细节扩充：写 2–4 句。 根据前文观点写 Evidence/Example/Fact/Detail，30–50 词的细节支撑！	
6	Conclusion		High school teachers are the last line of defense before students take on the world on their own, so it is imperative for teachers to recognize the specific problem a student may have and offer them corresponding assistance or find those who can help them.

◎ **Practice Ⅲ**：根据下面的要求进行翻译

1	Topic Sentence	尽管 Jordan 和 Erica 都提出了好的想法，但他们的建议有一定的局限性。	**Although Jordan and Erica both present good ideas, their proposals have certain limitations.**
2	Rebut A	给学生建议并帮助他们规划未来是必要的，但这项工作应该留给学生辅导员，因为他们对学生有更全面的了解，而老师可能只看到学生在少数科目上的表现。 将句子译为英文：放右边	
3	Rebut B	至于独立学习的能力，这种能力是自主发展的，而不是通过教授获得的。有些人学习所看见的事物，有些人则凭经验学习，还有一些人可能在犯错的过程中学习。当学生逐渐长大成人，他们会发现适合自己的学习方法。 将句子译为英文：放右边	
4	New Idea C	在我看来，对于一名高中教师来说，最重要的是具有多样的技能，特别是识别每个学生的特殊问题并提供相应帮助。	In my opinion, the most important skill for a high school teacher is versatility, specifically, the ability to identify each student's distinct problem and provide help accordingly.
5	Supports	每个学生都有自己独特的方式，这也意味着他们会在不同的领域里遇到一些困难。例如，内向的学生可能难以与他人交流，有的学生可能会发现某些科目学习起来很累，也有的学生可能很难集中精力完成任务。 将句子译为英文：放右边	
6	Conclusion	高中教师是学生独立面对世界之前的最后一道防线，因此，教师必须认识到学生可能存在的具体问题，并为他们提供相应的帮助或找到能够帮助他们的人。	High school teachers are the last line of defense before students take on the world on their own, so it is imperative for teachers to recognize the specific problem a student may have and offer them corresponding assistance or find those who can help them.

◎ **Possible Sample**

1	Topic Sentence	尽管 Jordan 和 Erica 都提出了好的想法，但他们的建议有一定的局限性。	**Although Jordan and Erica both present good ideas, their proposals have certain limitations.**
2	Rebut A	给学生建议并帮助他们规划未来是必要的，但这项工作应该留给学生辅导员，因为他们对学生有更全面的了解，而老师可能只看到学生在少数科目上的表现。	Giving advice and helping students plan their future is necessary, but that job should be left to student counselors since they have a more complete perception of the students, whereas, teachers may only see student performance in a few subjects.
3	Rebut B	至于独立学习的能力，这种能力是自主发展的，而不是通过教授获得的。有些人学习所看见的事物，有些人则凭经验学习，还有一些人可能在犯错的过程中学习。当学生逐渐长大成人，他们会发现适合自己的学习方法。	And as for the ability to learn independently, this ability is rather self-developed than taught. Some are visual learners, some learn through experience, and others may learn by making mistakes. Students discover their suitable method of learning as they mature into adults.
4	New Idea C	在我看来，对于一名高中教师来说，最重要的是具有多样的技能，特别是识别每个学生的特殊问题并提供相应帮助。	In my opinion, the most important skill for a high school teacher is versatility, specifically, the ability to identify each student's distinct problem and provide help accordingly.
5	Supports	每个学生都有自己独特的方式，这也意味着他们会在不同的领域里遇到一些困难。例如，内向的学生可能难以与他人交流，有的学生可能会发现某些科目学习起来很累，也有的学生可能很难集中精力完成任务。	Each student is unique in their own way, which also means they experience difficulties in different areas. For instance, an introverted student may have difficulty communicating with others, a student may find certain subjects very exhausting to learn, or perhaps, a student may have a hard time concentrating on a task.
6	Conclusion	高中教师是学生独立面对世界之前的最后一道防线，因此，教师必须认识到学生可能存在的具体问题，并为他们提供相应的帮助或找到能够帮助他们的人。	High school teachers are the last line of defense before students take on the world on their own, so it is imperative for teachers to recognize the specific problem a student may have and offer them corresponding assistance or find those who can help them.

很多人学会了框架与结构，展开思维顺畅了，但还是写不出文章，或者能写出来却写不好。学过同样课程，悟性和吸收能力也都差不多，但成绩却有高有低。归根结底，这些无法取得高分的人是在写作语言的三个维度（1. 语言逻辑；2. 句子扩展与句式使用；3. 恰当地使句子内部意群具有逻辑性）上没有把能力提升上来。本章将着重讲解如何从文章结构、句、词的角度提升语言能力。

Goal: To make our sentences more informative and logic.

2.1 语言逻辑

好作文里任何一个词或句子都有它的写作目的与作用！

★ 句内逻辑

好句分析

句子内部以单词和短语为单位，按组织规则将它们串起来，让它们具备内在的逻辑，从而准确地表达思想。我们可以通过下面选自满分例文的句子来理解意群之间内在的逻辑性。

© **Sample Sentence 1**

In contrast, if the same mistake was made at a company with a superior without any close family ties, he would react assertively, which would imprint the mistake on me, reducing the likelihood of repeating the same error.

句内逻辑链分析：

从句子内部来看，可分为四大意群：

In contrast, if the same mistake was made at a company with a superior without any close family ties, [前提] he would react assertively, [事件] which would imprint the mistake on me,[结果] reducing the likelihood of repeating the same error. [影响]

A. if 句引导的从句是一个条件，也是后面动作发生的原因。

B. 前面的条件导致后面主句所述 "he would react assertively" 这一动作（事件）发生。

C. 非限定性定语从句（, which…）引导结果——对 "我" 产生影响（imprint the mistake on me）。

D. 伴随状语（V-ing）引导结果——减少重复犯错的可能。

从用词等小意群角度来看，句中每一个词都对句子的中心含义有或大或小的贡献。

In contrast, if the same mistake was made at a company with a superior without any close family ties, he would react assertively, **which would** imprint the mistake on me, reducing the likelihood of repeating the same error.

A. 通过 in contrast 这一短语我们能明白这句话的内容应跟前文形成对比。

B. same 说明前文必然提过一个 mistake，但导致的结果可能跟本句的结果相反。

C. with a superior without any close family ties 说明在这种情况下可能发生的事，也跟前文涉及的某个相反的情况形成对立，也就是说前文必然提及 sb. with any close family ties。

© **Sample Sentence 2**

For example, if people with eccentric or offensive dress preferences do not confine their taste to the privacy of their homes or designated venues, they may leave a bad impression on the people around them, which could lead to consequences, such as losing their occupation or an opportunity for promotion.

句内逻辑链分析：

从句子内部来看，可分为三大意群：

For example, if people with eccentric or offensive dress preferences do not confine their taste to the privacy of their homes or designated venues, [前提] they may leave a bad impression on the people around them, [事件] which could lead to consequences, [结果] such as losing their occupation or an opportunity for promotion.

A. "若不限定行为的地点"是前提条件，也是原因。

B. 导致事件发生——给人留下不好印象。

C. 产生严重后果。后文是列举。

从用词等小意群角度来看，句中每一个词都对句子的中心含义有或大或小的贡献。

For example, if people with eccentric or offensive dress preferences do not confine their taste to the privacy of their homes or designated venues, they may leave a bad impression on the people around them, which could lead to consequences, such as losing their occupation or an opportunity for promotion.

A. for example 说明前文会有观点，这句话大概率是一个例证（evidence），用于支撑前文的观点。

B. the privacy of their homes or designated venues 限定了行为的地点，超出这个范围则会导致下面的结果，不超出便不会。

C. the people around them 限定了人群范围，即不是所有人，也不是远方的人，而是周围的人。当然这个片段的作用是让句子不至于空泛，对核心意义的作用比起其他部分稍微小一点。

D. 最后，为了让结果（consequences）更加言之有物，增加说服力，列举了 losing their occupation or an opportunity for promotion。并列是为了扩大范围，加大信息量。

◎ Sample Sentence 3

So, by working together with parents or other adults, older siblings can receive support and guidance in caring for their younger siblings, which can help mitigate the stress and burden of this responsibility.

句内逻辑链分析：

从句子内部来看，可分为三块大意群：

So, by working together with parents or other adults, [起因] older siblings can receive support and guidance in caring for their younger siblings, [事件] which can help mitigate the stress and burden of this responsibility. [结果]

A. 通过 "与父母协作" 的方式，可以导致事件发生，这个方式状语是后面事件发生的起因。

B. 主干讲述事件发生——大孩子可得到支持与指引。

C. 非限定性定语从句（, which…）引导结果——帮助他们减轻压力与负担。

从用词等小意群角度来看，句中每一个词都对句子的中心含义有或大或小的贡献。

So, by working together with parents or other adults, older siblings can receive support and guidance in caring for their younger siblings, which can help mitigate the stress and burden of this responsibility.

A. So 表明该句跟前文有因果逻辑关系。

B. in caring for their younger siblings 限定了 old siblings 接受帮助的范围，突出了重点，让内容更细化，言之有物，增强了文字的说服力。

C. of this responsibility 指出压力和负担是由什么带来的。此外，this 表特指，因此前面一定要有所指（caring for their younger siblings），这样句子内部会更有条理。

实战练习

◎ Practice 01

分析下列句子的逻辑链，指出它们有多少个大意群，并且明确大意群之间的关系。

> 1. Other incentives such as extra vacation days, gift packages, or reduced healthcare rates not only give workers satisfaction from doing their job but also help them balance their personal lives, which puts them in a better mental and physical state to tackle future challenges.

2. Not many parents can afford the time to supervise their children doing homework since they have many other obligations, such as work and household chores, so this method is impractical for many families.

3. And when it comes to launch events, many flaws of a product would be omitted by the host company, since exhibiting the shortcomings of a new product to the marketplace contradicts corporate interests.

4. However open and diverse the universities today have become, they are, compared with the all-inclusive society, still ivory towers inside which the beings cannot obtain a bird's-eye view of themselves, so they might hold Utopian thoughts about the roles they would play in society.

5. Because of their young age and lack of experience and wisdom, juveniles may easily make mistakes, so their grandparents can help them avoid making mistakes in their daily lives or their studies at school.

6. Thus, let's give ourselves the advantage of the time by finishing our schooling in a reasonable timeframe, because without time, talents would be wasted and potential would be lost.

★ <u>文内逻辑</u>

案例分析 **TG 41**

Sample Response of Full Score	文内语言逻辑分析
With their enriched living experience of life's ups and downs accumulated throughout their lives,【1】grandparents can give constructive advice and appropriate guidance to their grandchildren.【2】Even though the world changes gradually over time, some core values do not shift, as Terrance suggests.【3】Since grandparents have gone through a lot, their knowledge and perception accumulate, which is practical for the younger generation. 【4】Because of their young age and lack of experience and wisdom, juveniles may easily make mistakes, so their grandparents can help them avoid making mistakes in their daily lives or their studies at school. 【5】They can teach them how to improve their studies or behave properly in social life so that they can improve their academic performance or be accepted in their social interactions.【6】The young generations can hardly know everything at a young age so they need to learn, and their grandparents are available for them to consult with.【7】With advice from their grandparents, they may broaden their perspectives and deepen their understanding in case they face difficulties or have tasks to tackle.【8】With the knowledge and understanding of the past, younger generations can be enlightened so they can develop into well-rounded adults who can lead more balanced lives.	【1】介词短语 with 引导的修饰成分其实是后面主句中 grandparents 能给出建议的原因，跟主句形成因果关系。 【2】Topic Sentence. 【3】even though 引导的内容表让步，承认"世界改变"这个事实，但核心价值观并不会改变，以此来回应并强化前文"grandparents 可以给后辈建议"这个主题。从下文开始列举事实，对"grandparents 可以给后辈建议"的主题进行支撑。 【4】从这句话中我们可以看到有三个大意群：第一，经历多；第二，导致知识足；第三，这是后辈可效仿的。 【5】承接上文，进一步延伸解释。这句也同样有三个大意群：第一，后辈缺乏经验；第二，导致容易犯错；第三，祖辈能帮上忙。 【6】进一步承接上文，给出更多细节支撑。句内用 so that 对前文进行逻辑扩张；后面两个意群用 or 串起来，表示两种可能的结果。 【7】开始列举另一个事实进行主题支撑。该句有三个大意群：第一，后辈有不懂的地方；第二，需要学习；第三，祖辈可以帮助他们。 【8】本句承接上文，进一步支撑主题。该句一共有五个意群：第一，拥有祖辈的建议；第二，使后辈开阔视野；第三，使后辈深化认知；第四，补充条件一：万一遇到困难；第五，补充条件二：万一有任务要完成。本句是由一个原因、两个结果和两个条件组成的句子。

【9】It is common to see a successful old businessman sharing his life experience with his grandchild while having dinner.【10】	【9】进一步列举另一个事实，对主题进行支撑。本句有四个大意群：第一，后辈从祖辈那儿获得知识，with 引导的介词短语跟后文有隐性的因果逻辑关系；第二，结果是得到启发；第三，使后辈成长为"多面手"；第四，后辈会过上更加安定的生活。该句的四个意群有着非常明显而强大的因果逻辑内核，这将它们串在一起。
	【10】该句列举事例，进一步支撑上文句子，同时支撑主题。主要有两个意群：第一，成功人士教后辈的例子，用于支撑上文"知识的传承"这一观点；第二，饭桌的常见场景，让句子更言之有物，增强说服力。

实战练习

◉ Practice 02

根据上面案例分析的方法，对本文进行文内语言逻辑分析。

要求：

1. 指出每个句子在全文结构中属于哪部分。

2. 指出每个句子在上下文中的逻辑关联。

3. 指出每个句子内部有几个大意群，以及各意群之间的逻辑关系。

Sample Response of Full Score	文内语言逻辑分析
Protecting the environment, in my opinion, is a more pressing concern to society, so making efforts that contribute to this area would be the best choice.【1】With the current rate of various forms of pollution like air pollution, water pollution and land pollution, numerous severe ecological catastrophes are imminent, such as rising sea levels, irregular weather patterns, and mounting ocean plastics.【2】Any of these issues would fatally impact the world, wiping out human settlements or killing wildlife.【3】So to ensure the future of humanity on this planet, each of us should make the effort to alleviate environmental problems in a certain respect.	

【4】The idea of decreasing carbon footprint is conducive to preventing global warming, but its benefit is limited by the fact that most people in our society, under the current model, depend on motor vehicles to facilitate travel. 【5】Hence this method cannot be applied on a large scale. 【6】A more feasible approach for almost everyone is to cultivate the habit of reusing and recycling their daily items to lower non-biodegradable pollution. 【7】For instance, if everyone properly separates and returns different recyclable waste to processing plants, it can be manufactured into new products and would avoid leaking into natural habitats.

2.2 语言输出

写作过程中，大部分学生无法自如使用句子进行顺畅而流利的写作。究其原因，主要还是句子储备不足。为什么会这样？除一部分人是没有内容可写外，大部分人即便有了内容，也来不及在有限时间里将其完整写出来。这一问题其实是所有英语学习者都会遇到的，只有更深入、细致地学习句式写作，才能最终解决。笔者认为写作好的学生需要熟练运用各种句式进行输出，虽然意义是以词和意群为单位的，但文章是以句子为单位的。我们经过大量教学实践与研究，从高分例文中总结出几种常用的句式和句子内部扩充方式，以下将为大家一一呈现。

★ 句子扩充

通过语法扩张句子有非常多的方法，但我们如果意图把一整本语法书吃透并应用出来的话，一来不切实际，二来效率低。笔者教学团队经过多年托福写作教学实践与研究，对使用频率高且效果好的句式进行了归纳总结。只要对这些句式掌握得足够熟练，就可以完成限时高速写作，从而自如应对考试。

句子扩充模式：

核心语意 + 细节扩充 = 主干 + 修饰

句子扩充的顺序：

1. 简单句

2. 修饰

3. 介词短语

4. 从句

5. 逻辑扩张

◎ **Sample 1**

简单句：The North conflicted with the South.

扩张句：During the American domestic war, the North, the newborn capital force, conflicted with the South that represented the landlords of the old times on the issue of slavery institution. However, they chose to deal with the confliction by war, which was proved wrong by the subsequent devastating loss and pain.

During the American domestic war, **the North**, the newborn capital force, **conflicted with the South** that represented the landlords of the old times on the issue of slavery institution. However, they chose to deal with the confliction by war, which was proved wrong by the subsequent devastating loss and pain.

主干：表达最核心信息。

主句：The North conflicted with the South.

修饰：要在程度上或大或小强化主干的内容或补充相关细节。

成分 A： During the American domestic war 交代了事情发生的时间，让南北冲突有了背景，从而更加合理。

成分 B： the newborn capital force 和 that represented the landlords of the old times 分别修饰 the North 和 the South，显示它们是以完全不同甚至对立的阶层为代表的两大阵营，更加自然地引出主题"南北冲突"。

成分 C： on the issue of slavery institution 指出南北冲突的具体原因。虽然所有的修饰成分描述的内容各有不同，但它们存在的目的都是强化主句的内容。

成分 D： 扩张句子的过程中，不管句子内部怎么合理延伸，都会有结束的时候，于是开始顺承写后面的句子，句子间是承上启下的关系。但对上文的承接思考会远大于下文。当写第二个句子时，多考虑跟上文的逻辑联系。例句中，第二个句子用转折词 However 跟上文衔接，表示转折关系，也暗示着对下文用战争（war）的方式解决冲突的质疑。However 的作用是表达"应该用别的方式来解决冲突，却用了战争这种不该用的方式"。

成分 E： they chose to deal with the confliction by war 是主句，指出用了不该用的方式来解决冲突，预示着这必然导致严重的后果。

成分 F： which was proved wrong 是在进行评价与论述，议论性文章需要对事件进行评价来说明道理正确与否。

成分 G： by the subsequent devastating loss and pain 说明前文用战争的方式解决问题是错误做法的原因，指出战争导致毁灭性的后果和伤害。

◎ Sample 2

主干：Over one million people died.

修饰：As is estimated, **over one million people died** during the war period, which was even more than the total number of casualty in all other wars Americans ever encountered, bringing the whole nation to extreme suffering and regret.

成分 A：As is estimated 充当状语，让事实更有理有据一些。

成分 B：介词短语 during the war period 表时间。交代时间背景也为前面"超过百万人丧生"提供了背景信息支撑。

成分 C：非限定性定语从句，延伸说明死亡人数，并通过对比的形式凸显出数量之巨，进一步体现战争带来的罪恶。

成分 D：Americans ever encountered 是省略了 that 的定语从句，修饰 wars（限定为美国人曾遇到的战争），以此来对比内战的惨烈程度。

成分 E：V-ing 形式充当伴随状语，引导最后的严重后果——使全国陷入痛苦与悔恨之中。

◎ Sample 3

主干：Exercises have effects on human body.

修饰：**Exercises have** positive **effects on human body**, especially on respiration and metabolism of cells, which makes an individual feel a kind of refreshment and release, making his body to recover **and** getting ready for next intense tasks.

成分 A：形容词，修饰 effects。

成分 B：插入语，列举例子。

成分 C：非限定性定语从句，揭示结果——能让人放松。

成分 D：V-ing 形式充当伴随状语，表示结果——身体恢复。

成分 E：V-ing 形式并列充当伴随状语，表示结果——为难度更大的工作做好准备。

◎ Sample 4

主干：I find real relaxation and peace.

修饰：Jogging slowly on the smooth and endless road, listening to bird singing in a peaceful pace, **and** feeling the warmness of the glazing ray of the setting sun shining through the green leaves, **I find real relaxation and peace** in heart while surrounded in such a tranquil atmosphere.

成分 A：V-ing 形式充当伴随状语。

成分 B：V-ing 形式充当伴随状语。

成分 C：V-ing 形式充当伴随状语。这里三个现在分词短语表明做这三件事会使身心放松。句子细节更丰富，更有说服力。

成分 D：过去分词结构 surrounded...atmosphere 充当状语，表明环境背景信息。

建立观点

主题句需要满足两个条件：

1. 回应题目 Professor/Dr. 所讲的问题。

2. 是一个观点句式。

主题句可以比较简单：

TG 03　I think there are fundamental flaws with Ray and Mary's suggestions.

TG 05　I am a firm believer that friends can easily learn from each other.

TG 16　Personally, I would prefer employment at a company without any family ties.

TG 50　In my opinion, I would prioritize making friends with intelligent people.

以上主题句来自我们收录的高分例文。本书所持的观点是作文成绩的高低不会只由某个句子决定，如果主题句写得相对简单，但是其他地方都写得很好，也是可以得高分的。下面我们列举几个建议采用的句式。

◎ 直接提观点

doing sth. 充当主语的句式在主题句中的使用。[注意：谓语需"三单"]

TG 01　**Protecting the environment**, in my opinion, is a more pressing concern to society, so making efforts **that contribute to this area would be the best choice.**

TG 07　**Completing a college education** numerous years ahead of time gives an individual a big advantage in their future careers, **which can lead to success, fortune and status.**

TG 15　**Improving traffic conditions** is definitely one of the conundrums perplexing administrators of a fast-growing urban area.

> **注意：**
>
> 　　V-ing 形式充当主语的句式在议论性文体中非常实用。我们在后面的实战专栏中会进行集中练习。

"It is beneficial for sb. to do sth." 与相关句式的互换见下例。

TG 36	Working and sharing ideas with others is a better choice **when people are required to think creatively about solutions to problems in a work or school situation.**
转化	It is beneficial for people to work and share ideas with others **when they are required to think creatively about solutions to problems in a work or school situation.**
TG 41	With their enriched living experience of life's ups and downs accumulated throughout their lives, grandparents can give constructive advice and appropriate guidance to their grandchildren.

转化	It is beneficial for the grandparents to give constructive advice and appropriate guidance to their grandchildren because they have enriched living experience of life's ups and downs accumulated throughout their lives.

◎ Practice 03

将下列句式改为 "**It is beneficial for sb. to do sth.**" 句式。

TG 29 In my opinion, volunteering at a local community center or charity organization is the best choice for university students to make a positive impact in their community.

TG 38 Reading or watching the news presented by those whose views are different is a better choice since they broaden people's horizon and prevent them from making mistakes because of their knowledge limitations.

TG 39 Doing physical exercises is a better way to improve one's health because it strengthens the muscle and the body so that people can recover from high pressure and intense work more efficiently.

"**sb. should do sth.**" 句式与 "**It is beneficial for sb. to do sth.**" 句式的转化见下例。

TG 10	In my opinion, students should be involved in the decision-making process, not only because they represent the majority, but also because they provide crucial data that can improve the decision.
转化	It is beneficial for student to be involved in the decision-making process, not only because they represent the majority, but also because they provide crucial data that can improve the decision.

◎ Practice 04

将下列句式改为 "**It is beneficial for sb. to do sth.**" 句式。

TG 11 There are so many essential qualities parents could teach their children during their early juvenile years, but the most important one they should share with them is kindness.

TG 18 In my opinion, professional product reviews by credited individuals or organizations like a magazine or newspaper would be ideal sources of information for me to decide whether or not to make a large purchase.

TG 21 Internship compensates the shortage of school education that lacks practical skill cultivation and offers a chance for students to anticipate what a successful career needs.

TG 33 The government should prioritize spending its budget on repairing old buildings and streets in order to make the tourism destination more attractive.

TG 35 The government should prioritize spending its budget on building infrastructures like swimming pools and playgrounds in order to elevate the basic welfare and living standards of most citizens.

◎ 间接提观点

It seems that… but/however, ...

Even though/although…, …

TG 02 Even though patronizing local businesses or lowering personal carbon footprint is beneficial in their distinct ways, many people cannot afford the higher prices small local businesses offer or have the luxury of time to travel with less efficient means.

TG 34 Even though giving a helping hand to troubled students is warm-hearted and practical for them temporarily, support and guidance are not infinitely available; students eventually must face the world independently.

TG 36 Even though working or studying alone may prevent one from being interrupted by others or help develop one's independence, there are limitations and shortcomings in one's ability and performance that should be considered.

TG 38 Even though reading and watching the news that is similar to one's view is easy for him to accept and reinforces his beliefs, it also limits the development of his understanding of the world.

TG 17 Whether it is a childhood playmate, a high school buddy, or a close colleague, social connections play an irreplaceable role in our lives, and losing these ties can severely impact our lives. However, I do not believe relocating to another city or country is a reasonable step to take when people lose these connections.

注意：

让步与转折句式在 Academic Discussion Writing 中运用得非常广泛，我们在后面的实战专栏中会进行集中练习。

◎ 假设的观点

TG 40　It is beneficial for people to maintain an intimate relationship if they stay close to each other.

TG 12　If I had to choose between sharing a good time and communicating about personal problems to improve a friendship, I would choose the former.

TG 19　If I were to judge a person's character based on the way he dresses, I might gain some limited insight into his hobbies, interests, or preferences, since people tend to wear clothes that accommodate to their lifestyle. Nevertheless, a person's true nature cannot be observed by merely glancing at his outfit.

TG 32　Having rules about the types of clothes that people wear in certain areas, in my opinion, if I were a policymaker, is important.

> **注意：**
>
> 　　假设句式由于有推理和假设的特殊作用而被广泛应用于 Academic Discussion Writing 中，我们在后面的实战专栏中会进行集中练习。

实战练习 1 【V-ing 形式充当主语】

在 Academic Discussion Writing 中，经常需要讨论一个动作要不要做，于是会用到 V-ing 形式充当主语的句式。其应用广泛，应加大练习量。

Sample:

中文：在我看来，保护环境是社会更迫切关注的问题，因此，努力为这一领域做出贡献将是最好的选择。

英文：Protecting the environment, in my opinion, is a more pressing concern to society, so making efforts that contribute to this area would be the best choice.

◎ Practice 05

用 V-ing 形式充当主语的句式将下面的句子翻译成英文，注意句法的准确性。

1.	将不同的废料放入指定的垃圾箱有助于保持城市环境整洁，并减少垃圾填埋场的体积。
2.	把时间花在扩大社交网络上有助于推动一个人进一步努力。
3.	花时间熟悉所述领域的环境，并接触那些有类似追求的人或经验丰富的专业人士，可以带来许多优势。
4.	让学生在此类事务中有发言权，不仅表明管理委员会的诚意和责任，也为取得更令人满意的结果铺平了道路，使各方都受益。
5.	对某人的外表进行客观评价可能会伤害对方，孩子这样做可能会被认为不在意对方感受或者不礼貌。

6.	能够唤起如此美好的回忆也让我们继续保持良好的关系，即使我们生活在不同的国家。
7.	改善交通状况无疑是困扰快速发展的城市地区管理者的难题之一。
8.	优化公共交通是更好的方法，即使没有新建道路。
9.	在修复旧友谊前搬到一个新的地方可能会对个人的心理健康留下挥之不去的影响，随着时间的推移而恶化，并不断伤害一个人的心灵。
10.	在户外用餐可能非常方便和令人兴奋，但我大多数时候更喜欢自己做饭。
11.	向公司征税以停止向环境进一步排放污染物似乎是可行的，但它没有考虑到个人，因为个人也对环境造成巨大的污染。
12.	远离父母生活可以帮助一个人意识到母亲或父亲的关怀和牺牲，使其更感激这种关系。
13.	在当地社区中心或慈善组织做志愿者是大学生在社区产生积极影响的最佳选择。
14.	在进入特定环境（如宗教场所）时，衣着得体有时被视为一种尊重的表现。
15.	帮助学生具备制订合适计划的能力将对他们的一生产生积极影响。
16.	与他人一起工作或学习可以避免错误或误解，因为当有缺陷的想法被提出时，很可能会通过集体努力被纠正。
17.	向他人咨询自己不知道的事情是与同学或同事一起学习或工作带来的另一个好处。
18.	分享想法会激励他们更有创造性地思考，这样他们就可以为自己的项目或任务想出新的、更好的想法。

实战练习 2 【反驳】

◎ Practice 06

根据中文提示，用反驳的方式将下列中文部分翻译成英文，注意确保全句语法准确。

1. I think Mike and Denise both made good proposals, however, _____
_____. [他们忽略了一个重要方面——可持续性]

2. _____ on the total amount of carbon emission,
thus this is one reason why the policy is flawed. [飞行频率的小幅降低不会对碳排放总量产生重大影响]

3. _____ to take when
people lose these connections. [我认为搬到另一个城市或国家是不合理的]

4. If I were to judge a person's character based on the way he dresses, I might gain some
limited insight into his hobbies, interests, or preferences, since people tend to wear
clothes that accommodate to their lifestyle. Nevertheless, _____
_____. [一个人的真实本性不能仅仅通过看一眼他的衣着观察到]

5. Unlike what Leo said, _____
_____. [我认为实习不会干扰学生的学业]

6. _____ when visiting somewhere during his or her gap year poses a concern. [我不认为学生可能面临的危险]

7. _____ that movies have to do. [我不认为教育是必须的事情]

8. At first glance, taxing companies to stop further emitting pollution into the environment seems practical, but _____, who also contribute a lot to pollution. [它没有考虑到个人]

9. Different from Brad, _____ _____, which can only be felt by close reading, so it's better to read the book first. [我认为追求效率并不适用于欣赏故事的精妙、美丽和魅力]

10. Contrary to Michael's view, _____ when a friend does something that crosses you. [这并不总是一种不尊重或蔑视的表现]

★ 意群扩充

表示目的 …to do…

1. To ensure the future of humanity on this planet, each of us should make the effort to alleviate environmental problems in a certain respect.

2. A more feasible approach for almost everyone is to cultivate the habit of reusing and recycling their daily items to lower non-biodegradable pollution.

3. The man creates the perception of wealth, generosity, and attentiveness (of course, this may be genuine) to increase his chances of winning over the girl.

4. To survive and thrive in this challenging environment, I believe businesses (if they are to expand to a large scale) must invest an adequate amount of capital in advertisement.

5. Students can also attend functions and events that are related to their studies (i.e. an art student visits an art exhibition), so they can meet people with common interests, not only to make new friends but also to make acquaintances with potential collaborators.

6. In conclusion, while teachers did hold significant influence in the past, the evolving nature of education has provided new opportunities for teachers to have an even greater impact on their students.

7. In times of crisis, for example, a leader may need to make quick decisions to ensure the safety and well-being of their team.

8. These programs can provide students with opportunities to explore new subjects and develop new skills, while also preparing them for the upcoming school year.

表示拥有　with...

1. **With the current rate of various forms of pollution like air pollution, water pollution and land pollution**, numerous severe ecological catastrophes are imminent, such as rising sea levels, irregular weather patterns, and mounting ocean plastics.

2. **With kindness**, a child can cultivate a stronger sense of sympathy and empathy, which helps him assess the consequences of his actions.

3. **With the development of the global marketplace**, an increasing number of products are promoted in the market, leading to a fiercely competitive atmosphere in the business world.

4. **Along with other benefits** (lower costs, no need to find parking, etc.), many would abandon driving for taking public transportation, creating better city road environments, and making it more convenient and safer for all residents.

5. **With their enriched living experience of life's ups and downs accumulated throughout their lives**, grandparents can give constructive advice and appropriate guidance to their grandchildren.

6. **With advice from their grandparents**, they may broaden their perspectives and deepen their understanding in case they face difficulties or have tasks to tackle with.

7. **With the knowledge and understanding of the past**, younger generations can be enlightened so they can develop into well-rounded adults that can lead more balanced lives.

8. People are unique individuals **with different values, beliefs, and personalities**, and it is natural that conflicts may arise from time to time.

表示方式　by doing

在议论性文体 Academic Discussion Writing 中，"通过……方式，做了……事，达到了……结果，产生了……影响"这种句式表达很常用。

例如，通过在合理的时间范围内完成我们学业的方式，我们获得了时间的优势，因为如果没有时间，才能会被浪费，潜能也会丢失。

可以表达为：Let's give ourselves the advantage of the time **by finishing our schooling in a reasonable timeframe**, because without time, talents would be wasted and potential would be lost.

> **注意：**
>
> 方式状语 by doing sth... 句式在 Academic Discussion Writing 中被广泛使用。我们在后面的实战专栏中会进行句式操练。

© Practice 07

将下面的句子翻译成含方式状语的英文句子，注意句法的准确性。

1. 比如说，如果我在特定任务中犯了错误，作为亲属的上级可能会试图通过接管任务的方式来帮助我，而不是发出警告或惩罚。

2. 然而，我们不能仅仅通过看一个人的着装而了解这个人的本性。

3. 此外，真正成功的人都倾向于通过穿着朴素保持低调。

4. Diana 认为，距离可以为个人提供机会去反思所爱之人的重要性，通过这种方式可以改善人际关系。

5. 相比之下，Frederic 认为距离会减少共同的兴趣、知识和记忆，通过这种方式削弱人际关系。

6. 无人知晓天下事，所以与他人合作的人可能会通过获得建议或帮助来拓宽视野和加深理解，而这在他们面临困难时是非常有用的。

7. 一群科学家通过与队友讨论他们的想法和计划以解决难题是很常见的。

8. 通过与父母或其他成年人合作，年长的兄姐可以在照顾年幼的弟妹方面得到支持和指导，这有助于减轻这种责任带来的压力和负担。

9. 通过缩小班级规模，教师能够给每个学生更多一对一的关注，这就能够确保每个学生都能得到支持，从而取得成功。

10. 抗生素确实通过挽救无数人的生命和治疗曾经致命的传染病而彻底改变了医疗保健。

11. 通过严格跟随父母的步伐，孩子们可能会在不经意间扼杀自己的创造力，并限制他们接触其他更符合他们激情和天赋的领域。

12. 通过从事不同的职业，人们为他们各自的领域带来各种经验、想法和观点。

13. 通过走自己独特的道路，人们可以让自己过上更充实的生活，并为周围的世界做出有意义的贡献。

14. 通过创造积极和包容的课堂环境，教师可以塑造学生的性格，灌输对学习的热爱，并激励他们成为对社会有积极贡献的人。

15. 通过参考一个人喜欢的书籍和电影，人们可以了解这个人的兴趣。

16. 通过观察一个人喜欢的杂志和电影的所有细节，人们可以确切地总结出这个人的兴趣是什么，因为一个人的兴趣往往和他最喜欢的内容联系在一起。

17. 通过使用这种方法，人们还可以了解一个人的性格。

18. 通过做研究和与消费者交谈，他得到了产品的真实反馈和市场持续存在的问题。

19. 完善设施也可以通过提高大学声誉的方式使其受益，从而吸引更多有才华的学生。

20. 去一个不同的、完全陌生的地方，他们可以亲自了解不同的文化，这是通过看视频或读小说无法实现的。

21. 自己的经历有助于他们通过不同的、更客观的视角来批判性地思考许多事情。

22. 通过实习，学生可以学到很多东西，比如如何与客户沟通，如何与同事合作，如何处理工作上的任务，以及如何在空闲时间提高自己以满足工作要求。

23. 如果孩子们被要求做家务，通过牺牲玩耍的时间洗碗，在饭前半小时做饭，每周毫无怨言地打扫地板，他们就能站在父母的立场上理解他们，但是这也不可避免地会耗费他们的闲暇时间。

24. 通过规范城市污水中的重金属含量，各行业必须使用化学溶液去除污水中的金属元素，以降低人类和海洋动物被有毒物质杀死的风险。

25. 通过惩罚不遵守这些法律的公司，其他公司将会意识到污染空气和水的环境和经济后果，使它们更有可能使用环保的原材料生产商品。

26. 通过制定法律去减少污染源，可以很大程度上减少排放到自然中的污染物。

表示伴随 V-ing 形式充当伴随状语

在托福 Academic Discussion Writing 这种文体的写作过程中，V-ing 形式有两个主要用法，除前面讲过的充当主语外，就是充当伴随状语，表示动作与主语动作同时发生。在逻辑性较强的句子里，V-ing 形式经常用于表示事件的结果与影响。由于非常适用于表达因果逻辑关系，该句式被广泛使用于议论性文体。

Sample 1

这些问题中的任何一个都将对世界产生致命的影响，摧毁人类定居点或杀死野生动物。

Any of these issues would fatally impact the world, **wiping out human settlements or killing wildlife**.

Sample 2

一位数学老师可以为班级配备五到六套练习题，并把这些练习题分散到学生中，这使得学生不方便互相抄袭。

A math teacher can assign five or six sets of practice to his class and scatter the sets among all the students, **thus making it much more inconvenient for students to copy one another**.

Sample 3

在专业背景中，尤其在企业领域，很多人都试图塑造一个给人留下深刻印象的形象，从开豪车到在高档餐厅用餐。

In professional settings, especially in the entrepreneurial sector, many are trying to create an image to impress, **ranging from driving expensive cars to dining at high-end restaurants**.

Sample 4

他们可能不愿透露自己的真正强项，也不愿透露自己如何获得某些能力，这使得其他人很难真正从中学习。

They may be reserved about revealing their true strengths or how they came to obtain certain abilities, **making it difficult for others to truly learn from them**.

Sample 5

朋友们可能会下意识地模仿对方的动作和言语，或风格和品味，因为这可以拉近人们之间的距离，建立不可分割的纽带。

Friends may subconsciously mimic each other's movements and speech or style and taste because it can bring people closer to each other, **creating inseparable bonds**.

◎ Practice 08

根据中文提示，用 V-ing 形式充当伴随状语的形式将下列中文部分翻译成英文，注意确保全句语法准确。可参考前文 V-ing 形式充当伴随状语的例句。

1. Green energy can also flourish as a vibrant new industry, _____
   _____. [创造新的商机和就业机会，并使它在财政上具有可行性]

2. He left college prematurely to pursue his dream in the IT business, _____
   _____. [从事不同的职业，同时努力让苹果公司在父母的车库里运转]

3. The school can conduct a survey on the cafeteria's food quality, _____
   _____. [定期从在餐厅用餐的人（主要是学生）那里收集真实的意见]

4. If the school ignores or neglects the voice of the students, the chances of making a decision that might be viewed as impractical or senseless would increase, _____
   _____. [引发新的问题并导致不满]

5. With the development of the global marketplace, an increasing number of products are promoted in the market, _____. [导致商业世界竞争激烈]

6. The resiliency of a business largely relies on its ability to turn a profit, thus, when publicity is absent or insufficient, its capacity to prosper into a lucrative operation diminishes, _____. [从而阻碍其成功的道路]

7. Road space would be used with more efficiency; larger forms of transportation occupy less space per passenger compared to private vehicles, thus the streets would be less crowded with cars, _____. [从而减少或缓解交通拥堵]

8. Along with other benefits (lower costs, no need to find parking, etc.), many would abandon driving for taking public transportation, _____
   _____. [创造更好的城市道路环境，并且让所有居民都更方便、更安全]

9. This way, many abilities are refined, and more experience is gained, _____
   _____. [为更成功的职业生涯铺平道路]

10. Leaving it all behind may sound like a relief at first glance, but ultimately, the melancholy of missing old friends and the urge of wanting to reconnect would gradually eat away at one's spirit, _____. [导致负面情绪，如抑郁、沮丧和悲伤]

11. If I were to buy a car, a magazine like *Top Gear* can provide me with information on a car's capacity, including mileage, horsepower, safety, road performance, and so on, ___
   _____. [让我可以客观地对不同的车型进行比较]

12. A con artist might package himself with an expensive suit and ostentatious accessories, _____. [让自己看起来很体面，并且制造出拥有财富和地位的假象]

13. Apart from making policies, the government should also be an executor, _____ _____. [把收入再投资于发展新能源及消除废物排放对自然环境的负面影响]

14. Living away from parents can help an individual realize the care and sacrifice of a mother or father, thus _____. [帮助一个人更感激这种关系]

15. There is a risk that university students may become overburdened with this specific project, _____. [导致倦怠或缺乏参与]

16. Banning companies or factories from discharging waste might be the most effective measure to prevent pollution, but it only cares about the aspect of the environment, ____ _____. [不关心它对经济产生的影响]

17. In this situation, the fierce competition in these jobs would eliminate a large number of applicants, whereas less favorable ones will open their arms, _____ _____. [使他们更容易获得]

18. Since its initiation, the movie theater has kept satisfying human desires to imitate and imagine, _____. [满足源自人类特性的内在需求]

19. In this way, a once-for-all solution must be devised to terminate this dilemma, _____ _____. [结束人类对自然的寄生关系]

20. When individuals are far away from one another, they may not have so much to talk about or share with one another, _____. [导致亲密度下降]

21. She may draw complaints from parents and even the public, _____ _____. [将她的工作置于危险的境地]

22. If the buildings and streets lack repair or maintenance, the shabby walls and cracked pavement would arouse contempt and discomfort among tourists, _____ _____. [导致曾经备受青睐的目的地衰落，从游客的视野中消失]

23. A long-term plan guarantees students to fight through the adversities and obstacles they will face in their studies, _____. [培养勤奋感，并且降低他们放弃梦想的可能性]

24. Teachers can lead students to learn how to make detailed plans, according to which they realize future goals and finally fulfill their expectations, _____ _____. [从而获得成功的人生]

25. Playing with others enables children to cooperate with each other when they have to team up for a task in games, _____. [让每个参与者都受益]

26. The students are able to make comparisons with reports that consist of different angles

and details, _____. [让他们更好地了解内容]

27. Their previously shared memories may fade away with the passage of time and the decline of communication, ultimately _____.
[最终导致他们的关系破裂]

28. The contribution made by older children when they care for their younger siblings reduces the pressure on parents in many less affluent families since, in many cases, both parents are obligated to work excessive hours to provide for the family, _____
_____. [剥夺了他们照顾年幼子女的时间]

29. People would not have to worry about each other's food preferences since they can simply order their own dishes, hence, _____.
[更加关注面前的人]

30. The rise of antibiotic resistance poses a significant challenge, _____
_____. [使得一些抗生素的疗效随着时间的推移降低]

31. Electricity has undoubtedly transformed the way we live, _____
_____. [为我们的家庭、工业和技术设备供电]

32. Researchers are constantly pushing boundaries, _____
_____. [为紧迫的问题找到新的解决方案，并且发现新的可能性]

33. Choosing similar jobs can also lead to a lack of diverse experiences, _____
_____. [阻碍个人发展，并可能使个人成就无法实现]

34. They teach students how to evaluate sources, analyze information, and think critically, _____. [使他们能够作出明智的决定并且形成全面的观点]

35. If the same mistake was made at a company with a superior without any close family ties, he would react assertively, which would imprint the mistake on me, _____
_____. [减少重复同样错误的可能性]

★ 从句扩充

这里我们重点讲在 Academic Discussion Writing 中常用的 that 从句 [偶尔用到的同位语从句和经常用到的定语从句] 和 which 引导的限定性、非限定性定语从句。

that 引导的同位语从句

Sample 1

The fact _____ clearly says that most people watch to entertain. [这些频道受到公众青睐的事实]

Sample Answer 1

The fact that these channels are favored by the public clearly says that most people watch to entertain.

Sample 2

There is a risk _____, as private companies may have less incentive to invest in improving their infrastructure and technology. [提供免费互联网可能会导致服务质量下降]

Sample Answer 2

There is a risk that providing free Internet access could lead to a reduction in the quality of services, as private companies may have less incentive to invest in improving their infrastructure and technology.

◎ **Practice 09**

用 that 引导的同位语从句将下列中文部分翻译成英文，注意确保全句语法准确。

1. The idea of decreasing carbon footprint is conducive to preventing global warming, but its benefit is limited by the fact _____

    _____. [在目前的模式下，我们社会中的大多数人必须依靠某种形式的机动车来实现便利出行]

2. It is an indisputable fact _____

    ____. [由于经验和知识跨度有限，没有人能对真相一览无余]

who/that/which 引导的限定性定语从句

who 引导的定语从句用于修饰人。

Instead of making me laugh, I prefer the ones who can give me more insights and more inspiration.

Even though a person's outfit has an impact on people less conspicuously than smoking and littering in public or running a red light, people who dress inappropriately impose a negative influence on the people around them.

that/which 引导的限定性定语从句用于修饰物。

It may become one tool that/which opens windows to the world, unlocks doors to opportunities, and expands our minds to new ideas.

A strict workplace environment without any special treatment is more likely to encourage a worker to stride in a direction that/which would lead to success, since many of his qualities would be tested, such as patience, diligence, or attentiveness.

Besides, physical exercise helps people avoid sedentary lifestyles that/which lead to unhealthy conditions such as obesity or coronary diseases.

which 引导的非限定性定语从句

非限定性从句用于修饰前方句子，有利于加强句内意群之间的逻辑关系。该句式被广泛应用于议论性文体中。

1. The advent of the Internet has created an explosion of information accessible to the public, which provides a platform for innumerable news outlets, both mainstream and independent.

2. Modern audiences have access to the Internet, which broadens their perspective, so they are more sensitive to biased reports or misinformation.

3. Encircling and managing a large natural area requires substantial investment of finances and labor; strict environmental laws cut into the profit of large companies, which could lead to economic crises.

4. Completing a college education numerous years ahead of time gives an individual a big advantage in their future careers, which can lead to success, fortune, status, and so on.

5. Only a limited number of channels dedicate themselves to regular news programs, thus the traffic of viewers is directed to these channels, which explains the high ratings.

◎ Practice 10

根据中文提示，用 which 引导的非限定性定语从句的形式将下列中文部分翻译成英文，注意确保全句语法准确。

1. A law student can apply for an internship or a basic-level part-time job at a law firm, ___
_____. [这让他了解这些机构的运作方式，并帮助他结识有趣的人，这些人可以为他提供未来的就业机会]

2. If the only conversation between friends revolves around problems and difficulties, too much negative energy would accumulate, _____.
[这会让朋友们日渐疏远，因为花时间在一起总是有压力的]

3. If the same mistake was made at a company with a superior without any close family ties, he would react assertively, _____, reducing the likelihood of repeating the same error. [这会使得这种错误在我身上留下烙印]

4. No emission into the natural environment also means no production inside factories, ___
_____, so this measure is too radical and thus infeasible to some extent. [这必然对人们的经济生活造成巨大损害]

5. Better as it would be if student-targeted movies contain some teaching significance, it cannot ensure that children can really learn something from them, _____
_____. [这可以归因于人类对电影的固有观念]

6. They may be able to organize events or coordinate volunteers, _____
_____. [这可以帮助他们在项目管理和领导方面获得宝贵的经验]

7. There is a danger that treating the Internet as a public service could lead to government censorship and control over online content, _____.
[这可能会对言论和表达自由产生负面影响]

8. Negligence of religious dress codes can put one at risk and in harm's way, as in some corners of the world, this behavior is considered sacrilegious, _____
_____. [甚至可能会导致死刑]

9. A long-term plan guarantees students to fight through the adversities and obstacles they will face in their studies, cultivating diligence, _____.
[这会降低他们放弃梦想的可能性]

10. It will be wasteful to build art museums and concert halls before completing fundamental infrastructure because, under such conditions, the basic living demands of the average citizen cannot be guaranteed; let alone appreciate art, _____
_____. [这是富人和特权阶层的第二选择]

11. No one knows everything, so people working with others may broaden their perspectives and deepen their understanding by gaining advice or assistance, _____
_____. [万一他们面临困难，这是有用的]

12. I believe pursuing efficiency doesn't apply to the appreciation of the subtlety, beauty, and glamour of a story, _____, so it's better to read the book first. [这只有细读才能感受到]

13. It allows parents to share the responsibility of caring for their children with their older siblings, _____. [这对大家庭尤其有帮助]

14. A comprehensive summer school program consisting of various courses can accommodate the interest of students of all majors, _____. [这使他们为即将到来的高等教育挑战做好准备]

15. Positive learning habits are usually cultivated during high school education, such as note-taking, study schedules, and attentiveness, _____
_____. [这使大学的学习进程更加得心应手]

★ 并列细节扩充

【扩充】并列细节

The proposed factory would almost certainly have adverse effects on the local environment, particularly in regards to pollute the water, air and land.

With the current rate of various forms of pollution like air pollution, water pollution and land pollution, numerous severe ecological catastrophes are imminent, such as rising sea levels, irregular weather patterns, and mounting ocean plastics.

Some knowledge, such abstract subjects as history, philosophy, fundamental mathematics and calculus, has to be learned from, or primarily from books.

For instance, a man pursuing a woman would buy her gifts that successful women with good taste may favor, such as a certain fashion label, exquisite confectionery, or luxurious accessories.

It may become one tool that opens windows to the world, unlocks doors to opportunities, and expands our minds to new ideas.

◎ Practice 11

用并列细节的形式将下列中文部分翻译成英文，注意确保全句语法准确。

1. It is necessary for everyone to read _____. [富有想象力的文学作品，如诗歌、小说或神话]

2. As we all know, field trip is essential to children's development because during the process, children can learn _____ ____. [做很多事情，比如观察昆虫、研究野花、享受他人的陪伴]

3. _____ [更好的生活质量、更低的压力和更清新的空气] are dragging people from the centers of the cities to the place surrounded by __ _____. [清澈的水、无边的绿野和看似可触摸的浅蓝色天空]

4. Almost all the critical advancements that make our lives easier, such as _____ _____, come from the creative ideas and hard work of scientists. [我们出国旅行的飞机，我们工作或娱乐时使用的电脑，以及帮助我们做饭或打扫房子的家用电器]

5. What have been _____ mean far more than just words or symbols since they are the condensed nutrition of soul and spirit of human beings. [写在纸上、刻在石头上、记录在羊皮纸上的东西]

6. Those scientific discoveries and innovations _____. [使我们的工作更加高效，购物更加方便，生活更加安全]

7. As a nation's leader, I would urge the government to fund the research, development, and popularization of green energy, _____. [如太阳能、风能或水力发电]

8. They are unanimously entertainment channels like HBO, Netflix, Star, etc, which mainly offer the audience shows _____. [戏剧、喜剧或动画等节目]

9. Besides reflection, other advantages of taking a gap year, _____ _____, can be easily obtained during college or work without having to waste a year. [如放松自己、开阔视野或设定目标]

10. This can also help foster a sense of teamwork and cooperation among siblings and provide opportunities for older siblings to develop vital life skills _____ _____. [如责任感和领导力]

11. Employers need to take steps to minimize these distractions, _____ _____ [例如提供降噪耳机，创建指定的安静区域，并给突如其来的事务和会议制定明确的规则]

12. Other incentives _____ not only give workers satisfaction from doing their jobs but also help them balance their personal lives, which puts them in a better mental and physical state to tackle with future challenges. [如额外的假期、礼包或降低医疗保健费]

13. Issues _____ cannot be solved through personal or familial efforts alone. [如环境退化、公共卫生危机和系统性不平等]

14. Positive learning habits are usually cultivated during high school education, _____ _____, which makes the later learning process in college much more proficient. [如记笔记、学习时间表和专注力]

15. If the degree of punishment is not cautiously calculated, punitive measures might inflict adverse effects on the students, _____. [如失去信心、自我怀疑或受到他人欺凌]

★ 逻辑扩充

因果句式展开

因果逻辑扩张是意群之间或者句子之间最为常见的扩充形式。除直接使用因果逻辑连词之外，还可以用介词短语、从句或者伴随状语等修饰成分表示因果逻辑。前面我们已经讲解了一些因果逻辑句式，本部分集中练习相对明显而简单的因果逻辑扩充句式，增强逻辑性，提升写作能力。

Sample 1:	Protecting the environment, in my opinion, is a more pressing concern to society, so _____. [努力为这一领域做出贡献将是最好的选择]
Answer:	Protecting the environment, in my opinion, is a more pressing concern to society, so making efforts that contribute to this area would be the best choice.

Sample 2:	Experiencing a gap year for college graduates vacillating between prospects can help them conduct productive reflections because _____ _____. [他们可能比高中毕业生更成熟、老练，从而能够自我发现]

Answer:	Experiencing a gap year for college graduates vacillating between prospects can help them conduct productive reflections because they are more likely to possess the maturity and sophistication to carry out self-discovery than high school graduates.

Sample 3:	In the past, most average citizens lacked the means to obtain different sources of information, thus _____ _____.［他们对本国以外的事件、环境和文化了解较少］
Answer:	In the past, most average citizens lacked the means to obtain different sources of information, thus they were less aware of the events, circumstances, and cultures outside of their native country.

Sample 4:	In addition, ideas from different viewpoints inspire people to think more so that _____.［提出新的创造性想法］
Answer:	In addition, ideas from different viewpoints inspire people to think more so that they may come up with new and creative ideas.

Sample 5:	With the development of the global marketplace, an increasing number of products are promoted in the market, leading to _____ _____.［商业世界竞争激烈］
Answer:	With the development of the global marketplace, an increasing number of products are promoted in the market, leading to a fiercely competitive atmosphere in the business world.

◎ Practice 12

用因果关系的形式将下列中文部分翻译成英文，注意确保全句语法准确。

1. A math teacher can assign five or six sets of practice to his class and scatter the sets among all the students, thus _____ _____.［使得学生们不方便互相抄袭了］

2. Through building stronger friendships, people enhance their state of survival since ____ _____. ［他们可以获得从情感支持到经济援助等广泛的好处］

3. The absence of global knowledge made people less critical of the news conveyed to them by the press since _____ _____.［他们往往不了解新闻报道更大的背景］

4. School policies and facilities function to promote a student's educational experience and

campus lifestyle, so _____
_____. [学生对这些方面的反馈或批评可以帮助行政部门制定更好的决策]

5. For any friendship to be enduring or unbreakable, an injection of positive energy is desired, because _____
    _____. [它能创造美好的回忆和共同的经历，成为朋友们一生讨论的话题]

6. Since _____
    ___, the government should adjust and devise a more feasible notion. [飞机不可取代并且对飞机征税只会给旅行者带来经济负担]

7. Therefore, since _____
    _____, it would be worthwhile and rational for the government to promote their construction. [游泳池和游乐场几乎每天都有较多的市民光顾，以改善他们的健康或丰富他们的日常生活]

8. Cooperative will and ability are essential characteristics to a successful career in the modern world since _____
    _____. [在专业环境中经常遇到团队合作的情况]

9. Even though they may seem to have identical personalities because _____
    _____, people sharing the same memory and experience can really enhance their relationship. [当他们变得更亲密，他们会有共同的兴趣和爱好]

10. Firstly, since _____, their knowledge and perception accumulate, which is practical for the younger generation. [祖父母经历了很多]

11. They can teach them how to improve their studies or behave properly in social life so that _____
    _____. [提高学习成绩或者在社交中被人们接受]

12. With the knowledge and understanding of the past, younger generations can be enlightened so _____
    _____. [成长为全面发展的成年人，过上更加安定的生活]

让步句式扩充

Academic Discussion 是对主讲人和两位发言人之间的话题与观点进行讨论，因此观点之间的碰撞会比较多。让步与对比是这一过程中最为常用的句式，能使 Academic Discussion 更为客观，在写作中经常用到。

Sample:

中文：尽管在孩子青少年时期父母有很多重要品质要教会他们，但是父母需要跟他们分享的最重要的品质是友善。

英文：There are so many essential qualities parents should teach their children during their early juvenile years, but the most important one parents should share with them is kindness.

© Practice 13

用让步转折句式将下面的句子翻译成英文，注意语法的准确性。

1. 尽管有内容丰富的节目和频道，如晚间新闻、历史节目，但是人们观看电视的总体时间还是花在给他们带来欢笑、放松和兴奋等的节目上。

2. 尽管光顾当地企业或降低个人碳足迹有其独特的益处，但是许多人负担不起当地小企业提供的更高价格，或者没有充裕的时间用效率较低的方式旅行。

3. 尽管适度的困难可以促进一段关系，但是积极性应该是友谊中的主导因素。

4. 尽管学生在上大学之前有一年的时间为成年生活做准备，但是他（她）也没有多少经历可以去反思，所以这样的反思也不能带来对将来重要的结论或计划。

5. 尽管目前似乎不可能，但是可降解材料让我们相信，在不久的将来，我们可以实现从环境中获取和排放东西的多重闭环。

6. 尽管学生确实需要自己的时间来做一些可以将他们从学校作业中转移出来的事情，但是他们的父母应该对孩子如何做这些事情划定一个界限。

7. 尽管一个人的着装对人们的影响不如在公共场合吸烟、乱扔垃圾或闯红灯那么惹人注目，但是着装不当的人会对周围的人产生负面影响。

8. 尽管向有问题的学生伸出援助之手对他们来说暂时是热心的、实用的，但是支持和指导并不是无限的，所以学生最终还是必须要独立面对世界。

9. 尽管独自工作或学习可以防止被他人打扰，或有助于培养自己的独立性，但是也应该考虑到自己的能力和表现有局限性和不足之处。

10. 尽管人类进入电子时代是不可逆转的，人们接触电子设备和电脑也是不可避免的，但是在电脑上玩游戏或在手机上刷视频对小孩子的身心发展是不利的。

11. 尽管阅读和观看与自己观点相似的新闻很容易让他接受并强化他的信念，但这也限制了他对世界认知的发展。

12. 尽管放松活动在一定程度上有缓解压力的效果，但是这些活动对人的健康的影响是有限的。

13. 尽管随着关系越来越近，他们会产生相同的兴趣爱好，因而也可能会拥有相同个性，但是相同记忆和经历才能真正增进感情。

14. 尽管世界随着时间的推移而逐渐变化，但是一些核心价值观并没有改变。

15. 尽管良好的幽默感肯定会让生活更加愉快，并且有助于缓解压力和紧张，但是聪明才智可以带来很多其他的益处。

16. 尽管 Jordan 和 Erica 都提出了好的想法，但是他们的建议都有一定的局限性。

17. 尽管抗生素确实通过挽救无数人的生命和治疗曾经致命的传染病而彻底改变了医疗保健，但是抗生素耐药性的上升带来了重大挑战，随着时间的推移，一些抗生素的疗效会降低。

18. 电力无疑已经改变了我们的生活方式，为我们的家庭、工业和技术设备提供动力，但是可再生能源的发展，如太阳能、风能，正在重塑能源格局。

19. 尽管他薪水不错，但是由于接触不到大自然，他一点也不快乐。因此，保护野生动物和荒地对下一代的普遍幸福意义重大。

20. 尽管城市的急剧发展改善了许多人的经济状况，但是实际上整个社会的幸福感普遍削弱了。

21. 尽管工作缓慢可能会花费更多的时间，但是在仔细考虑每一个细节的情况下，项目和任务都可以更好地完成。

22. 尽管很多人认为一份安稳的工作意味着更小的工作压力和更多的休闲时间，但是实际上，无论是什么工作，它都有助于提高一个人的工作技能，比如与他人沟通的能力、使用软件的能力和合理安排时间的能力。

23. 尽管这些工作并不令人满意，但是一个想提高自身竞争力的人也仍然会愿意通过它们来学习技能，继而找到更满意的工作。

24. 尽管许多人可能会认为花一年时间工作或旅行是在浪费时间，但是这对许多尚未确定目标并且对未来感到困惑的学生来说是有益的。

25. 尽管有些人可能会说，做无聊的家务只会浪费时间，而这些时间本该用来学习或玩耍，但是做家务的利远大于弊。

26. 尽管现代技术提供的便利不容忽视，但是我们也需要承认，优点出现的同时也伴随着缺陷。

27. 尽管这听起来可能有道理，但人们可能会忽视这样一个事实，即年轻人仍然需要花更多时间在完成学校作业或参加社区活动上。

28. 这些人没有考虑到，尽管开支可能巨大，但不保护野生环境造成的长期影响可能会给子孙后代带来更大的问题，而这会需要更大的开支。

if 句式扩充

表示假设的 if 句式在议论文中有重要的作用，可以用于论述完之后的总结式反推，也可以作为观点，表示对未来的猜测与假设。

Sample:

中文：如果惩罚的程度没有被谨慎地预估，惩罚的措施可能会对学生产生负面影响，例如失去信心、自我怀疑或受到他人欺凌。

英译：If the degree of punishment is not cautiously calculated, punitive measures might inflict adverse effects on the students, like losing confidence, self-doubt, or bullying from others.

◎ **Practice 14**

参考例句，用 if 句式将下面的句子翻译成英文，注意语法的准确性。

1. 举个例子，如果一个人的朋友圈里有很多喜欢阅读的人，那么这个人更有可能养成阅读的习惯，因为这会给他提供更多共同的聊天话题，帮助他增进与朋友的关系。

2. 此外，如果城市和工业地区保持清洁能源的使用，其排放量也将降至最低水平。

3. 如果乔布斯几年后才踏上自己的道路，那么他也许会错过关键的机会之窗，并且他的故事也会被改写。

4. 相反，如果学校忽视学生的声音，就很大可能会作出不切实际或毫无意义的决定，从而引发新的问题并且导致不满。

5. 如果我必须在共享美好时光与交流个人问题以增进友谊之间作出选择，我会选择前者。

6. 另一方面，如果朋友之间唯一的对话围绕着问题和困难展开，那么会积累太多的负能量，这就会让朋友们渐行渐远，因为在一起的时间始终是有压力的。

7. 为了在这种充满挑战的环境中生存和发展，我认为企业（如果要大规模扩张）必须在广告上投入足够的资金。

8. 两双质量和设计相同的运动鞋，如果其中一双侧面印有某著名品牌的标志，而另一双没有，那么它们的价格就会形成鲜明的对比。

9. 比如说，如果我在特定任务中犯了错误，作为亲属的上级可能会试图通过接管任务的方式来帮助我，而不是发出警告或者实施惩罚，因此我犯的错误不会给我留下深刻印象，并且我可能会重复这个错误，这对提升技能是不利的。

10. 相反，如果同样的错误发生在一个没有任何亲密家庭关系的上司的公司，他就会果断做出反应，这就会使得这种错误在我身上留下烙印，从而减少重复相同错误的可能性。

11. 例如，如果我要买车，像 *Top Gear* 这样的杂志可以为我提供有关汽车性能的信息，包括里程、马力、安全性、在道路上的表现等，这使我能够客观地比较不同的车型。

12. 如果我根据一个人的穿着来判断他的性格，我可能会对他的爱好、兴趣或偏好了解得很有限，因为人们往往会穿适合自己生活方式的衣服。

13. 然而，如果一个人根据骗子的外表去判断这个人，他就不会意识到在迷人的外表下这个人是一个骗子。

14. 如果我们总是吝惜在制造新事物上投入的时间和金钱，那么我们以前的努力就确实是白费了。

15. 如果以学生为目标对象的电影包含一些教学意义那就更好了，但是这也不能保证孩子们能真正从中学到一些东西，这可归因于人类对于电影的刻板印象。

16. 例如，如果一个学生对音乐充满激情，并决定加入乐队，那么他不仅会学到音乐理论和表演，还会学到协作、沟通和团队精神。

17. 同样，如果一个学生对志愿工作感兴趣，他可能会培养出同理心、同情心和领导能力。

18. 例如，如果有古怪或冒犯性着装好的人把自己的穿衣习惯带到了自己家或指定场所这样的私人空间以外的地方，他们可能会给周围的人留下不好的印象，这可能会导致一些后果，如失去工作或晋升的机会。

19. 如果人们想生活在舒适圈，去一个陌生的城市或国家旅行对他们来说就不是一个明智的选择；相反，他们应该留在自己的社区，根本不用想着离开。

20. 然而，如果建筑和街道缺乏维修或维护，那么破旧的墙壁和开裂的路面势必会引起游客的鄙视和不适，从而导致曾经备受青睐的目的地衰落，淡出游客的视野。

21. 如果教师的专业能力能够得到提高，他们将能够进行更有见地的授课，更有效地解决学生的问题，以及更自信地指挥课堂。

22. 虽然经济收益是好的，但如果这是对员工的唯一奖励，可能会导致过度疲劳，因此员工可能会忽视工作的其他宝贵意义：成就感和自我价值。

23. 如果该行为是微不足道的或无意的，也许值得和你的朋友共同探讨，并且一起寻找解决方案。

24. 然而，如果这个行为严重破坏信任或者违背价值观，这就可能有必要重新评估友谊了，看它是否仍然合理并且有益于双方。

25. 如果该地区变得繁荣，那么来自贫困地区的人们就会去那里找工作。

26. 虽然说，如果使用适量，这些添加剂不会对人体造成伤害，但例外情况仍有可能突然或逐渐发生。

27. 每次她点餐时，如果有什么她不知道的，比如菜的原料是什么，或者为什么有些菜如此受欢迎，她就会问她那些土生土长的印度同事。

28. 如果我们吃的东西是在如此恶劣的环境中生长的，并且有如此令人生畏的化学物质，我们怎么能说今天的食物比过去健康得多呢？

29. 当他去看医生时，他被告知如果他没有选择这种新发明的含有某种有害物质的香料，就不会发生这些事情。

30. 如果她仍然过着忙碌的生活，生活在老板的高压以及消费者不断变化的偏好下，这样的事情就不会发生。

31. 如果我的表姐没有电影和电视的陪伴，而是保持她原有的生活方式，这些都不会发生。

32. 如果 Jerry 没有为这个错误承担责任，那么这些宝贵的价值就不会得到认可，如此一来公司就不可能成功。

33. 如果不是他在公司迅速适应，他永远无法在如此友好和温暖的环境中工作；他也不会这么快得到晋升。

34. 如果政府可以把钱花在保护现有的历史遗迹或房屋上，而不是没完没了地建新建筑，北京的环境肯定会更适合人们居住。

并列句式 not only...but also...

　　句内并列成分是扩充句子细节的一个非常有效的方法，可以让句子的信息量更大，更言之有物，从而增加可信度。

看下列句子的句内并列表达：

环境保护不仅是一个迫在眉睫的问题，而且也是一个棘手的问题。

Environmental protection is **not only** an imminent problem, **but also** a tricky one.

如果有足够多的人参与，这种小小的责任之举不仅会对我们当前的环境产生重大影响，而且还会确保子孙后代拥有一个宜居的星球。

This small act of responsibility, when engaged by sufficient people, **not only** has a significant impact on our current environment **but also** ensures a livable planet for future generations.

学生应该参与决策过程，不仅因为他们代表大多数人，还因为他们提供了可以改进决策的关键数据。

Students should be involved in the decision-making process, **not only** because they represent the majority, **but also** because they provide crucial data that can improve the decision.

◎ **Practice 15**

用并列细节的形式将下列中文部分翻译为英文，注意确保全句语法准确。

1. Giving students a say in such affairs _____

_____. [不仅表明了管理委员会的诚意和责任，而且为取得更令人满意的结果铺平了道路，使各方都受益]

2. Commercials _____, _____

_____, which inflates the intrinsic value of any product produced by a

company. [不仅让公众接触到某种产品，而且树立了一个公司的形象和品牌]

3. The environment is important _____

_____. [不仅对生态系统的平衡很重要，而且对人类的可持续发展也很重要]

4. Tremendous changes have been witnessed by us all over the past decades, and these changes _____

_____. [不仅发生在我们的生产方式上，也发生在我们看待世界的方式上]

5. It can cultivate a strong sense of kinship between the siblings, which _____

_____. [不仅使他们的童年更加和谐，而且有助于提升他们未来的人际交往技能]

6. Other incentives such as extra vacation days, gift packages, or reduced healthcare rates

_____

_____, which puts them in a better mental and physical state to tackle with future

challenges. [不仅能让员工对工作感到满意，还能帮助他们平衡个人生活]

7. If I were a counselor, I would organize my students to visit history museums or historical sites because I believe they chose my university _____ _____. [不仅是因为大学本身,也是因为学校所在的城市]

8. It involves facing _____ _____. [不仅涉及更困难的学术工作, 还涉及相对独立的生活方式]

9. Embracing diverse career choices _____ _____. [不仅有助于个人成长,也丰富了我们社会结构]

10. I would say a different job from their old ones _____, _____ _____. [不仅可以让孩子们像 Daniel 提到的那样追求自己的激情或兴趣, 还可以促进一个多元化的社会]

2.3 答案汇总

Practice 01 Answers: Omit

Practice 02 Answers: Omit

Practice 03 Answers

TG 29 It is beneficial for university students to make a positive impact in their community if they volunteer at a local community center or charity organization.

TG 38 It is beneficial for people to read or watch the news presented by those whose views are different since they broaden people's horizon and prevent them from making mistakes because of their knowledge limitations.

TG 39 It is beneficial for people to improve their health if they do physical exercises because it strengthens the muscle and the body so that they can recover from high pressure and intense work more efficiently.

Practice 04 Answers

TG 11 It is beneficial for parents to share kindness with their children even though there are so many essential qualities parents could teach them during their early juvenile years.

TG 18 It is beneficial for me to decide whether or not to make a large purchase if I refer to the professional product reviews by credited individuals or organizations like a magazine or newspaper as ideal sources of information.

TG 21 It is beneficial for people to compensates the shortage of school education that lacks skills cultivation and to anticipate what a successful career needs if they take internships.

TG 33 It is beneficial for the government to prioritize spending its budget on repairing old buildings and streets in order to make the tourism destination more attractive.

TG 35 It is beneficial for the government to prioritize spending its budget on building infrastructures like swimming pools and playgrounds in order to elevate the basic welfare and living standards of most citizens.

Practice 05 Answers

1. Putting different waste materials in their designated bins helps maintain a clean urban environment and reduces the volume of landfills.

2. Spending time on expanding social networks can help further one's endeavors.

3. Taking the time to be familiar with said field's milieu and reaching out to those with similar pursuits or seasoned professionals can deliver many advantages.

4. Giving students a say in such affairs not only shows the sincerity and responsibility of the administration board but also paves the way for more satisfying results that benefit all parties involved.

5. Stating an objective observation of someone's physical appearance can be hurtful to the listener, and it could be perceived as inconsiderate or impolite for a child to do so.

6. Being able to reminisce such endearing memory has allowed us to maintain a wonderful relationship, even though we live in different countries.

7. Improving traffic conditions is definitely one of the conundrums perplexing administrators of a fast-growing urban area.

8. Optimizing public transport is the better method, even if no new roads are built.

9. Moving to a new place before repairing old relationships can leave a lingering effect on an individual's mental health, festering with time and continuously damaging one's psyche.

10. Eating out at a venue can be very convenient and exciting, but I would prefer to prepare my own food for the majority of my meals.

11. Taxing companies to stop further emitting pollution into the environment seems practical, but it does not consider the individual, who also contribute a lot to pollution.

12. Living away from parents can help an individual realize the care and sacrifice of a mother or father, thus helping one appreciate the relationship more.

13. Volunteering at a local community center or charity organization is the best choice for university students to make a positive impact in their community.

14. Being presentable is sometimes viewed as a sign of respect when entering particular settings, such as houses of religion.

15. Helping students to equip themselves with the ability to make suitable plans will influence their whole life positively.

16. Working or studying with others can avoid mistakes or misunderstandings since when flawed ideas are proposed, they are likely to be corrected by the group effort.

17. Consulting others about what one doesn't know is another benefit that studying or working with classmates or colleagues brings about.

18. Sharing ideas inspires them to think more creatively so that they may come up with new and better ideas for their projects or tasks.

Practice 06 Answers

1. they neglected an important aspect—sustainability

2. A minor diminution of flight frequency does not have a significant impact on the total amount of carbon emission

3. I do not believe relocating to another city or country is a reasonable step

4. a person's true nature cannot be observed by merely glancing at his outfit

5. I don't think internships would be a distraction to students' academic affairs

6. I don't think the possibility of danger a student may face

7. I don't think teaching people is a necessary thing

8. it does not consider the individual

9. I believe pursuing efficiency doesn't apply to the appreciation of the subtlety, beauty, and glamour of a story

10. it is not always a sign of disrespect or contempt

Practice 07 Answers

1. For instance, if I make a mistake during a particular task, a superior who is a relative may attempt to assist me by taking over the assignment instead of issuing a warning or punishment.

2. Nevertheless, a person's true nature cannot be observed by merely glancing at his outfit.

3. Furthermore, genuinely successful people tend to keep a low profile by dressing modestly.

4. Diana argues that distance can improve relationships by providing individuals with a chance to reflect on the importance of their loved ones.

5. In contrast, Fredric believes that distance weakens relationships by reducing common interests, knowledge, and memories.

6. No one knows everything, so people working with others may broaden their perspectives and deepen their understanding by gaining advice or assistance, which is useful in case they face difficulties.

7. It is quite common to see a group of scientists fight through difficult situations by discussing their ideas and plans with their teammates.

8. By working together with parents or other adults, older siblings can receive support and guidance in caring for their younger siblings, which can help mitigate the stress and burden of this responsibility.

9. By reducing class sizes, teachers are able to give more individual attention to each student, which can help ensure that each student receives the support they need to succeed.

10. Antibiotics have indeed revolutionized healthcare by saving countless lives and treating once-deadly infections.

11. By strictly adhering to parental footsteps, children may inadvertently stifle their own creativity and limit their exposure to alternative fields that could better align with their passions and talents.

12. By pursuing different professions, individuals bring a variety of experiences, ideas, and perspectives to their respective fields.

13. By following their own unique paths, individuals can lead more fulfilling lives and make meaningful contributions to the world around them.

14. By cultivating a positive and inclusive classroom environment, teachers can shape students' character, instill a love for learning, and inspire them to become active contributors to society.

15. By referring to the books and movies a person like, people can understand that person's interests.

16. By observing all details of magazines and movies a person likes, one can surely conclude what that person's interest is, because the interest of a person and his favorite content are often linked together.

17. By using this method, one can also learn about a person's personality.

18. By doing researches and talking to the consumers, he got the true feedbacks of his products and ongoing problems of the market.

19. Improving the facilities can also benefit the university by raising its reputation so it attracts more talented students.

20. Going to a different and totally strange place, they get to know different cultures personally, which would otherwise not be achieved by watching videos or reading novels.

21. The experience of their own helps them to think critically about many things by using a different point of view that is more objective.

22. By working in an internship, students can learn many things like how to communicate with customers, how to cooperate with workmates, how to deal with work tasks and how to improve themselves in leisure time to meet the requirements in the work.

23. If children are required to do housework, they are able to stand in their parents' shoes by sacrificing their time for playing to wash dishes, doing cooking half an hour before the meal and cleaning the floor every week without complaint, which inevitably drains up their leisure time.

24. By regulating the amount of heavy metal in municipal sewage, the industries must use chemical solutions to remove the metal elements from the sewage, reducing the risk that people and marine animals get killed by toxic materials.

25. By punishing the companies that do not follow the laws, other companies will be aware of both environmental and economic consequences of polluting the air and water, making them more likely to use environmental-friendly raw materials to produce goods.

26. By making a law to reduce the source of pollution, the amount of pollutants entering the nature can be largely reduced.

Practice 08 Answers

1. creating new businesses and employment, and making it financially feasible

2. working different occupations while struggling to keep Apple running in his parent's garage

3. gathering honest opinions from those (mainly students) who dine at the facility on a regular basis

4. instigating new problems and leading to discontent

5. leading to a fiercely competitive atmosphere in the business world

6. hampering its trajectory to success

7. reducing or alleviating traffic congestion

8. creating better city road environments, and making it more convenient and safer for all residents

9. paving a path for a more prosperous career

10. leading to negative emotions, such as depression, frustration, and misery

11. allowing me to objectively compare different models

12. making himself presentable, and creating the illusion of wealth and status

13. reinvesting its revenues in the areas of developing new energy and neutralizing the negative effects of waste emission on the natural environment

14. helping one appreciate the relationship more

15. leading to burnout or a lack of engagement

16. paying no attention to the impact it will have on the economy

17. making them easier to obtain

18. fulfilling intrinsic needs that stem from human nature

19. ending humankind's parasitic relationship with nature

20. leading to a decline in closeness

21. putting her job on the line

22. leading to the decline of a once-favored destination, fading from the tourists' view

23. cultivating diligence and lowering the possibility of them giving up their dreams

24. resulting in a successful life

25. benefiting every participant

26. giving them a better picture of the context

27. leading to the disintegration of their relationship

28. depriving them the time to care for the young ones

29. giving more attention to the people in front of them

30. rendering some antibiotics less effective over time

31. powering our homes, industries, and technological devices

32. finding new solutions to pressing problems, and uncovering novel possibilities

33. hindering personal development and potentially leaving individuals unfulfilled

34. enabling them to make informed decisions and form well-rounded perspectives

35. reducing the likelihood of repeating the same error

Practice 09 Answers

1. that most people in our society, under the current model, must depend on some form of motor vehicles to facilitate travel

2. that nobody has a panoramic view of the truth due to their limited experience and knowledge span

Practice 10 Answers

1. which gives him insight into how these establishments operate and helps him meet interesting people who could present him with future career opportunities

2. which would drive friends to drift apart since spending time together is consistently stressful

3. which would imprint the mistake on me

4. which must cast huge damage to people's living economically

5. which can be attributed to the predisposed conception of movies by humans

6. which can help them gain valuable experience in project management and leadership

7. which could have negative implications for freedom of speech and expression

8. which could even result in capital punishment

9. which lowers the possibility of them giving up their dreams

10. which is a secondary option for the affluent and privileged

11. which is useful in case they face difficulties

12. which can only be felt by close reading

13. which can be especially helpful in large families

14. which prepares them for the upcoming challenges of tertiary education

15. which makes the later learning process in college much more proficient

Practice 11 Answers

1. imaginative literature, such as poetry, novels, or mythology

2. to do a lot of things such as observing the insects, studying the wild flowers, and enjoying the companionship of others

3. Better quality of life, lower pressure, and more refreshing air…limpid water, boundless green fields, and seemingly touchable light blue sky

4. the airplane we take to travel abroad, the computers we use whether for work or for entertainment, and the home appliances which help us cook our meals or clean our houses

5. written on the paper, carved on the stone and documented on the parchment

6. make our work more efficient, our shopping more convenient, and our lives more secure

7. such as solar energy, wind energy, or hydroelectricity

8. such as dramas, comedies, or animations

9. such as relaxing oneself, broadening horizon, or setting goals

10. such as responsibility and leadership

11. such as providing noise-canceling headphones, creating designated quiet areas, and establishing clear guidelines for interruptions and meetings

12. such as extra vacation days, gift packages, or reduced healthcare rates

13. such as environmental degradation, public health crises, and systemic inequality

14. such as note-taking, study schedules, and attentiveness

15. like losing confidence, self-doubt, or bullying from others

Practice 12 Answers

1. making it much more inconvenient for students to copy one another

2. they gain a wide range of benefits, from emotional support to financial assistance

3. they often failed to acknowledge the greater context of a news report

4. the feedback or criticism from students regarding such aspects can assist the administration to formulate better decisions

5. it creates fond memories and common experiences that can be the topic of discussion for friends to share over their lifetime

6. airplanes are irreplaceable, and taxing them merely imposes an economic burden on travelers

7. swimming pools and playgrounds are commonly patronized by a larger population almost every day to improve their health or enrich their daily life

8. it is common to encounter teamwork situations in professional settings

9. they share the same interests and hobbies as they grow closer

10. grandparents have gone through a lot

11. they can improve their academic performance or be accepted in their social interactions

12. they can develop into well-rounded adults that can lead more balanced lives

Practice 13 Answers

1. Despite the existence of informative shows and channels, such as the evening news or the history program, the overall time people spend viewing television is on programs that give them laughter, relaxation, excitement, and so on.

2. Even though patronizing local businesses or lowering personal carbon footprint is beneficial in their distinct ways, many cannot afford the higher prices small local businesses offer or don't have the luxury of time to travel with less efficient means.

3. Although a healthy dose of hardship can contribute to a relationship, positivity should be the dominant factor in a friendship.

4. Even when a student was given a year to get ready for adult life before college, he or she would have got too little experience to reflect on, so such a reflection yields no significant conclusion or plans for the future.

5. Although it seems impossible at present, degradable materials make us believe that in the near future, we can achieve multiple closed loops of what we take from and discharge to the environment.

6. Students do need their own time to do something that can shift them away from their school assignments, but there should be a line drawn by their parents on how their kids should do those things.

7. Even though a person's outfit has an impact on people less conspicuously than smoking and littering in public or running a red light, people who dress inappropriately impose a negative influence on the people around them.

8. Even though giving a helping hand to a troubled student is warm-hearted and practical for them temporarily, support and guidance are not infinitely available, so students eventually must face the world independently.

9. Even though working or studying alone may prevent one from being interrupted by others or help develop one's independence, there are limitations and shortcomings in one's ability and performance that should be considered.

10. Even though it is irreversible for human beings to enter the electronic era and it is also inevitable for people to get into contact with electronic devices and computers, playing games on computers or swiping through videos on cell phones are detrimental for children in the process of their physical and mental development.

11. Even though reading and watching the news that is similar to one's view is easy for him to accept and reinforces his beliefs, it also limits the development of his understanding of the world.

12. Even though relaxation activities have effects to a certain degree when it comes to relieving stress, their impact on one's health is limited.

13. Even though they may seem to have identical personalities because they share the same interests and hobbies as they grow closer, people sharing the same memory and experience can really enhance their relationship.

14. Even though the world changes gradually over time, some core values do not shift.

15. Although a good sense of humor can certainly make life more enjoyable and help alleviate stress and tension, intelligence can provide a wealth of other benefits.

16. Although Jordan and Erica both present good ideas, their proposals have certain limitations.

17. Although antibiotics have indeed revolutionized healthcare by saving countless lives and treating once-deadly infections, the rise of antibiotic resistance poses a significant challenge, rendering some antibiotics less effective over time.

18. Electricity has undoubtedly transformed the way we live, powering our homes, industries, and technological devices, but the development of renewable energy sources, such as solar and wind power, is reshaping the energy landscape.

19. Although he earns a good salary, he is not happy at all due to the loss of natural environment, so, protecting wild animals and wildernesses is significant for the general happiness of the next generation.

20. Although the drastic growth of cities has improved economic conditions for many people, the happiness is actually weakened generally throughout the society.

21. Although working slowly may cost more time, the projects and tasks can be finished better with every detail considered carefully.

22. Although many people considered that a secure job means less working pressure and more leisure time, it's true that no matter what job it is, it can help improve one's working skills, such as the communication skill with others, the ability of using software and the capacity to make schedule reasonable.

23. Although the jobs are not satisfying, it couldn't prevent one from learning skills from the jobs if he wants to enhance his competitiveness and then find a more satisfying job.

24. Although many people may think that spending one year working or traveling may be a kind of wasting time, it is beneficial for many students who haven't yet determined their goals and feel confused about the future.

25. Although some people may say that it will be nothing but a waste of time, which are supposed to be used for studying or playing, to perform boring household chores, the benefits provided by doing housework simply outweigh the drawbacks.

26. Even though convenience provided by the modern technology cannot be ignored, we need to admit that at the same time the flaws also come with the advantages.

27. Even though it may sound plausible, people may neglect the fact that young people still need to finish their school assignments or to take part in community activities they will spend far more time on.

28. These people fail to consider that though the spending maybe huge, long-term effects caused by doing nothing to protect the wild environment might causes bigger problems to the future generations, which requires more spending.

Practice 14 Answers

1. For example, if a person's friend circle consists of many who love to read, that person would be more likely to develop a habit of reading since it would help him improve his relationship with his friends by giving him more common topics of conversation.

2. In addition, if urban and industrial regions are maintained with clean energy, their emissions would also be reduced to minimal levels.

3. Had Jobs set off on his path a few years later, perhaps he would have missed crucial windows of opportunity, and his story would have been rewritten.

4. In contrast, if the school ignores or neglects the voice of the students, the chances of making a decision that might be viewed as impractical or senseless would increase, instigating new problems and leading to discontent.

5. If I had to choose between sharing a good time or communicating about personal problems to improve a friendship, I would choose the former.

6. On the other hand, if the only conversation between friends revolves around problems and difficulties, too much negative energy would accumulate, which would drive friends to drift apart since spending time together is consistently stressful.

7. To survive and thrive in this challenging environment, I believe businesses (if they are to expand to a large scale) must invest an adequate amount of capital in advertisement.

8. Two pairs of sneakers with identical quality and design would have a sharp contrast in their prices if one pair had a logo of a prestigious brand imprinted on the side, while the other pair did not.

9. For instance, if I make a mistake during a particular task, a superior who is a relative may attempt to assist me by taking over the assignment instead of issuing a warning or punishment, thus the mistake I made would not leave a deep impression on me, and I would likely repeat the mistake, which would be detrimental to advancing a skill.

10. In contrast, if the same mistake was made at a company with a superior without any close family ties, he would react assertively, which would imprint the mistake on me, reducing the likelihood of repeating the same error.

11. For instance, if I were to buy a car, a magazine like *Top Gear* can provide me with information on a car's capacity, including mileage, horsepower, safety, road performance, and so on, which allows me to objectively compare different models.

12. If I were to judge a person's character based on the way he dresses, I might gain some limited insight into his hobbies, interests, or preferences, since people tend to wear clothes that accommodate to their lifestyle.

13. However, if one base his judgment of the conman on his appearance, he would not realize the person underneath the glamorous coating is but a liar.

14. If we are always stingy about the time and money invested in making new things, our previous efforts would have been wasted indeed.

15. Better as it would be if student-targeted movies contain some teaching significance, it cannot ensure that children can really learn something from them, which can be attributed to the predisposed conception of movies by humans.

16. For example, if a student is passionate about music and decides to join a band, he will not only learn about music theory and performance but also collaboration, communication, and teamwork.

17. Similarly, if a student is interested in volunteer work, he may develop empathy, compassion, and leadership skills.

18. For example, if people with eccentric or offensive dress preferences do not confine their taste to the privacy of their homes or designated venues, they may leave a bad impression on the people around them, which could lead to consequences, such as losing their occupation or an opportunity for promotion.

19. If people want to live in a safety bubble, traveling to an unfamiliar city or country is not a smart choice for them; instead, they should stay in their community without ever thinking about leaving.

20. However, if the buildings and streets lack repair or maintenance, the shabby walls and cracked pavement would arouse contempt and discomfort among tourists, leading to the decline of a once-favored destination, fading from the tourists' view.

21. If teachers' professional capability can be enhanced, they will be able to conduct more insightful lectures, resolve students' issues more productively, and command the classroom more assertively.

22. While financial gains are favorable, if it's the only reward for employees, it may lead to exhaustion, thus workers may lose sight of other valuable meanings of their jobs: the sense of accomplishment and self-worth.

23. If the action was minor or unintentional, it may be worth discussing with your friend and working together to find a resolution.

24. However, if the action was a serious breach of trust or values, it may be necessary to reevaluate the friendship to see whether it is still healthy and beneficial for both parties.

25. If the area becomes prosperous, people from poorer regions would go there looking for work.

26. Though it is said that such additives will not do harm to the human body if they are used in the appropriate amounts, it's still likely that exceptions might happen, suddenly or gradually.

27. Every time she ordered food, if there was something she didn't know, such as what the ingredients of the dishes were or why some dishes were so popular, she could ask her colleagues, native Indians.

28. If what we eat are grown in such damaged environment and covered with such intimidating chemicals, how can we say the food today is much healthier than that in the past?

29. When he went to the doctor, he was told that none of this would happen if he hadn't picked this newly invented flavor that includes certain harmful substance.

30. Such things would never happen if she still led a busy life, living under high pressure from her boss as well as the ever-changing preferences of consumers.

31. None of these would ever happen if my cousin maintained her original lifestyle without the company of movies and televisions.

32. Had Jerry not accepted the responsibility for the mistake, these precious values would not have been recognized, and so the success of the company would have never been realized.

33. Had it not been his quick accommodation in the company, he would never be able to work in such a friendly and warm environment; nor would he have gotten promotion so fast.

34. Suppose that the government could spend the money on preserving the already existing historic sites or homes instead of endless new buildings, Beijing's environment is surely going to be nicer for people to live in.

Practice 15 Answers

1. not only shows the sincerity and responsibility of the administration board but also paves the way for more satisfying results that benefit all parties involved

2. not only expose the public to a certain product, but also build a company's image and brand

3. not only for the balance of the ecosystem but also for the sustainable development of humankind

4. not only happen in how we produce but also in the way we see the world

5. not only makes their childhood more harmonious but also facilitates their interpersonal skills in the future

6. not only give workers satisfaction from doing their job but also help them balance their personal lives

7. not only for the university itself but also for the city where the school is situated

8. not only more difficult academic work but also a relatively independent lifestyle

9. not only fosters personal growth but also enriches the fabric of our society

10. not only allows children to pursue their own passions or interests like Daniel mentioned, but it can also promote a diverse society

Integrated Writing Task 综合写作

TEST Procedure

	Procedure	Time
1	Directions	1 minute
2	Reading	3 minutes
3	Listening	2 minutes
4	Writing	20 minutes

Features of Integrated Writing

◆ Academic Style

◆ An Essay Presenting the Relationship Between the Reading and Listening

◆ No Personal Opinion but Objective Description

◆ Reading Not Available When Listening

◆ Reading Available When Writing

◆ Official Requirement: 150–225 words

◆ Suggestion Based on Real Full-score Writings: 320 words

综合写作需要写多少词?

　　如果对分数的要求不高(20分左右),对词量的要求就不会很严格,而且词量相对少也并不意味着不能得高分,主要看文章的质量。我们在这里讨论的是在语言功底相对普通的情况下,遵循写作规律,结合官方评分偏好和笔者团队带过的学生的写作速度与特征,所给出的针对不同层次学生的可行性建议。300–320词的文章在28–30分的分数区间内最为常见,也有个别文章词量略多或略少。此外,若文章涉及听力部分的还原,阅读部分用尽可能少的词写出重点即可,把主要篇幅留给听力部分。

Integrated Writing Task Strategies

Be extremely familiar with the writing procedure.

Make every step of the writing process perfect.

Pay attention to note-taking skills.

Be logically and meaningly loyal to the sources, particularly the listening.

Review useful language expressions.

Practice every step in the procedure and make it skillfully autonomous.

3.1 综合写作流程

综合写作要综合评估阅读、听力和写作三个方面的能力。与 Academic Discussion Writing 相比，综合写作更注重实际操作性。我们可以将综合写作的过程分解为厘清阅读框架、做笔记、理解阅读细节、听力和做笔记、笔记的还原以及写作等环节，只有每个环节都做到最好，才能产出优质的作文。接下来，我们将逐一呈现每个步骤的写作要领，通过分解步骤来攻克写作中会遇到的难题。

★ Step 1： 阅读处理

在阅读环节中，首先要抓住并理解重点，同时将其记录下来；然后，全面理解文章的细节以及其与框架的关系。这将为接下来的听力环节做好准备。

阅读部分信息，要抓住七个要点：

(1)主题；

(2)三个分论点；

(3)三个细节支撑。

> **说明：**
>
> 虽然有一些题目只需要抓住主题和三个分论点的主旨，但大多数文章的阅读部分需要应用上述七点进行处理。我们可以在作文中概括这些要点，以体现文章的支撑关系，从而使逻辑更加清晰，论述更加深入。

案例分析与例文 1 EX 01

> **说明：**
>
> 在考试中，阅读的时间限制为 3 分钟。因此，在平时的训练中，我们要严格按照要求进行限时阅读训练。我们应该充分利用这 3 分钟的时间，重点抓住文章的框架支撑关系，并且全面理解文章的内容。这种方式有利于提高听力的准确性，以便最终在写作上获得高分。

笔者团队不同意行业中"只须读懂主题和三个分论点"这一观点。首先，这样做没有充分利用好时间。其次，在阅读文章中经常会出现一些较难的内容或生僻词汇，而在其中往往有相关的词汇或描述，有了提示之后会更容易理解，接下来的听力也会更容易。

◎ 阅读下面文章

The sand dunes at the edge of the Newland Desert, located in western Uganda, are eroding due to forceful wind and violent rainfall, causing them to diminish in size rapidly. This raises concerns for the surrounding towns since the dunes act as a protective barrier, shielding the towns from destructive windstorms. Experts have proposed several methods to prevent further erosion of the dunes.

The first solution is to build a sandbar at sections of the dune where the wind is fierce. Sandbars can block high-velocity winds that sweep up large quantities of sand, thus maintaining the integrity of the dunes. In addition, sandbars reduce the overall speed of the wind, so in places of weaker wind, the sand will remain better intact. In this way, the rate of erosion will be significantly reduced.

Since only sand in certain areas along the edge of the dunes is being eroded, some experts suggest that it is possible to replace the lost sand by transporting sand from neighboring regions of the desert. There is a sizeable sand slope 10 miles north of the dunes, which can be accessed by local workers for excavating and transporting sand to replenish the dunes. Thus, regular routines of transporting sand from the slope can effectively offset the damage brought on by the weather.

Another solution is to replace the sand with artificial materials like metal or plastic beads. A major advantage of using beads is they can be produced to the size and weight that can withstand even the strongest wind or rainstorm. In addition, these materials can be stockpiled in large quantities so that they are readily available anytime the dunes require refilling. This proposal for maintaining the desert dunes has gained support from many experts in recent years.

◎ 阅读重点信息标记

The sand dunes at the edge of the Newland Desert, located in western Uganda, are eroding due to forceful wind and violent rainfall, causing them to diminish in size rapidly. This raises concerns for the surrounding towns since the dunes act as a protective barrier, shielding the towns from destructive windstorms. Experts have proposed several methods to prevent further erosion of the dunes.

The first solution is to build a sandbar at sections of the dune where the wind is fierce. Sandbars can block high-velocity winds that sweep up large quantities of sand, thus maintaining the integrity of the dunes. In addition, sandbars reduce the overall speed of the wind, so in places of weaker wind, the sand will remain better intact. In this way, the rate of erosion will be significantly reduced.

Since only sand in certain areas along the edge of the dunes is being eroded, some experts suggest that it is possible to replace the lost sand by transporting sand from neighboring regions of the desert. There is a sizeable sand slope 10 miles north of the dunes, which can be accessed by local workers for excavating and transporting sand to replenish the dunes. Thus, regular routines of transporting sand from the slope can effectively offset the damage brought on by the weather.

Another solution is to replace the sand with artificial materials like metal or plastic beads. A major advantage of using beads is they can be produced to the size and weight that can withstand even the strongest wind or rainstorm. In addition, these materials can be stockpiled in large quantities so that they are readily available anytime the dunes require refilling. This proposal for maintaining the desert dunes has gained support from many experts in recent years.

◎ 重点信息抓取

主题：methods to prevent erosion of the dunes

分点 1：build a sandbar

支撑 1：block high-velocity winds and maintain integrity

分点 2：replace the lost sand by transporting sand

支撑 2：transporting sand from regions 10 miles away can effectively offset the damage

分点 3：replace the sand with artificial materials like metal or plastic beads

支撑 3：materials can withstand wind or rainstorm and are available anytime

★ Step 2：听力与笔记

听力录音参考 EX 01。[见配套]

◎ 笔记

R. Prevent erosion dunes

1. Build sandbars
   - block fierce wind (Sweeps sand)

2. Transport sand from elsewhere
   - nearby slope
     ↓
   use local workers

3. Replace sand W. beads
   - produce size, weight
     ↓
   withstand storm
   - can stockpile

L. X solutions ineffective

1. work for short time
   exp. do not cover all
        fixed in places w. strong wind
        ↓
   wind redirected, new areas
                    damaged

2. impractical
   ① - sand being lost in whole region
        ↓
      run out soon
   ② - damage local ecosystem
       - destroy micro-habitats
         ↓
       native species ↓

3. Bad idea
   - manufacturing cannot keep up
     - millions of tons disappear
   $ → factories or import
         ↓
       both ✗
   - heavy financial burden

◎ 延伸 1 听力材料：**Script of the Listening EX 01**

Now, listen to a part of the lecture on the topic you've just read about.

Unfortunately, none of the solutions you've read in the passage effectively solve the problem of the sand dunes deteriorating and decreasing in size.

First, about building sandbars to prevent sand from being blown away. It's true that sandbars may reduce the rate of erosion shortly after they are placed. But, over time, their effectiveness will reduce and problems will quickly return. You see, the sandbars do not cover the entire boundary of the dunes, instead they are simply fixed in places where winds are usually stronger. This means that winds would be directed to the gaps between the sandbars, concentrating their speed and power. So new areas of the dunes would be damaged, and sand may still be blown to the towns, which severely impacts the residents.

Second, it is impractical to transport sand from the nearby sand slope. Sand is not only being lost at the dunes, but the worsening weather conditions are also blowing and washing away sand in the entire region. So the amount of sand surrounding the dunes will be depleted very quickly, and workers won't be able to find alternative sources to keep filling the dunes. Furthermore, excavating the land for sand damages the local ecosystem. The desert provides a unique home for organisms that have evolved to adapt to various micro-habitats, pockets of habitat insulated from fluctuations in the ambient climate. Digging and transporting sand will destroy the habitats of native species, leading their numbers to decline.

And third, the proposal from experts to use metal or plastic beads to replace the sand is also not a good idea. This is simply because the scale of manufacturing beads cannot keep up with the millions of tons of sand disappearing each year. To meet this demand, the local government must invest a substantial amount of capital to set up manufacturing facilities capable of producing millions of tons of beads every year. Or they can import the beads from abroad, which would cost even more. Both options are neither feasible nor sustainable since they would impose heavy financial burdens on the government and taxpayers. Therefore, the solution of using beads to replace the sand is unwise.

◎ 延伸 2 框架：**Structure of the Integrated Writing**

文章写四段。

第一段：[1 句概括] 话题 + 主题：阅读讲了什么…… [1 句] 听力反驳

第二段～第四段：[1 句] 阅读说…… [多句] 听力反驳 + 听力理由

说明：

关于开头段的写法，业内有老师建议采用三句的写法：第一句是话题句，第二句表述阅读观点，第三句则是听力反驳。对于这种写法，只要内容准确无误，我们是可以接受的。然而，我们主要推荐两句的写法，即将话题和阅读观点融合在一个句子中。对于非采分点，我们建议用尽可能少的词来完成所需写作内容，保证语言精练且无误。我们要将篇幅和时间精力放在采分点上，也就是听力部分的内容。

◎ 延伸 3 框架与思路相关表达

Typical Expressions

阅读	听力
◆ The reading	◆ The listening
◆ The author of the passage	◆ The speaker of the lecture
◆ The writer of the text	◆ The lecturer in the speech
◆ The article	◆ The professor

Typical Expressions

说	驳
◆ Say	◆ Hold a totally different view
◆ Claim	◆ Argue against
◆ Reveal	◆ Rebut
◆ Suggest	◆ Rebut
◆ Describe	◆ Refute
◆ Indicate	◆ Oppose against
◆ Maintain	

Typical Expressions

因果	转折
◆ Because	◆ However
◆ Due to	◆ But
◆ Due to the reason that…	◆ Nonetheless
◆ Since	◆ Nevertheless
◆ For	◆ On the contrary, …
◆ Considering…	

★ Step 3: 成文

Sample Response of Full Score

The reading proposes several solutions to address the erosion of sand dunes in the Newland desert, **while** the listening dismisses each proposal by pointing out their flaws.

First, the passage suggests that sandbars can be built in sections of the dunes that experience high-velocity winds, which can reduce overall wind speed, slowing down the erosion. **Nevertheless**, the lecturer asserts that this solution can only work temporarily and that the problem will return soon after. Since the sandbars do not cover the entire dunes, but only in places with strong wind, the winds would be directed to and concentrated in the gaps between the sandbars, thus, other areas of the dune would be damaged and eroded.

Second, the author states that the issue can be solved by transporting sand from a nearby sand slope to replace the eroded sand. **On the contrary**, the professor insists that this is an impractical method. He explains that sand is being eroded in the entire region, meaning that sand would soon be depleted in neighboring sources, which makes the solution unsustainable. In addition, excavation damages the local ecosystem; it would destroy many micro-habitats that many local species depend on for survival. Consequently, the population of native species would decline along with the digging and shipping of sand.

The third solution from the reading is to replace the missing sand with plastic or metal beads. **However**, the listening sees this again as a bad idea. To specify, the rate of manufacturing beads simply would not be able to keep up with the millions of tons of sand disappearing each year. If the government were to obtain sufficient sand, they could either invest capital in establishing more factories or import beads from abroad. Both options will impose heavy financial burdens on the government and taxpayers, making them unfeasible.

3.2 信息抓取与笔记

三标记笔记策略

根据笔者十多年托福写作教学的心得，做笔记是综合写作中最重要却也经常被忽视的环节。许多人认为"综合写作只是听力问题，只要听到就可以了"，于是他们在这一步就停了下来，没有考虑如何更好地理解所听到的内容。实际上，那些认真听了但无法写好作文的学生，要么根本没有听懂内容，要么就是无法在听懂的情况下对信息进行"准确和全面"的还原。综合写作的方法看似容易，但实际操作的要求非常高。那么，该怎样做笔记呢？

简单地说，要想还原 95% 的信息（满分作文的信息量），大部分学生都需要进行笔记和信息还原的训练。除了那些运气好或实力极其过硬的少数学生，在多年的教学生涯中，我发现听力超过 25 分的学生中，即便是那些上课听得很好的学生，在第一次听后就能达到要求的也寥寥无几。多数学生需要经过笔记和信息还原的训练，才能做到准确和全面。

在课堂上，我们建议大家使用一种叫作"三标记要求"的方式来进行笔记和信息还原的训练。首先，学生在第一次听时边听边做笔记。因为很少有人能够一次听全，所以我们放慢训练脚步，确保信息的准确性。然后，在第二次听时，学生对笔记进行补充。如果仍然有不完整的部分，再听一次，并继续对笔记进行补充。该练习的最终目标是让学生在上考场时，只需听一遍就能达到高分或满分要求，这也是我们训练的方向。课堂上只是树立标准、指出问题并确立操练模式。而课后，学生还有一定量的笔记练习。随着时间的推移和技能的提升，需要补充的笔记内容会减少直至完全没有需要补充的内容，学生将能够做到只听一次就能记下来大部分内容。

注意：

如果经过三次仍然无法完全听懂，学生可以查看听力文本，看是否有生词或者内容超出了自身知识储备。如果这种状态长期持续，那么学生就需要特别关注听力，多做听力练习，因为很有可能是因为听不懂才无法做笔记，更不用说还原要求了，当务之急是提高听力能力。

"笔记案例"部分展示的笔记带有作者个人风格，其主要是服务于后续写作，不追求拼写的完整、准确。读者领会记笔记的方法即可。

三标记笔记案例

TPO 16

R
archaeology = A
problems & limitations

1. artifacts lost
2. construction

2. financial support inadequate
   government & grants

3. difficult career
   uni / government agency

L 1990
new rules & guidelines adapted
        change fidal UK
reprove situation
   construction

1. bf site examined by A
   itt / caline?
   builders & goverment officials
        A   A
   plan preserve artifacts
   excavate + document properly
   bd aramid

   any work
2. paid by construct
   initial examination × govern
   hand source all the work
   fund → greater range of site

   provide
2. paid work 4 A
   experts A hire all stage
   4 examine value
   drop plan preserve
   do research scientific purpose
   process data
   write article & reports
   highest no. of A ↑

TPO 18

R Torreya taxifoha = T

  Torreya = T extract

  evergreen

1. reestablish

  microclimate Florida

  cool damp

2. move

  forests N cool

  relocate

  "assured migration"

  research center

3. preserve resent centers

  monitored

  protect species

  conduct research

L save ×satisfactory

         solution

1. reestablish · same location

  ×success

  coolest dampest areas

N F microurmore

  change laying ilm

  GW T↑

  C

  mallards drained

  drier

  ×condition

2. relocate far

  black locess Bl→N

    locust now environ

  spread quickly

  kill off plants & trees

      ↙

  danger already

  unpredictably outcome

  new environ

3. ppl ×resist disease

  relatively

large diverse qun

×capacity ← research conter

×large ppl. ×diverse

    wild. ✓

reading	listening
△: critic: ethanol ✗ a good replacement	△: aotaull is rep
for gapline	✗3 convince
	1. ✗ add to GW
h ✗golve global warming	✓ release carborn when burned
↑	↳ E made from plant such as corn
E release carlon dioxide	process grow P countereace
	grow: absorb CO_2 as part of nutritional
	∴ remove ↾
2. ↓ the aurhme of plant qvailable ofher than fuel	2. ✗ have to reduce food available for animal
eg. corn	↑
	☑ use ceilulose to produe E
	(✗ ontenby animal)
	✗ part that are eaten
	∴ could produe energy without reduce ani's food
3. ✗ compete on price	3. will be able to compete
now ✗	✓ cheaper ← subsidy
↳govornment help	↳ ✗always be needed
	wore by ⟹ ↑ production
	⟱
	generally price ⟱ ∴ price ↓ when available
	price
	⟨3✗times, drop 40%⟩

R. Prevent erosion dunes

1. Build sandbars
   - block fierce wind (Sweeps sand)

2. Transport sand from elsewhere
   - nearby slope
          ↓
      use local workers

3. Replace sand W. beads
     - produce size, weight
              ↓
        withstand storm
     - can stockpile

L. X solutions ineffective

1. work for short time
exp. do not cover alli
      fixed in places w. strong wind
                    ↓
  wind redirected, new areas
              damaged

2. impractical
   ① - sand being lost in whole region
                      ↓
              run out soon
   ② - damage local ecosystem
        - destroy micro-habitats
                    ↓
            native species ↓

3. Bad idea
   - manufacturing cannot keep up
       - millions of tons disappear
   $ → factories or import
                ↓
          both x
       - heavy financial burden

R^x Painting
① dress^x inconsist

② light, shadow^x

③ pack of woods^x △

prue, but ↓
        exam ✓ R

① x-rey, andlysis, pigment
  fur collar^x + top 100 y 后
  ? vallue ↑ → formal portait
                  arit lady

② remove, original paint sean
  simple collar of light color
                    clothe
                refleat light
                    iuminate
                      face
∴ partially shadow
       realistic → original
              R ✓

③ collar + wood + top, sides
     granol ↗ value ↗
   → single piece wood
            expect → R's
B. researoh founal
   woods → same true
   secf pontrai hat

```
chacou house use                              convincing ✗

1. residential          1. outside ✓
                           imside ✗ → live there
                           if 100人 → ♪
                           fire place - daily cooking
                        → few ↑
                        大 room → 10 fine place vs 100 family
                           ∴ resident ✗

2. storage food         2. grain maize - ✗ support
                           seems reasable → larg empty
                                                room
                                                 ↓
                                              storage
                           excauation ✗ {trace? maize
                                        {remain, container

                           {if storage
                           {spew arain maize → floor
                           {remain i container

3. ceremorioul center   3. beside pots i other materioul
                                               ↓
                                      stuff → ✗ expeat ↓
                                               ceremony
                           building materioul ↓
                               sand, stone constru tools
                           trash heap ✗ use up → throw
                                                    away
                           B pots ↓
                           regular brash → left meals
                                               ↓
                                            workers
                           ∴ ✗ ceremonial center
```

```
R. adv-vertical farming      L. ✗ shortcomings

1. Benefit farmers           1. disadv 4 farmers
- indoor → no seasons           - Hidden costs
         ↓                        - assemlding farms
    more produce                  - acquire building
        +                         - est. 4✗ more than traditional
    higher return
    lower risks

2. Less pollution            2. More pollution
  - shorter transport distance   - artificial lighting 4 farming
         ↓                                      ↓
    less emissien                - consume ↗ electricity
                                           ↓
                                   generated by
                                      burning fossil fuel
                                               ↓
                                 * even though    more pollution
                                   reduce food-miles

3. relieve farmland scarcity 3. Not practical solution
   - use buildings; less land    - buildings in shortage
     higher production/land ratio - expanding urban population
                                            ↓
                                   only small scale
                                   other solutions ✓
                                     - increase yielol ←
                                     - educate consumers
```

笔记案例 01 EX 02

阅读与听力录音参考 EX 02 [见配套]

阅读部分信息，要抓住七个要点：

（1）主题；

（2）三个分论点；

（3）三个细节支撑。

> 主题：doubt whether a painting was painted by Rembrandt
>
> 分点 1：inconsistent dress
>
> 支撑 1：a cap only for servants yet the coat she is wearing has a luxurious fur collar that she could not afford
>
> 分点 2：light and shadow do not fit together
>
> 支撑 2：her face was illuminated by light but the fur collar was dark that cannot reflect but absorb light
>
> 分点 3：panel made of several pieces of wood
>
> 支撑 3：Rembrandt never used panel made of woods glued together

© **Sample Notes**

```
R^x  Painting                    prue, but ↓
①  dress^x inconsist                  exam ✓ R
                                 ①  x-rey, andlysis, pigment
                                    fur collar^x +  top  100 y 后
                                 ? ⌠vollue ↑ → formal portait⌝
                                   ⌞          arit lady    ⌟
②  light, shadow^x               ②  remoue, original paint sean
                                    simple collar of light color
                                                    clothe
                                              refleat light
                                                  iuminate
                                                      face
                                    ∴ partially shadow
                                         realistic → original
                                                   R ✓
③  pack of woods^x               ③  collar +  wood +  top, sides
                                       granol ↗ value ↗
                                    → single piece wood
                                          expect → R's
                                 B.  researoh founal
                                     woods → same true
                                     secf pontrai hat
```

笔记案例 02 EX 03

阅读与听力录音参考 EX 03 [见配套]

阅读部分信息，要抓住七个要点：

(1)主题；

(2)三个分论点；

(3)三个细节支撑。

主题：possible usage of the great house found in the Chaco Canyon

分点 1：residential

支撑 1：similarity to the apartment buildings at the Tao

分点 2：storage of food

支撑 2：reasonable because of its size that is suitable to store the grain maize for long

分点 3：ceremonial centers

支撑 3：broken pots that might be used in the ritual as tools

◎ **Sample Notes**

chacou house use   *convincing* ×

1. *residential*

2. *storage food*

3. *ceremorioul center*

1. outside ✓
   imside × → live there
   if 100人 →)
   fire place - daily cooking
   → few ↑
   大 room → 10 fine place vs 100 family
   ∴ resident ×

2. grain maize - × support
   seems reasable → larg empty
                              room
                                ↓
                              storage
   excauation × {trace? maize
                 {remain, container

   {if storage
   {spew arain maize → floor
   {remain i container

3. beside pots i other materioul
                      ↓
              stuff → × expeat ↓
                         ceremony
   building materioul ↓
          sand, stone constru tools
   trash heap × use up → throw
                           away
   B pots ↓
   regular brash → left meals

                        workers
   ∴ × ceremonial center

笔记案例 03 EX 06

阅读与听力录音参考 **EX 06** [见配套]

阅读部分信息，要抓住七个要点：

（1）主题；

（2）三个分论点；

（3）三个细节支撑。

主题："Let It Burn" policy leads to damage so that it should be replaced

分点 1：damage trees and vegetation

支撑 1：a third of Yellowstone Park became scorched and devastated wasteland

分点 2：wildlife was affected

支撑 2：disruption of food chain happened since smaller animals died while predators escaped

分点 3：tourist attraction was compromised

支撑 3：local economy was affected since the tourist season was cut short

---

◎ **Sample Notes**

笔记√ ↓ → ↑	
Let. Policy x	Eco. cycle; distruc. , creative √
1. vegetat. x Plant scorched, devastated wasteland	1. even, Yello, damage x; Scorch area → colonize e.g. fire → chance → small plant 　　　open, unshaded → diverse B. seed → heat → generate
2. Wildlife, affect Animal flee, x escape Hibitat x, food chains x	2. Small plant ↑ ideal habitat → animal, rabit, hare 　　　　↑ → predator ↑ 　　　　food chain ↑
3. Tourist, economy, x Tour. reason, short Visitor x Business, affect	3. problem √ , if fire ↑ ; but x Combina. Rain fall 小 , wind 大 , accumu. undergrowth 多 → fire, massive 1988 后 , tourist. back each y.

注意：

　　根据纸质笔记进行转录，内容展示更清晰！

笔记案例 04 EX 04

阅读与听力录音参考 EX 04 [见配套]

阅读部分信息，要抓住七个要点：

(1)主题；

(2)三个分论点；

(3)三个细节支撑。

主题：new regulations are unnecessary

分点 1：regulations exist

支撑 1：require company to use liner while building landfills and ponds

分点 2：concerns about recycling coal ash

支撑 2：consider them too dangerous and give up buying and using products of coal ash

分点 3：cost increases

支撑 3：lead electricity bill to increase

◎ **Sample Notes**

笔记√ ↓ → ↑	
Coal ash, new regulations, x need	New regu √
1. Effe., envi. Regula. √ Use liner, new pond, landfill	Old regu, use liner, x suffic. liner → new landfil, pond; x older one Chemicals leak, groundwater, conta. Drink, water new → x environ. damage
2. Discourage, recycling Concern, recycled, danger	2. x stop, recycled products. Mercury, hazardous material, strict rule. recyc 50 y. Few concern, x fraid, buy
3. Disposal, handling cost ↑ eletri. price ↑	3. true, cost ↑ → worth Cost, company ↑ Do math, average consumer, bill ↑ 1% cleaner environ.

注意：

根据纸质笔记进行转录，内容展示更清晰！

综合写作模板 延伸

In the article the author puts forward the theories about _____. However, the speaker in the listening suggests that none of the theories is convincing.

First of all, the passage proposes that _____ due to the reason that _____. By contrast, the professor rebuts it since even though _____, it doesn't mean that _____. _____. Therefore, _____ _____.

What's more, the author suggests that _____ since _____ _____. Nevertheless, the professor refutes it by arguing that _____, although it is true that _____ _____. _____.

Finally, the writer of the reading claims that _____ considering that _____. In the contrary, the professor rebuts this opinion and claims that _____. _____. Therefore, _____.

关于托福综合写作模板使用的问题

首先，我们并不否认中低分层的学生可以通过背模板来快速学习文章的框架和固定表达，从而初步提升写作速度和语法准确性。然而，模板内容是通用的，不包含题目的主要信息。要想获得高分，必须紧扣与试题相关的重点内容，这是无法通过背模板实现的。

其次，模板的词数是有限的，过度延伸和扩充只会导致文章质量低下。虽然文章看起来变长了，但分数不一定高。要想获得高分，就需要在长度和质量之间取得平衡，写出信息量充足且质量高的文章，而不是简单地依靠模板。

另外，长期使用模板虽然轻松，但可能会使学生过度依赖模板。在达到中分层后，如果想提升到高分层，就必须摆脱机械化使用模板的习惯，学会灵活运用模版，进而渐渐舍弃模板中的惯用语。总之，模板对于学习框架是有帮助的，但我们的最终目标是能够灵活运用，从而让文章的内容质量更高。应该努力写出高质量的文章，而不是过度依赖模板。

如果仔细观察上面的模板，可以发现它只是一个结构框架，大部分的内容仍然需要根据阅读重点和听力内容进行提取。自由组合语料形成的框架会比死记硬背来得更好，这样可以避免每次写作都出现雷同的情况。

笔者与一些写作老师进行了讨论，发现有些学生并没有使用线上或出版物中的模板，但分数却越来越低，排除了其他原因后，我们认为这可能是因为他们都总结了一个自己的模板，每次都进行套用以加快写作速度。而 ETS 在评改作文时会将考生的作文录入语料库，如果发现自我雷同的情况过多，可能会被识别为雷同或抄袭，从而得到低分。因此，不建议背诵模板，而是要记住思路框架，并在每次写作中以自然的方式进行语料组合，通过替换表达来避免这一问题。

综上所述，建议读者通过自由组合语料的方式来灵活运用上面的模板。

3.3 信息还原度

全面与精准

我们在还原听力信息时需要做到两点：全面还原和忠实于听力原文。要尽可能地还原出原文中提及的细节。在多年的教学实践中，笔者发现许多学生无法确定是否已经全面还原听力信息，因此需要进行系统的训练。在这一部分我们展示了信息还原全面与精准的一些案例，这样写作更容易获得高分和满分。值得注意的是，精准还原并不要求将听力的所有内容逐词抄写，只要将绝大部分细节精准地还原，并确保意义和逻辑与原文高度一致即可。要达到这一点，学生需要听清听力部分的内容，并能够有效地做笔记，从而精准地还原原文。

案例分析与例文 1 EX 03

阅读与听力录音参考 EX 03。[见配套]

© Sample Notes

---

chacou house use   convincing ✗

1. residential

2. storage food

3. ceremorioul center

1. outside ✓
   imside ✗ → live there
   if 100人 → }
   fire place - daily cooking
   → few ↑
   大 room → 10 fine place vs 100 family
   ∴ resident ✗

2. grain maize - ✗ support
   seems reasable → larg empty
                          room
                           ↓
                        storage
   excauation ✗ {trace? maize
                {remain, container

   { if storage
   { spew arain maize → floor
   { remain i container

3. beside pots i other materioul
                          ↓
          stuff → ✗ expeat ↓
                        ceremony
   building materioul ↓
          sand, stone constru tools
   trash heap ✗ use up → throw
                          away
   B pots ↓
   regular brash → left meals
                        workers
   ∴ ✗ceremonial center

◎ Sample Essay

第一段：

第一句：In the reading passage, the author says that the Chaco House was used for residence, storage of foods and ceremonial center.

第二句：However, the lecturer in the listening material holds a totally different view and claims that none of the statements given in the text is convincing.

第二段：

第一句：First of all, the author of the text describes that the house in the Canyon was used as an apartment building due to its similarity to the residential houses at the Taos.

第二句：But it is refuted by the professor because from the outside it looks like an American old house but from the inside it can not prove that many people lived there.

第三句：For example, in the biggest room, the number of the fireplaces is only enough for less than 10 families for their daily cooking instead of 100 households, whereas the space of the room is large enough for more than 100 families.

第三段：

第一句：Second, the passage indicates that great house was used to store foods, considering that the crops need a large and suitable place to store.

第二句：However, the speaker in the lecture rebuts it due to the reason that there was no grain maize or remains of maize containers that were discovered during the process of excavation, even though it sounds possible because of its large and empty rooms.

第三句：If the house was used for the storage of grain maize, there should be some remains of them spewing on the ground or some remains of big containers.

第四段：

第一句：Finally, the writer of the reading suggests that the massive stone building was used as a ceremonial center for there are some broken pots in the house that might be used in ritual.

第二句：But the lecture opposes against this opinion since, besides the piles of broken pots, there are also other materials including sands, stones and construction tools that may be just a trash heap that was not used up while the Chaco House was built.

第三句：Moreover, those piles of broken pots might also be regular trash that was used by the construction workers in their meals and then thrown away while they built the Chaco House.

案例分析与例文 2 EX 04

阅读与听力录音参考 EX 04。[见配套]

◎ **Sample Notes**

笔记√ ↓ → ↑	
Coal ash, new regulations, x need	New regu √
1. Effe., envi. Regula. √ Use liner, new pond, landfill	Old regu, use liner, x suffic. liner → new landfill, pond; x older one Chemicals leak, groundwater, conta. Drink, water new → x environ. damage
2. Discourage, recycling Concern, recycled, danger	2. x stop, recycled products. Mercury, hazardous material, strict rule. recyc 50 y. Few concern, x fraid, buy
3. Disposal, handling cost ↑ eletri. price ↑	3. true, cost ↑ → worth Cost, company ↑ Do math, average consumer, bill ↑ 1% cleaner environ.

◎ **Sample Response of Full Score**

Introduction

笔记√ ↓ → ↑	
Coal ash, new regulations, x need	New regu √
1. Effe., envi. Regula. √ Use liner, new pond, landfill	
2. Discourage, recycling Concern, recycled, danger	The author of the text indicates that new regulations of disposing coal ash are not necessary and could even bring negative results. On the contrary, the professor argues that there should definitely be new rules restricting the storing and handling of coal ash.
3. Disposal, handling cost ↑ eletri. price ↑	

Body Ⅰ

笔记√ ↓ → ↑	
Coal ash, new regulations, x need	New regu √
1. Effe., envi. Regula. √ Use liner, new pond, landfill	Old regu, use liner, x suffic. liner → new landfill, pond; x older one Chemicals leak, groundwater, conta. Drink, water new → x environ. damage
2. Discourage, recycling Concern, recycled, danger 3. Disposal, handling cost ↑ eletri. price ↑	First of all, the reading material points out that there are already existing regulations such as one restriction of the use of liner while building disposal ponds or landfills. **By contrast**, the speaker of the lecture rebuts that the existing rules are not sufficient enough. For instance, the rules about the usage of liner only regulated the companies that build new landfills and ponds. However, the old landfills were not restricted. As a result, they cause significant problems that some chemicals leaked into the soil and ground-water and polluted the drinking water source. So, new regulations are needed to require both new and old sites to use liner on coal ash disposal.

Body Ⅱ

笔记√ ↓ → ↑	
2. Discourage, recycling Concern, recycled, danger	2. x stop, recycled products. Mercury, hazardous material, strict rule. recyc 50 y. Few concern, x fraid, buy
3. Disposal, handling cost ↑ eletri. price ↑	In addition, the writing suggests that these new regulations would discourage the recycled products of coal ash since people would consider them too dangerous. **However**, the listening material rebuts it by saying that new laws do not necessarily stop the usage of the recycled products. For example, the use of mercury, a chemical ingredient that is harmful to human body, was restricted by regulations. Nonetheless, it has been still safely and successfully used for nearly 50 years, and consumers did not feel afraid to use the recycled products of mercury. Hence, the use of recycled products of coal ash would not decrease too.

Body Ⅲ

笔记√ ↓ → ↑	
3. Disposal, handling cost ↑ eletri. price ↑	3. true, cost ↑ → worth Cost, company ↑ Do math, average consumer, bill ↑ 1% cleaner environ.
	Furthermore, the author of the passage indicates that new regulations would cause a significant increase in the cost of disposal for the power companies so that the price of electricity is likely to increase. **By contrast**, the lecturer in the speech refutes that even if this price might increase, it is worth the cost. The increase of the expense for handling the coal ash might sound a lot; however, if we divide the cost to each household that uses electricity, we will find that each individual only needs to pay 1 percent more for the electricity bill. Thus, this is not a big problem in comparison to the cleaner environment they have.

案例分析与例文 3 EX 05

阅读与听力录音参考 EX 05。[见配套]

© **Sample Notes**

真↓
poem → ideality poet
① John
　　wothrest → John
　　poem → produce
　　honolwrting

② Huyln
　　subject Crowarn
　　style Aurtn

③ Severd othor
　　same rejin
　　eollection

× Cowing
① true
　　hondwtry
　× some
14ᵗʰ copieel books √
　　handconity × original
　　same copyist

② √ Gowein
　　　Aurter
　× same peogle
　　diff. dialeot
　diffe place olrfile
H aplane
P differ
× Same

③ diffcer plance
Saue VovaGu → diffce wrdos
　some uncommon 2 + poem
　　L × other literit
　× diffcer writer
　　　same words
　　　√ potes

◎ Sample Essay of Full Score

The article puts forward the theories about the possible identities of Pearl Poets for the four finest poems in a fourteenth-century handwritten book. However, the speaker in the listening suggests that none of the theories is convincing.

First of all, the passage proposes that Pearl Poet must be John Massey because John Massey lived in Northwest England where the Pearl manuscript was produced and their handwritings matched each other well. In the contrary, the professor rebuts it. Even though the manuscript of John's poem has the same handwriting as that of the four poems by Pearl Poet, it doesn't mean that they are the same person. Copied books were very popular in the 14th century and many books with the same handwriting were not original but made by the same copyists. Therefore, the same handwriting may only prove that the four poems were copied by the same copyist.

What's more, the author suggests that Hugh authored the four poems because he shared with Pearl Poets the same subject matter like Sir Garwain and the same usage of alliteration. Nevertheless, the professor refutes it by arguing that they are not the same person, although it is true that Hugh created his works with the character Sir Gowain and the use of alliteration. People from different places in England differ in their use of diverse dialects and Hugh wrote his poems by using the spoken dialect in Yorkshire, which is quite different from that the pearl poets used from other region in England.

Finally, the writer of the reading claims that the four poems were written by several authors because the only thing in common is that the places mentioned in the poems are in the same region of England. Nonetheless, the professor rebuts this opinion and claims that it is a single poet who wrote the four poems. They have more similarity besides the places they mentioned. There are same vocabulary in different works and some of uncommon words were used in more than two poems but never found in other literature. It is impossible that various writers would use the same rare and unique words in their poems at the same time.

案例分析与例文 4 EX 06

阅读与听力录音参考 EX 06。[见配套]

◎ Sample Notes

笔记√ ↓ → ↑	
Let. Policy x	Eco. cycle; distruc. , creative √

1. vegetat. x Plant scorched, devastated wasteland	1. even, Yello, damage x; Scorch area → colonize e.g. fire → chance → small plant open, unshaded → diverse B. seed → heat → generate

2. Wildlife, affect
 	
Animal flee, x escape
 	
Hibitat x, food chains x
	2. Small plant ↑ ideal habitat → animal, rabit, hare
	
	               ↑ → predator ↑
	
	            food chain ↑

3. Tourist, economy, x Tour. reason, short Visitor x Business, affect	3. problem √ , if fire ↑ ; but x Combina. Rain fall 小 , wind 大 , accumu. undergrowth 多 → fire, massive 1988 后 , tourist. back each y.

Practice EX 06

给下列作文打分并指出它的不足之处。

In the reading passage, the author argues that "Let it Burn" policy brings about more negative effects rather than positive ones. However, the lecturer points out that the argument is actually unconvincing.

First of all, the author of the passage says that this policy will cause irreversible destruction to the vegetation and plants. However, the speaker disputes this statement. Even though the fire happened in the Yellowstone Park destroyed many plants and lands, compared to the destruction brought about by the fire, the benefits outweigh the damages. Small plants and vegetation can colonize these lands where massive fire once occurred, and this increases the number and diversity of the creatures because seeds of certain plants will not germinate unless they are put in relatively high temperature.

Secondly, the writer claims that wildlife will be seriously affected. However, the professor holds a totally opposite view in his speech due to the reason that the number of the animals can recover, or even increase since fire creates a new habitat more suitable for some animals like rabbits and hares. Once the rabbit thrive, the population of predator will grow too, and therefore the food chain will remain as strong and intact as possible.

Finally, the writing material suggests that the tourist attraction will decline consequently. But the lecturer refutes the writer's point that the fire brought about great loss and impact to the Yellowstone Park, since it is extremely difficult to reach the conditions for the fire, like low rainfall, strong wind and dry climate. On the other hand, the visitor came back to the Yellowstone Park the next year after the disastrous fire. So the tourist industry will not be influenced by the fire.

◎ 延伸：评分标准 **3—4 分**

上方的例文可得：3.5 分【3—4 分】

Ⅰ minor important information missing

Ⅱ inaccuracy, vagueness, imprecision of some content and connections between reading and listening

Ⅲ frequent or noticeable errors of language use

Ⅳ occasional lapse of clarity

Ⅴ not logically connected

Ⅵ fake information that is not from the prompt

看似不错，成绩却一般的文章：

文章约有 280 词，原文的很多关键词也都重现了，为什么拿不到高分呢？下面几点要特别注意:

1. 综合写作是复述，不是分析！复述应尽可能忠于原文。

2. 避免缺信息，特别是重要信息。

3. 避免逻辑混乱（忠于原文意义，忠于听力原文逻辑）。

4. 不根据原文的内容进行推理和延伸！

◎ **Sample Response Analysis**

Introduction

In the reading passage, the author points out that "Let it Burn" policy brings about more negative effects. However, the lecturer argues that the idea is unconvincing.

基本上符合要求。

Body Ⅰ

First of all, the author of the passage says that this policy will cause irreversible [A] destruction to the vegetation and plants. [B] However, the speaker disputes this statement. Even though the fire happened in the Yellowstone Park destroyed many plants and lands, compared to the destruction brought about by the fire, the benefits outweigh the damages. [C] Small plants and vegetation can colonize these lands where massive fire once occurred, [D] and this increases the number and diversity of the creatures because [E] seeds of certain plants will not germinate unless they are put in relatively high temperature. [F]

A 多余：阅读部分中 irreversible 这个词用得比较重，假如全文只有这个词用重了，问题不大，但精益求精的话，将它去掉更准确。

B 可完善：阅读部分如果想再抓一点重要信息作为支撑，可以将 Yellowstone Park 三分之一被烧成焦地（wasteland）补充进来。这样阅读部分的信息就比较完善了。

C 多余：原文的听力部分并没有表达 "相较于破坏而言，带来的好处更大一些" 这样的信息，这完全是作者自己的概括与延伸，建议删除。

D 缺信息：听力中讲到大火将 "大树烧掉，就会有开阔而无遮蔽的地方让低矮植物成长"，要将它还原出来。

E 逻辑混乱：这里前后是两个例子，并非因果关系，文章强行将它们串起来，反而使信息的准确度大大降低，建议断开，各自写成完整的例子。

F 可完善：可补充原文听力里提到的 "火灾之后，就会有大量新的物种出现" 这个信息。

Body Ⅱ

Secondly, the writer claims that wildlife will be seriously affected. [G] However, the professor holds a totally opposite view in his speech due to the reason that the number of the animals can recover, or even increase since fire creates a new habitat more suitable for some animals like rabbits and hares. Once the rabbit [H] thrive, the population of predator will grow too, and therefore the food chain will remain as strong and intact as possible.

G 可完善：可补充 "食物链断裂" 这个结果。

H 语法错误：the rabbit thrive, 加复数 -s。

Body Ⅲ

Finally, the writing material suggests that the tourist attraction will decline consequently. [I] But the lecturer refutes the writer's point that the fire brought about great loss and impact to the Yellowstone Park, [J] since it is extremely difficult to reach the conditions for the fire, like low rainfall, strong wind and dry climate. [K] On the other hand, the visitor [L] came back to the Yellowstone Park the next year after the disastrous fire. [M] So the tourist industry will not be influenced by the fire.

I 可完善：阅读里可以把 "当地经济会受影响" 这个结果写出来。

J 缺信息：把 "如果每年都发生火灾，那确实会带来巨大的损害，但并没有" 这个让步信息添加进去。

K 信息错：不是干燥的天气，而是 accumulation of dry undergrowth（累积较多的地表沉积物）导致容易发生火灾。

L 语法错误：visitor 要加复数 -s。

M 信息错：正确的信息是 "那年 visitors 回来了，而且每年都回来"。

© **Sample Response**

In the reading passage, the author points out that "Let it Burn" policy brings about more negative effects. However, the lecturer argues that the idea is unconvincing.

First of all, the author of the passage says that this policy will cause destruction to the vegetation and plants and the fire in Yellowstone Park caused a third of the land to scorched area and wasteland. However, the speaker disputes this statement. Even though the fire happened in the Yellowstone Park destroyed many plants and lands, small plants and vegetation soon colonized these lands where the massive fire once occurred. The fire makes the plants and vegetation more diverse. It creates opportunities for those small plants that could not grow otherwise. When big trees are burned, there are open and unshaded place for the small plants to grow. Besides, seeds of some species need to be put in relatively high temperature to germinate, so after the fire there appear many new species of plants.

Secondly, the writer claims that wildlife will be seriously affected and food chain will be interrupted with small animals being killed and predators fleeing. However, the professor holds a totally opposite view in his speech due to the reason that the number of the animals can recover since fire creates a new ideal habitat for some animals like rabbits and hares. Once the rabbits thrive, the population of predators will grow too, and therefore the food chain will remain as strong and intact as possible.

Finally, the writing material suggests that the tourist attraction will decline consequently so that the local economy will compromise. But the lecturer refutes the writer's point that if fire happens every year it would be a problem but it does not. There is an unusual combination of situations that year to cause the fire that massive and it is extremely difficult to reach the conditions, like low rainfall, strong wind and dry undergrowth. On the other hand, after that year, there was no fire again and the visitors came back to the Yellowstone Park and the years after that. So the tourist industry will not be influenced by the fire.

◎ 延伸：评分标准 5 分

上方修改后例文得分：5 分！［我们的满分评定标准是：（1）满足官方评分标准 5 分的要求；（2）与过往考满分学生稳定发挥的文章质量相当。］

Ⅰ important information

Ⅱ coherent and accurate

Ⅲ relevant information between the lecture and the article

Ⅳ well organized

Ⅴ minor errors in language use that don't lead to inaccurate or imprecise presentation of content and connections

Practice EX 07

3 分钟完成下面阅读。

Vertical agriculture is well advocated by agriculturists in recent years since the rapid expansion of urbanization is leading to a sharp diminish of arable land. Under this mode of farming, crops are cultivated in buildings using vertical space and produced in the cities rather than in the countryside. Greenhouse agriculture has its advantages compared to traditional agricultural production.

Firstly, vertical farming is much more beneficial for farmers than traditional farming. Unlike farming in open fields, indoor environments are not subjugated to a particular season or climate, instead, crops can be cultivated all year round and in any city. Farmers can fit buildings with equipment that regulates temperature, humidity, and other weather conditions to grow produce that have a greater demand or give them higher economic returns. In addition, with this method of farming, farmers are less exposed to risks brought on by unpredictable weather, which is a leading cause of bankruptcy among many.

Second, vertical agriculture also produces less pollution to the environment. Traditionally, a well-developed transportation system is needed for sending crops to market with land farming. This produces environmental problem because the vehicles used for transport burn fossil fuels like petrol that emits large amounts of pollutants. However, vertical agriculture is located in cities, near the consumers. In this case, transportation distance is significantly reduced, which lowers the level of pollution created by the vehicles.

Lastly, the intensive problem of farmland scarcity will be relieved. Vertical agriculture is operated in large buildings where vertical farms are installed on each floor. As a result, only small plots of the land are needed. This minimizes the requirement for arable fields, meaning that the same quantity of crops produced in buildings need far less land than that are needed in traditional farming. As global population increases at a staggering rate, the problem of farmland shortage is becoming a major cause for concern. Experts believe that transitioning to vertical farming is the best solution to sustaining the growing food demand of the world population.

听力录音见配套音频。

Summarize the points made in the lecture, being sure to explain how they respond to the specific concerns presented in the reading passage. 20 minutes limited.

_____

_____

_____

_____

_____

_____

_____

© Script of the Listening

Now, listen to a part of the lecture on the topic you've just read about.

Well, even though vertical agriculture is somehow practiced in some cities, the reading takes it too optimistically. Unfortunately, there are shortcomings that the reading does not cover.

First, although it is true that vertical agriculture produces crops all year round, there are obvious disadvantages that make it hard to outcompete traditional farming. You see, there are hidden costs in this new form of agriculture. For instance, to begin farming in a building, a farm needs to be assembled in a tall building and it costs much more than traditional farms. More importantly, farmers also need to acquire a suitable building in the cities, which requires a large amount of investment, even if it's an old abandoned factory building. It is estimated that, for the same quantity of yield, it costs farmers 4 times more to practice vertical farming than traditional farming.

Second, about the idea that it causes less pollution than traditional agriculture. Well, that's unreasonable as well. You know, all plants require a source of light. But the crops that grow in tall buildings have less access to sunlight. Consequently, farmers need artificial ultra-violet lighting for the plants and vegetation. This consumes a lot of electricity. And electricity is generated by burning fossil fuels like coal, which produces large quantities of greenhouse gases and toxins. So, in fact, vertical agriculture generates more pollution because of the usage of artificial lights, even when food-miles are reduced due to shorter farm-to-market distances.

And finally, vertical agriculture isn't a practical solution for the shortage of arable land.

What the reading failed to mention is that population increase also leads to a shortage of living space, which means buildings would also be in shortage in many urban areas. This makes it difficult for vertical farming to expand to a scale large enough to counterbalance the growing demand for food production. Instead, other solutions such as crop modification to increase yield or educating consumers to switch their diet to subsist crops and livestock that require less land are much more effective.

◎ 笔记参考

R. adv-vertical farming   L. ✗ shortcomings

1. Benefit farmers   1. disadv 4 farmers
- indoor → no seasons   - Hidden costs
          ↓   - assemlding farms
   more produce   - acquire building
          +   - est. 4× more than traditional
   higher return
   lower risks

2. Less pollution   2. More pollution
   - shorter transport distance   - artificial lighting 4 farming
            ↓   ↓
   less emission   - consume ↗ electricity
                                                 ↓
                                         generated by
                                            burning fossil fuel
                                                 ↓
                                      * even though   more pollution
                                        reduce food-miles

3. relieve farmland scarcity   3. Not practical solution ⌐
   - use buildings; less land   - buildings in shortage
     higher production/land ratio   - expanding urban population
                                                 ↓
                                         only small scale
                                         other solutions √
                                            - increase yielol
                                            - educate consumers

The passage puts forth several advantages of vertical agriculture, a method of farming that uses tall buildings in urban settings. However, the listening casts doubt on the benefits and points out their respective shortcomings.

The author begins by claiming that farmers can benefit from this new farming method since indoor environments allow them to grow crops without seasonal restrictions, which has lower risks and can draw more profit. In contrast, the speaker points out several disadvantages that vertical agriculture imposes on farmers despite the advantage of being indoors. Specifically, this method has many hidden costs, including assembling farms on each building floor and the large sum of capital needed to acquire a building (even for abandoned buildings). An estimate indicates that vertical agriculture can cost up to 4 times more than traditional farming for the same quantity of yield.

In addition, the article suggests that vertical farming shortens the distance between farm and market, reducing carbon emissions, and thus is less harmful to the environment. The professor, conversely, rebuts this notion and asserts that vertical agriculture would, in fact, create even more pollution. In order to successfully harvest crops indoors, farmers must employ artificial ultra-violet lighting since buildings have less access to natural sunlight. This means that a farm needs to consume much more electricity, which is generated mainly by burning fossil fuels. Even though food miles are reduced, the higher consumption of energy in vertical farming will result in more pollutants and toxins released into the environment.

Lastly, the reading believes that vertical agriculture is an effective solution to the current farmland shortage problem since it can obtain higher yields by using less land. Oppositely, the listening argues that it's an impractical solution. He elucidates that available buildings for farming are often scarce in an urban area as city populations are expanding, and living space is in high demand. In this case, vertical farming can only be applied on a small scale, which is insufficient for the growing need for food production. Thus, other methods would be more feasible solutions, such as modifying crops to increase yield and educating consumers to purchase more food items that require less land to grow.

学术讨论例文

TG 01　Sociology

Your professor is teaching a class on Sociology. Write a post responding to the professor's question. In your response, you should:

• express and support your opinion

• make a contribution to the discussion

An effective response will contain at least 100 words. You will have 10 minutes to write it.

Dr. Cruz:

When people talk about being responsible members of society, they usually mention various ways in which people can contribute to their community, such as actions that benefit society in a particular aspect, like the economy, the environment, or security. The effects of these efforts can significantly improve the well-being of the residents in an area. So I want to ask you this question: What is the best way for an individual to contribute to society during their daily lives?

Lina:

I think buying locally grown or made products goes a long way in benefiting our fellow citizens. This ensures that cash flow remains within a community, allowing small businesses to flourish and securing employment opportunities for its residents. When a community is well off economically, there would be extra funding available for it to improve other amenities like libraries or parks.

Felix:

I know that environmental issues are becoming a major concern for everyone nowadays, so protecting the planet should be a priority for any responsible citizen. The best way to do so is to lower our daily carbon footprint by reducing the use of automobiles. For instance, you can commute to work or school by walking or riding a bike.

◎ Sample Response 1

Protecting the environment, in my opinion, is a more pressing concern to society, so making efforts that contributes to this area would be the best choice. With the current rate of various forms of pollution like air pollution, water pollution and land pollution, numerous severe ecological catastrophes are imminent, such as rising sea levels, irregular weather patterns, and mounting ocean plastics. Any of these issues would fatally impact the world, wiping out human settlements or killing wildlife. So to ensure the future of humanity on this planet, each of us should make the effort to alleviate environmental problems in a certain respect. The idea of decreasing carbon footprint is conducive to preventing global warming, but its benefit is limited by the fact that most people in our society, under the current model, must depend on some form of motor vehicles to facilitate travel. Hence this method cannot be applied on a large scale. A more feasible approach for almost everyone is to cultivate the habit of reusing and recycling their daily items to lower non-biodegradable pollution. For instance, if everyone properly separates and returns different recyclable waste to processing plants, it can be manufactured into new products and would avoid leaking into natural habitats.

◎ Sample Response 2

I think a better approach for the average citizen to contribute to society is something applicable to most people. Even though patronizing local businesses or lowering personal carbon footprint is beneficial in their distinct ways, many cannot afford the higher prices small local businesses offer or don't have the luxury of time to travel with less efficient means. However, almost everyone is a consumer, and thus we generate waste. So optimizing the disposal of our daily accumulated garbage, to which most can afford the time and energy, can go a long way in helping the environment when enough people participate. For example, putting different waste materials in their designated bins helps maintain a clean urban environment and reduces the volume of landfills. Furthermore, when more materials are recycled, ecologically harmful synthetics like plastic and battery acid are less likely to leak into natural habitats. This small act of responsibility, when engaged by sufficient people, not only has a significant impact on our current environment but also ensures a livable planet for future generations.

TG 02   Political Science

Your professor is teaching a class on Political Science. Write a post responding to the professor's question. In your response, you should:

- express and support your opinion
- make a contribution to the discussion

An effective response will contain at least 100 words. You will have 10 minutes to write it.

Dr. Singh:

As I mentioned in our previous class, the news we are exposed to from media outlets is often influenced by political or financial interests. For example, news agencies may polish the depiction of a current event to make it sound more interesting to attract more viewers, thus increasing network ratings. In this class, I would like you to discuss this question: Are people more concerned about the accuracy of news than in the past?

Henry:

I honestly believe that people cared more about news accuracy in the past. Think about the ways people received the news in the past. They were limited to only a few TV or radio channels, so it was essential for them to obtain correct information from these outlets.

Joyce:

I disagree with Henry that people cared more about the accuracy of news in the past. The average citizen today is much more critical of the information they receive from news agencies. This can be reflected by the advent of countless independent news critics who create content for the sole purpose of analyzing the legitimacy of mainstream media reports.

© Sample Response

The advent of the Internet has created an explosion of information accessible to the public, which, as Joyce suggests, provides a platform for innumerable news outlets, both mainstream and independent. I think this phenomenon does reflect that modern people care more about the accuracy of the news they receive. In the past, most average citizens lacked the means to obtain different sources of information, thus they were less aware of the events, circumstances, and cultures outside of their native country. The absence of global knowledge made people less critical of the news conveyed to them by the press since they often failed to acknowledge the greater context of a news report. In contrast, modern audiences have access to the Internet, which broadens the range of their perspectives, so they are more sensitive to biased reports or misinformation. As a result, they become more skeptical of the news and focus more on its accuracy because they know the news can be misleading or partial. Essentially, this enhanced understanding of the world induces modern citizens to be more concerned about the accuracy of the news.

TG 04　Marketing

Your professor is teaching a class on Marketing. Write a post responding to the professor's question. In your response, you should:

- express and support your opinion
- make a contribution to the discussion

An effective response will contain at least 100 words. You will have 10 minutes to write it.

Dr. Lim:

We are all consumers in the market economy and make purchases according to particular needs. But today's market offers so many products that it has led to a culture of hyper-consumerism, which blurs the line between what consumers need and what they want. For example, people may buy the newest model of a cell phone without any contemplation on its use. Before the next class, I would like you to discuss this question: Do people often buy products not because they need them but because others have them? Why?

Yumi:

I think this happens quite often. A lot of people buy into the idea of being successful, or at least they want to feel successful, and a quick way to gain this feeling is to own the same products as a successful person. For instance, when fans see their icon wearing a particular shirt, they might go out and buy the same shirt since they want to be like their icon.

Jeremy:

I agree that this behavior exists amongst consumers, but it doesn't happen as often as some might think. The evidence lies with finances. Only those with discretionary savings are more likely to buy products out of envy. And recent statistics show that, even in affluent countries, less than 20 percent of the population has disposable income.

◎ Sample Response

From my perspective, I agree with Yumi that people often buy things because others possess them. However, a more obvious reason for this behavior is not to feel successful, but rather to create a positive persona to others, or in a word, vanity. Why wear an uncomfortable suit, pay for expensive jewelry, or use a computer at only 10 percent of its capacity? Most people want others to see them as smart, sophisticated, attractive, rich, etc. For instance, a man pursuing a woman would buy her gifts that successful women with good taste may favor, such as a certain fashion label, exquisite confectionery, or luxurious accessories. The man creates the perception of wealth, generosity, and attentiveness (of course, this may be genuine) to increase his chances of winning over the girl. Likewise, in professional settings, especially in the entrepreneurial sector, many are trying to create an image to impress, ranging from driving expensive cars to dining at high-end restaurants. Many of us look up to those who have made it in the rat race, whose fortunes and possessions represent a symbol of status, so many tend to recreate themselves in their images not only to gain a sense of success but more importantly, to gain the respect and admiration from others.

TG 05 Psychology

Your professor is teaching a class on Psychology. Write a post responding to the professor's question. In your response, you should:

• express and support your opinion

• make a contribution to the discussion

An effective response will contain at least 100 words. You will have 10 minutes to write it.

Dr. Schwimmer:

As per our discussion from the last class, we spoke about the factors of social influence and its potential effects on individuals. For example, you may learn to like a song you previously did not enjoy because most people in your friend circle and the larger society like that song. So as you can see, we are influenced by others in one way or another and vice versa. For this week's discussion board, I would like you to discuss this question: Do people easily learn from friends who are close to them?

Mei Ling:

From where I stand, I think good friends do have the tendency to learn from each other. A strong friendship often involves friends participating in the same activities or having a common interest, and within them, they exchange thoughts, ideas, tips, and so on, which naturally leads to mutual learning.

Ed:

I disagree with Mei Ling that friends learn easily from each other. Don't forget there's also a degree of competitiveness within most friendships. So they may be reserved about revealing their true strengths or how they came to obtain certain abilities, making it difficult for others to truly learn from them.

◎ Sample Response

I am a firm believer that friends can easily learn from each other. Apart from the frequency of interaction that leads to mutual learning, human nature plays a vital role in this matter. We are all the product of our environment; what we are exposed to and who we interact with influence us to help shape who we are. Humans have the innate ability to imitate, which is programmed into our genes, and it is one of the traits that help us survive. For example, if a person's friend circle consists of many who love to read, that person would be more likely to develop a habit of reading since it would help him improve his relationship with his friends by giving him more common topics of conversation. Moreover, friends may subconsciously mimic each other's movements and speech or style and taste because it can bring people closer to each other, creating inseparable bonds. Through building stronger friendships, people enhance their state of survival since they gain a wide range of benefits, from emotional support to financial assistance. Therefore, learning from our friends is nothing but natural human behavior, and most of us are proficient at this act.

TG 06 Environmental Science

Your professor is teaching a class on Environmental Science. Write a post responding to the professor's question. In your response, you should:

- express and support your opinion
- make a contribution to the discussion

An effective response will contain at least 100 words. You will have 10 minutes to write it.

Dr. Ganas:

In the past few weeks, we've been examining global environmental issues and the various actions governments around the world have taken in an attempt to resolve them. For example, The Paris Agreement was a collaborative effort of 178 countries to control the rate of global warming. If you were a policymaker or the leader of a nation, what do you think is the most important action for the government to take to protect the environment?

Mike:

I think the government must establish nature reserves that protect habitats and wildlife. The main purpose of environmental protection is to save the diversity of lifeforms living on our planet, but if governments don't act fast, many plants and animals will become extinct very soon, which would be an irreversible loss.

Denise:

One of the biggest concerns today comes from pollution, particularly air and water pollution. So as a policymaker, I would push laws that limit the quantity of pollutants large corporations discharge or emit into the water or air. This would have a significant positive impact on urban and rural areas alike.

© Sample Response

Environmental protection is an imminent problem, but also a tricky one. I think Mike and Denise both made good proposals, however, they neglected an important aspect—sustainability. Encircling and managing a large natural area requires substantial investment of finances and labor; strict environmental laws cut into the profit of large companies, which could lead to economic crises. The government should focus its resources on a sustainable solution that, at the same time, has a significant impact. As a nation's leader, I would urge the government to fund the research, development, and popularization of green energy, such as solar power, wind power, or hydroelectricity. Provided that all forms of transportation were powered by sustainable electricity or a type of emission-free fuel, air pollution would be nearly eradicated. In addition, if urban and industrious regions are maintained with clean energy, their emissions would also reduce to minimal levels. Furthermore, green energy can also flourish as a vibrant new industry, creating new businesses and employment, and making it financially feasible. The energy industry is where many dire problems stem from, so if we want to truly eradicate environmental problems, we should address them at the core.

TG 07 Education

> Your professor is teaching a class on Education. Write a post responding to the professor's question. In your response, you should:
>
> • express and support your opinion
>
> • make a contribution to the discussion
>
> An effective response will contain at least 100 words. You will have 10 minutes to write it.

Dr. Lannister:

There are many things you should consider when choosing a major before enrolling in university. I'm sure all of you had to go through the process of weighing your options, trying to figure out what the best decision is. Among many, a factor that often can't be neglected is future employment prospects, so I want to know what you would choose between these two choices and why: a major that can be completed in a shorter time so you can enter the workforce sooner or a major that requires many years to finish, but it would offer many more job opportunities in the future.

Cersei:

I'd have to go with the first option. Entering the workforce sooner means earning an income sooner, which is important to so many students because they're burdened with expensive student loans. Debt carried by college students has become a serious social issue, and I just can't imagine myself still paying off a student loan in my forties.

Tyrion:

Contrary to Cersei, I insist on choosing the second option. Why? The answer is plain and simple—the pay gap. Most majors leading to high-paying jobs require students to study extensively, such as doctors. But once you become a doctor or a lawyer, the annual income you pull in is equivalent to multiple years of doing a job with an average salary. I think you can see where I'm going with this.

◎ Sample Response

I would make the same choice as Cersei, but not only because of student loans. Completing a college education numerous years ahead of time gives an individual a big advantage in their future careers, which can lead to success, fortune, status, and so on. Any profession can be lucrative; it depends on the effort and time one is willing to invest. One should marinate and gain experience for many years in society before expecting notable accomplishments. Take Steve Jobs for example. He left college prematurely to pursue his dream in the IT business, working different occupations while struggling to keep Apple running in his parent's garage. He devoted his energy and possessions to his passion, which eventually made him into the iconic figure we all know him to be. One critical factor that allowed Jobs' career to take off was time. Had Jobs set off on his path a few years later, perhaps he would have missed crucial windows of opportunity, and his story would have been rewritten. Thus, let's give ourselves the advantage of the time by finishing our schooling in a reasonable timeframe, because without time, talents would be wasted and potential would be lost.

TG 08　Media

Your professor is teaching a class on **Media**. Write a post responding to the professor's question. In your response, you should:

- express and support your opinion
- make a contribution to the discussion

An effective response will contain at least 100 words. You will have 10 minutes to write it.

Dr. Stark:

In the next few classes, we're going to focus on television programs. As you all know, the TV industry has grown exponentially in the past few years, giving viewers so many more choices than before. The average time people spend watching television, unsurprisingly, has also noticeably increased. Before we begin, I'd like everyone to discuss the motive for people to watch TV, which leads to this topic: Do most people watch television for entertainment or for gaining knowledge?

John:

To me, it's obvious. Most people watch TV for fun. Just look at the channels that are the most popular—none of them are educational stations. They are unanimously entertainment channels like HBO, Netflix, Star, etc., which mainly offer the audience shows such as dramas, comedies, or animations. The fact that these channels are favored by the public clearly says that most people watch to entertain.

Sanza:

I tend to disagree with John on this one. One thing he failed to mention is TV ratings in relation to the time of day. When we look at the data, the highest amount of traffic goes to news channels every day, especially during the evening news broadcast. Sure some of us watch TV because it's extremely entertaining, but I think the thirst for knowledge still trumps sitcoms and cartoons.

© Sample Response

Whether it is watching a classic film or the latest drama series, I think the primary purpose for people to watch TV is to entertain. Despite the existence of informative shows and channels, such as the evening news or the history program; the overall time people spend watching television is on programs that give them laughter, relaxation, excitement, and so on. Sanza argues that news broadcasts gain the highest ratings throughout the day and claims it to be proof that people are watching TV mainly to gain information. However, this phenomenon only accounts for an insignificant portion of the day, and if we examine the cause, we can find that it does not support her argument. Only a limited number of channels dedicate themselves to regular news programs, thus the traffic of viewers is directed to these channels, which explains the high ratings. Entertainment channels, on the other hand, have a more even distribution of viewership as the audience seeks a show out of hundreds of options that cater to their preference. In addition, it is no coincidence that the vast majority favor entertainment over learning: people need to set aside their obligations after a long day of school or a tough day at work. I would certainly be unwilling to overload my mind after undergoing a stressful test.

TG 09 Time Management

Your professor is teaching a class on Time Management. Write a post responding to the professor's question. In your response, you should:

- express and support your opinion
- make a contribution to the discussion

An effective response will contain at least 100 words. You will have 10 minutes to write it.

Dr. LeBlanc:

The efficient use of time has been our main topic of discussion for the past few weeks. We talked about the importance of exploiting free time to benefit personal well-being or that of others, for example, attending social gatherings to strengthen existing bonds or create new ones, which enhances a sense of community and expands your social resources. Here's the question for today's board: As a student in college, which activity during your spare time do you think would bring you the most benefit?

Phoebe:

I would spend my time participating in volunteer work that contributes to the local community. Knowing that I helped people in a certain way gives me a sense of pride, achievement as well as self-worth. But beyond that, I think it's a good way to get in touch with others and make new friends with a positive mindset, thus indirectly expanding your social network.

Matt:

I think I'd spend the time enriching myself by pursuing an interest or passion. Personally, it would be learning a musical instrument. Learning a new skill set is conducive to your future in multiple ways, whether in your private life or professional career. It can be a tool used for relaxation and enjoyment or a catalyst for interaction and communication.

◎ Sample Response

Spending time helping others or acquiring a skill is practical in some ways, but as a student, I would take a more pragmatic approach that has a pronounced impact on my future career instead—to specify, spending time on expanding social networks that can help further one's endeavors. Students undergoing tertiary education usually study a field of major that they one day wish will become their profession. So taking the time to be familiar with said field's milieu and reaching out to those with similar pursuits or seasoned professionals can deliver many advantages. For instance, a law student can apply for an internship or a basic-level part-time job at a law firm, which gives him insight into how these establishments operate and helps him meet interesting people that could present him with future career opportunities. Students can also attend functions and events that are related to their studies (i.e an art student visits an art exhibition), so they can meet people with common interests, not only to make new friends but also to make acquaintances with potential collaborators. Optimal social networking gives a head start to students when entering the society, instead of facing a completely new challenge; they will have a solid foundation on which they can build their future.

TG 10　Political Science

Your professor is teaching a class on Political Science. Write a post responding to the professor's question. In your response, you should:

- express and support your opinion
- make a contribution to the discussion

An effective response will contain at least 100 words. You will have 10 minutes to write it.

Dr. Fernandez:

Most of us, if not all, are subjects of a system established by the government that regulates the functioning of society. However, many are not involved in the policy or law-making process; it is mainly up to those in positions of power, especially in authoritarian regimes. Let's view our school as a miniature version of society, and I want you to think about this question: Should students be involved in making decisions that affect campus life, such as the food served in the cafeteria or opening hours of the library, or leave the decisions up to the school administration and experts?

Cole:

Students should definitely have a say in making school policies that affect their campus life, in my opinion, because they're the ones affected the most. Just look at the ratio of campus demographic. I'd say over 80 percent of our school's population consists of students, so it makes sense to involve the majority who are affected in the decision-making process.

Chantelle:

I don't think it's a great idea to involve too many students when it comes to making these policies. Don't get me wrong. I think the students' voices should be heard, but they shouldn't overpower the administration because most students are just not mature enough to give useful suggestions. Look at what at least half of the students do in their spare time—partying and playing video games.

◎ Sample Response

In my opinion, students should be involved in the decision-making process, not only because they represent the majority, but also because they provide crucial data that can improve the decision. School policies and facilities function to promote a student's educational experience and campus lifestyle, so the feedback or criticism from students regarding such aspects can assist the administration to formulate better decisions. For example, the school can conduct a survey on the cafeteria's food quality, gathering honest opinions from those (mainly students) who dine at the facility on a regular basis. With that information, the school can conclude whether they should continue to offer food services as it is or make any suitable changes. In contrast, if the school ignores or neglects the voice of the students, the chances of making a decision that might be viewed as impractical or senseless would increase, instigating new problems and leading to discontent. Therefore, giving students a say in such affairs not only shows the sincerity and responsibility of the administration board but also paves the way for more satisfying results that benefit all parties involved.

TG 12   Psychology

Your professor is teaching a class on **Psychology**. Write a post responding to the professor's question. In your response, you should:

• express and support your opinion

• make a contribution to the discussion

An effective response will contain at least 100 words. You will have 10 minutes to write it.

Dr. Goldstein:

Friendship is one of the fundamental expressive ties between people within our social construct. We value established cordial relationships because they fulfill many intrinsic human desires, such as love, community, and well-being. So it's expected that we carry out activities that strengthen the bond between friends. If you had to choose one of the following activities to improve a friendship, which would it be and why? 1. Having a good time together. 2. Talking to each other about problems and supporting each other.

Gemma:

Hanging out and enjoying good times together is fun and all, but the relationship tends to stay superficial. That's why I'd go with sharing problems and supporting each other. They allow friends to interact and communicate on a deeper level, just like my best friend and I. We've been mutually supportive for many years, and our friendship is rock solid.

Zeke:

I think, in general, positive common experiences have a greater impact on friendships. Think about how relationships are forged. Two strangers don't just come together and talk about personal issues. They go out and have fun! And during that process, they can learn a lot about each other: their interests, personalities, backgrounds, etc.

◎ Sample Response

If I had to choose between sharing a good time or communicating about personal problems to improve a friendship, I would choose the former. Apart from the types of interaction mentioned by Zeke, friends' participating in a positive event or activity is the cohesion that bonds two people together, and the more frequently these activities occur, the stronger the bond becomes. For any friendship to be enduring or unbreakable, an injection of positive energy is desired, because it creates fond memories and common experiences that can be the topic of discussion for friends to share over their lifetime. This is the exact case between my good friend and I. We often talk about the road trips we took that involved many interesting adventures and engaging encounters. Being able to reminisce such endearing memory has allowed us to maintain a wonderful relationship, even though we live in different countries. On the other hand, if the only conversation between friends revolves around problems and difficulties, too much negative energy would accumulate, which would drive friends to drift apart since spending time together is consistently stressful. Although a healthy dose of hardship can contribute to a relationship, positivity should be the dominant factor in a friendship.

TG 13 Marketing

Your professor is teaching a class on Marketing. Write a post responding to the professor's question. In your response, you should:

• express and support your opinion

• make a contribution to the discussion

An effective response will contain at least 100 words. You will have 10 minutes to write it.

Dr. Haus:

In the past few weeks, we spoke about several commercial advertisement methods and their effects on the consumer. Companies may employ celebrities or admired media personalities, craft catchy slogans or jingles, or design elaborate visual effects to catch the viewer's attention. But they all serve the same purpose of stimulating sales so that the company can meet the bottom line. Before we proceed to our next unit, I'd like you to respond to this question: To become a successful business, is it necessary to spend a large amount of funding on advertising?

Imran:

I believe media exposure plays an irreplaceable role in today's business arena. Considering that more and more people are accustomed to online consumerism, we gain information about a product mainly through social media, websites, or email. It'd be nearly impossible for a product to gain traction without exploiting these channels. So yes, substantial investment is required.

I hold a different opinion from Imran. I think publicity plays an active role in getting the message out there to the public, but it doesn't need a huge amount of investment. As long as the quality of a product is exceptional, word of mouth will do the rest. I know that iPhones are really popular in China, but there are rarely any Apple commercials in the Chinese media.

◎ Sample Response

With the development of the global marketplace, an increasing number of products are promoted in the market, leading to a fiercely competitive atmosphere in the business world. To survive and thrive in this challenging environment, I believe businesses (if they are to expand to a large scale) must invest an adequate amount of capital in advertisement. Commercials not only expose the public to a certain product, but a more glaring function is that they also build a company's image and brand, which inflates the intrinsic value of any product produced by a company. Consider this scenario. Two pairs of sneakers with identical quality and design would have a sharp contrast in their prices if one pair had a logo of a prestigious brand imprinted on the side, while the other pair did not. The brand itself accounts for this stark difference, which is established through years of persisting advertisement. The resiliency of a business largely relies on its ability to turn a profit, thus, when publicity is absent or insufficient, its capacity to prosper into a lucrative operation diminishes, hampering its trajectory to success.

TG 14 Administration Policies

Your professor is teaching a class on Administration Policies. Write a post responding to the professor's question. In your response, you should:

• express and support your opinion

• make a contribution to the discussion

An effective response will contain at least 100 words. You will have 10 minutes to write it.

Global warming is a major global concern because it leads to many critical environmental problems like rising sea levels and weather anomalies. One of the primary causes of rising temperatures I mentioned before is carbon emission, which can be largely attributed to industries such as manufacturing, energy production, and transportation. Airplanes, among all forms of transportation, leave the heaviest trail of carbon footprint. So for this discussion board, I'd like you to tell me whether or not you believe the following policy is a good idea, and why: Lower pollution by imposing an ecological tax on airplanes and use the tax revenue to develop low-pollution transportation.

Melissa:

I don't think this would have a noticeable effect on air pollution. Air travel is an essential form of transportation, thus it cannot be replaced. Taxing it would only make it more expensive to travelers, not decrease the frequency of its use. It's by far the most efficient way to travel overseas, so most people who intend to visit another country or continent can't afford the time to have a second option.

Elijah:

I agree with Melissa that airplanes are a necessary means of transportation, but making air travel more expensive can have a significant impact on reducing pollution. Airline companies would take measures to cut costs to offset the financial pressure imposed by the tax, and that could result in fewer flights. For instance, they would ensure flights reach their full passenger capacities, so empty flights or ones with only a few passengers would be canceled. Plus, funding for new innovations would be secured. It's a win-win situation.

© Sample Response

At first glance, one might perceive taxing air travel could reduce air pollution since it is possible to reduce the number of total flights. However, a minor diminution in flight frequency does not have a significant impact on the total amount of carbon emission, thus this is one reason why the policy is flawed. In addition, the tax would be reallocated to the passengers by the airlines, which means the government is indirectly taxing average citizens, which defeats the initial intention. Since airplanes are irreplaceable, and taxing them merely imposes an economic burden on travelers, the government should adjust and devise a more feasible notion. In my opinion, the tax should be modified to a corporate tax with a clause clearly stating that it cannot be exploited to inflate airfares. Subsequently, the revenue should go to developing clean fuel instead of a new form of transportation. And provided that the innovation succeeds, airplanes can switch to clean fuel, which then will generate a significant impact on lowering emission levels. Therefore, for the sake of saving citizens from financial burdens and avoiding investing in dead-ends, the government should fine-tune its policy into a more pragmatic and effective strategy.

TG 15 Transportation

Your professor is teaching a class on Transportation. Write a post responding to the professor's question. In your response, you should:

• express and support your opinion

• make a contribution to the discussion

An effective response will contain at least 100 words. You will have 10 minutes to write it.

Dr. L'amour:

For our next unit, we're going to look at urban transportation. A highly urbanized area cannot function without a sophisticated road network and public transit systems. However, with the rapid growth of city population, the traffic system of many dense urban areas are under increased pressure. To alleviate this problem, some propose to lower gas prices and build more roads so more people can drive private vehicles, while others believe it's better to encourage people to take public transportation by increasing the number of bus and train routes. Which suggestion do you think is better for improving city traffic conditions? And Why?

David:

To me, one of the biggest issues of city transportation is traffic congestion. And the leading cause of traffic jams is the overwhelming number of private motor vehicles on the streets. So, encouraging more citizens to travel via public transport is the better method to improve traffic conditions. If more routes were added to the point that it's more convenient to travel by bus or train, more people would abandon driving, thus reducing overflowing traffic.

Saoirse:

I don't believe a more complex public transportation system would improve traffic conditions. The reason is actually quite obvious. Increasing the number of routes based on an existing road network only adds fuel to the fire. Imagine the same road space but with many more large vehicles like buses. It would create worse congestion. So building more roads and lowering gas prices is the more effective approach.

◎ Sample Response

Improving traffic conditions is definitely one of the conundrums perplexing administrators of a fast-growing urban area. From my perspective, optimizing public transport is the better method, even if no new roads are built. More bus routes or subway lines that can reach more corners of the city mean that more commuters are able to reach most of their destinations, which has a variety of advantages. Road space would be used with more efficiency; larger forms of transportation occupy less space per passenger compared to private vehicles, thus the streets would be less crowded with cars, reducing or alleviating traffic congestion. In addition, some forms of public transport are not subjected to road conditions, such as traffic lights, line-ups, and so on, so travelers can usually arrive at their destinations punctually. This is achievable without investing in a more complex and extended road system since the existing infrastructure of a mature city already reaches most of the city's regions, and subways or trains can exploit space above or under the ground. Along with other benefits (lower costs, no need to find parking, etc.), many would abandon driving for taking public transportation, creating better city road environments, and making it more convenient and safer for all residents.

TG 17　Social Studies

> Your professor is teaching a class on Social Studies. Write a post responding to the professor's question. In your response, you should:
>
> • express and support your opinion
>
> • make a contribution to the discussion
>
> An effective response will contain at least 100 words. You will have 10 minutes to write it.

Dr. Nardone:

As I mentioned in class, our social network plays a significant role in our lives, whose value is reflected by the various benefits it provides, such as companionship, a sense of security and belonging, and perhaps, even wealth. It takes time and effort to establish meaningful and fruitful relationships. So the loss of such relationships is not only emotionally devastating, but you also lose a degree of their perks. The question I'd like you to discuss this time is whether it is a good thing for people to move to a new town or country because of their loss of old social connections.

Nathan:

I mean, sometimes we're so used to the people around us that we take them for granted. I wouldn't uproot myself and move to a new city or foreign country merely because I drifted apart from my connections. Why not just reconnect with them? You'd have to make new friends and go through the process of social networking again at a new place, which probably wouldn't hold the same weight as your old friends. So no, I don't think it's a good thing.

Aubrey:

I don't completely agree with Nathan on this one. I think people need a fresh start sometimes. There must be a reason for people losing their social connections, for instance, an irresolvable conflict of interest or some kind of deep misunderstanding. No one likes to live with a chip on his shoulder, getting awkward glances or overhearing critical gossip. Being in such an environment can be suffocating. Therefore moving to a new place is a positive step to take.

◎ Sample Response

Whether it is a childhood playmate, a high school buddy, or a close colleague, social connections play an irreplaceable role in our lives, and losing these ties can severely impact our lives. However, I do not believe relocating to another city or country is a reasonable step to take when people lose these connections. Moving to a new place before repairing old relationships can leave a lingering effect on an individual's mental health, festering with time and continuously damaging one's psyche. Humans are emotional creatures with powerful memory; the jubilant events and delightful experiences with close ones are etched into our minds permanently, and so is the case with unresolved misunderstandings and disputes. Leaving it all behind may sound like a relief at first glance, but ultimately, the melancholy of missing old friends and the urge of wanting to reconnect would gradually eat away at one's spirit, leading to negative emotions, such as depression, frustration, and misery. New social connections would fail to fill the void inside as bonds only gain strength with the presence of time. Thus, rather than turn a blind eye to deteriorating relationships, one should at least try to mend or revive these meaningful connections.

TG 18 Consumerism

> Your professor is teaching a class on Consumerism. Write a post responding to the professor's question. In your response, you should:
> - express and support your opinion
> - make a contribution to the discussion
>
> An effective response will contain at least 100 words. You will have 10 minutes to write it.

Dr. Finch:

The market economy encourages us to consume products, and we often buy things without too much thinking. But when it comes to making a major purchase like a car or a laptop, most people would think twice before buying, and they'd gather all the information available to make a more rational decision. Given today's abundance of product information, if you were to make such a large purchase, which source of information would influence your decision the most? Why?

Han:

I'm thinking online user reviews. Most of them are genuine post-purchase user experiences without the motive of promoting the product they've bought. So it's safe to say that they're mostly objective, offering credible reference. I based the purchase of my new smart phone on the reviews I had read, and I'm very satisfied with the result.

Felicia:

As for me, I would be more influenced by product launch events. Although these events serve the purpose of promoting a product, they are surprisingly informative. I can gain a more comprehensive understanding of a product through the introduction of its specs and the demonstration of its functions. These events can provide the most detailed information on a product, and I can use it to decide whether or not the product suits my needs.

© Sample Response

In my opinion, professional product reviews by credited individuals or organizations like a magazine or newspaper would be ideal sources of information for me to decide whether or not to make a large purchase. The people writing the articles about a specific product are mainly experts in the industry, and they can offer professional insight into the applications and specifications of the product. For instance, if I were to buy a car, a magazine like *Top Gear* can provide me with the information on a car's capacity, including mileage, horsepower, safety, road performance, and so on, which allows me to objectively compare different models. All of the information depicted in the magazine is written by recognized individuals in the automobile industry, and the knowledge they convey is meticulously vetted before publication. On the other hand, independent consumer reviews can be biased as people have different demands for a product. And when it comes to launch events, many flaws of a product would be omitted by the host company, since exhibiting the shortcomings of a new product to the marketplace contradicts corporate interests. Therefore, the best approach for me to gain useful information and make a rational purchase is through reading professional reviews.

TG 20   Consumerism

Your professor is teaching a class on **Consumerism**. Write a post responding to the professor's question. In your response, you should:

- express and support your opinion

- make a contribution to the discussion

An effective response will contain at least 100 words. You will have 10 minutes to write it.

Dr. Hensley:

A large chunk of people's income goes into sustenance for the simple reason that we all have to eat to sustain life. This gives precedent to a vibrant restaurant industry in many places around the world. Some people like to buy and eat meals at restaurants, bistros, or eateries frequently, while others still prefer to prepare and enjoy their meals at home. Which option would you prefer? And explain the rationale behind your decision.

Finley:

I'm a big foodie, so I tend to eat out most of the time. The variety of foods I'm able to experience at a restaurant is much more abundant than what I can make at home. Some dishes are nearly impossible or at least extremely difficult to prepare at home because they involve an immense amount of prep time and exotic ingredients that are hard to obtain from the local market. Just think about brewing a stock for many hours only to make a bowl of Vietnamese Pho.

◎ Sample Response

Eating out at a venue can be very convenient and exciting, but I would prefer to prepare my own food for the majority of my meals. Firstly, it is the best way to maintain a healthy and balanced diet since I can control each step of making the meal, from shopping for ingredients to cooking. This way, the quality of the dish can be ensured as the produce, meat, and other items are carefully chosen from the market, and the seasoning that goes into the dish is safe to consume. Many restaurants serve food that is pre-made for efficiency or add additives to make the dish tastier or pleasing to the eye, which may contain harmful agents, such as carcinogens. Secondly, apart from the financial pressure that constantly dining out imposes on our wallets, the fun and excitement of the restaurant experience would significantly diminish when dining out becomes a routine. So for the sake of my health and to retain the novelty of dining experiences, I would choose to live a more domestic lifestyle.

TG 22　Environment Protection

Your professor is teaching a class on the Environment Protection. Write a post responding to the professor's question. In your response, you should:

- express and support your opinion

- make a contribution to the discussion

An effective response will contain at least 100 words. You will have 10 minutes to write it.

Lilian:

Together with the development of the economy and society, pollution also attracts people's attention. As we all know, the environment is important not only for the survival of the ecosystem but also for the sustainable development of humankind. As the environment becomes worse, it is essential for a nation's government to take action to help protect the environment. Which action do you think is the most important for a nation's government to take for protecting the environment? Why?

The right way to protect the environment is to launch a protection campaign on the environment and ecosystem, which can improve the living environment for many people. In addition, wildlife and plant species can be preserved by establishing nature conservation parks. For example, the number of endangered animals like tigers, pandas, or rhinos can be sustained.

I don't agree with Kevin since if pollution is not prevented, or at least reduced, its destruction of the environment will continue. The best way to protect the environment is to enforce laws to eliminate the source of pollution, such as air and water pollution emitted by large companies. This way, the problem can be solved at the core.

◎ Sample Response

Just like what Katherine has said, banning companies or factories from discharging waste might be the most effective measure to prevent pollution, but it only cares about the aspect of the environment, paying no attention to the impact it will have on the economy. No emission into the natural environment also means no production inside factories, which must cast huge damage to people's living economically, so this measure is too radical and thus infeasible to some extent. Therefore, the best way to protect the environment is to take both the economy and the environment into consideration, and in this case, the government should make attempts to find a balance between them and form milder policies. For example, the government can set a penalty threshold to manage factories' emissions of waste, and those who emit excessive amounts of waste shall be fined. Also, the limit should be adjusted higher or lower according to local conditions. Apart from making policies, the government should also be an executor, reinvesting its revenues in the areas of developing new energy and neutralizing the negative effects of waste emission on the natural environment.

TG 23 Technology

Your professor is teaching a class on Technology. Write a post responding to the professor's question. In your response, you should:

- express and support your opinion
- make a contribution to the discussion

An effective response will contain at least 100 words. You will have 10 minutes to write it.

Dr. Jackson:

As I have mentioned, the development of society has its negative and positive sides. And this is proven true in the development of scientific technology, such as how nuclear technology can be used to power cities or to build weapons of mass destruction. Some people claim the importance of searching for development since it changes and improves the living standards and welfare of citizens, while others point out that it is time-consuming and costly, and they think it is unnecessary to do so. Do you think humankind should exert so many costs to advance scientific research? Why?

Caterina:

It is the nature of human beings to search the unknown world. I think diligent scientific research, like space exploration, is necessary since it pushes the boundary of human potential. Just like the saying, no pain, no gain. If people don't invest, how can they get paid?

Anderson:

Even though scientific research draws benefits in successful cases, it is costly and energy-consuming. Since most of the cases people are exposed to are successful, it might mislead people into thinking that scientific progression is always beneficial. But actually, a larger proportion of scientific research ends up fruitless, which depletes a lot of public resources.

◎ Sample Response

When you're trying to shoot a basketball into the rim above you, it's full of odds for you to miss, but are the missed ones really a waste of time and energy? I would say they increase your shooting percentage in the future. As Anderson said, most of the cases people have seen were successful. That is sufficient for us to continue our forward march on scientific research. Even though there were considerable attempts ended up in failure, they still drove us ahead. Looking back on the marvelous achievements that we have made, they were not achievements from the beginning, but we have obtained them through failures and frustrations. When Thomas Edison searched for a suitable material as a filament for his bulb, he tried thousands of types of materials before he finally got to Japanese bamboo. Even after that, more suitable materials kept being found to perfect incandescent bulbs, but can we say that all those materials were wasted? Even if they were, their waste was worthwhile. If we are always stingy about the time and money invested in making new things, our previous efforts would have been wasted indeed.

TG 24 Education

Your professor is teaching a class on Education. Write a post responding to the professor's question. In your response, you should:

- express and support your opinion
- make a contribution to the discussion

An effective response will contain at least 100 words. You will have 10 minutes to write it.

Professor Kalman:

Education is considered the preparation for one's career. So the goal of universities is to cultivate more students who are suitable for the labor market. In this case, some universities encourage students to study fields in which significant job growth is expected, such as science, technology, engineering, and math. Do you think it is a good idea for students to study fields in which they can find a job easier, instead of learning what they are interested in? Why?

Mark:

People need to consider their career development since they need to earn a living for themselves and their families. When students learn skills or knowledge at a university, most of them connect their future careers and lives to what they choose to study. People live a better life because of the education they undergo, which is one of education's purposes.

Lily:

Even though I agree with Mark that education helps people build a better life, they should take into account their interests. If students pursue a major they are not interested in, they would lack the motivation to learn it well. So in the future, they lose a competitive edge and may have to put up with a job they find tedious.

◎ Sample Response

Interests are not necessarily incompatible with prospects. Many people are working on their interests: Walt Disney, an amateur painter before founding the world-renowned Disney; Zuckerberg, whose company, Facebook, originated from his own Facemash website during Harvard. I wouldn't owe their success to the luck that brought them the jobs which met their interests, but I would admire them for their persistence in their interests. In their cases, interest came first, and it was interest that gave birth to their lucrative businesses. Apart from that, our society is a construct consisting of various occupations, where favored jobs tend to be in the fields of business, technology, and engineering. In this situation, the fierce competition in these jobs would eliminate a large number of applicants, whereas less favorable ones will open their arms, making them easier to obtain. The income you are going to get, if you follow your interests, is probably higher than what you will get with so-called popular jobs since your interests will inspire you and keep you motivated. All balanced, it is not wise to let the consideration of prospects discourage your pursuit of interests.

TG 25　Education

Your professor is teaching a class on Education. Write a post responding to the professor's question. In your response, you should:

• express and support your opinion

• make a contribution to the discussion

An effective response will contain at least 100 words. You will have 10 minutes to write it.

Dr. Kagan:

Whether students should spend all their time on studying is under discussion in the current education milieu. Some even advise students to take a gap year before heading into university education. In what way do you think it is beneficial or harmful if a student graduating from high school takes a year's gap traveling or working before they go to university? Why?

Shirley:

Life is not always about studying, and there are other important things in one's life. A straight-A student does not necessarily have a successful career. It is beneficial for students to reflect on what they really want and how they can be competitive in the future, and this needs time. A gap year offers them the opportunity to do so.

Karson:

A gap year is a waste of time. On one hand, most students are not mature enough to control their desires before they get into university since they are still quite young. On the other hand, when they arrive in an unfamiliar environment during traveling they may put themselves at risk. What if they come across danger? Averting danger requires experience and wisdom.

◎ Sample Response

I don't think the possibility of danger a student may face when visiting somewhere during his or her gap year poses a concern. Everything has its risks, just like road accidents while driving, yet we still have to do them. The problem of a gap year does not lie in the potential dangers or temptations but lies in the timing. Even when a student was given a year to get ready for adult life before college, he or she would have got too little experience to reflect on, so such a reflection yields no significant conclusion or plans for the future. Besides reflection, other advantages of taking a gap year, such as relaxing oneself, broadening horizon, or setting goals, can be easily obtained during college or work without having to waste a year. Therefore I think a gap year before college would be an unnecessary thing to do, but under ideal conditions, I think a gap year can be conducive. For example, experiencing a gap year for college graduates vacillating between prospects can help them conduct productive reflections because they are more likely to possess the maturity and sophistication to carry out self-discovery than high school graduates.

TG 26 Entertainment

> Your professor is teaching a class on Social Study. Write a post responding to the professor's question. In your response, you should:
>
> • express and support your opinion
>
> • make a contribution to the discussion
>
> An effective response will contain at least 100 words. You will have 10 minutes to write it.

Dr. Stark:

As the pace of living accelerates over time, citizens live their lives under greater pressure. To relieve pressure, many turn to watching movies, which has bloomed into an enormous industry adored by people around the world. Currently, there is a plethora of different film genres and themes that cater to the diverse preference of the audience. However, the public always wants movies to be not only entertaining but also meaningful. So some may insist that only stories with profound lessons are worth watching. Do you think the main purpose of a movie should be to convey meaningful lessons? Why?

Langley:

Movies are very popular nowadays, and most children are interested in watching movies during their free time at night or on holidays. Some of them even spend a lot of time binge-watching. So if they have meaningful lessons, they would be worth watching because children learn in the process of enjoying movies. In addition, movies with meaningful messages help educate children, improve their knowledge, or establish their moral standards. It would be optimal to have this function.

Martin:

We cannot forget that the most obvious and original purpose of the motion picture industry is to entertain the audience. When modern society renders people's lives distressed, they need ways to relax. Movies are introduced to fulfill this demand, and when people are relaxed, they have higher efficiency to continue their studies or work. In addition, the entertainment industry creates a great economic benefit for society. So receiving education is not the main purpose for people who go to the cinema.

◎ Sample Response

I don't think teaching people is a necessary thing that movies have to do. At least films should not be blamed when they are not educating enough. The reason is simple: they were just fundamentally not invented for the sake of education. Since its initiation, the movie theater has kept satisfying human desires to imitate and imagine, fulfilling intrinsic needs that stem from human nature. Better as it would be if student-targeted movies contain some teaching significance, it cannot ensure that children can really learn something from them, which can be attributed to the predisposed conception of movies by humans. When it comes to watching movies, we all inherently think about fun, so even if some movies aim to teach a particular group of people, they will not be as efficient as a class or lecture because people tend to appreciate them in a recreational manner rather than looking for lessons. All things considered, the educational effect is merely a by-product of a movie, which we should not regard as a purpose.

TG 27   Business

Your professor is teaching a class on **Business**. Write a post responding to the professor's question. In your response, you should:

• express and support your opinion
• make a contribution to the discussion

An effective response will contain at least 100 words. You will have 10 minutes to write it.

Professor King:

As industries and businesses develop, the economy expands and proliferates. But they also wield a negative impact on the global environment. Many companies sell products or services but at the same time cause environmental damage. Some say it can be stopped by asking them to pay penalties, such as a higher tax when they cause environmental damage. Others say there are better ways to stop them from harming the environment. What do you think is the best way to prevent the environment from deteriorating? Why?

Sam:

Taxing the companies that cause environmental damage is an efficient way to reduce pollution. Most companies do not have a budget large enough to pay heavy fines repeatedly. So if they are punished by the government, to avoid further penalties, they will stop polluting the environment. In addition, when companies are penalized, they get a bad reputation that may affect their development. There's no point in that they do not stop polluting the environment.

Claudia:

Financial punishment may reduce the possibility of reoccuring polluting behavior, but damage to the environment has already happened. I think advertisement campaigns about the consequences of pollution can be created to inform companies about the severity of pollution damage and preventative measures. In addition, the government can launch a policy to ban the kinds of corporate activities that may inflict irreversible harm on the environment.

◎ Sample Response

At first glance, taxing companies to stop further emitting pollution into the environment seems practical, but it does not consider the individuals, who also contribute a lot to pollution. It is a hard truth that I rarely see anyone who would live their lives in an environmentally-friendly way, including myself. We wouldn't wait for a second to turn on the AC when we feel hot, and we wouldn't pay attention to the exhaust made by our cars either. The reason we wouldn't do those things is that we have no alternatives. With increased living standards comes an inevitable shift of convenience and comfort from being a luxury to a basic need. To meet such demands, however, the sacrifice of the environment is required, and this is the fundamental contradiction between humans and nature—one consuming the other. In this way, a once-for-all solution must be devised to terminate this dilemma, ending humankind's parasitic relationship with nature. Although it seems impossible at present, degradable materials make us believe that in the near future, we can achieve multiple closed loops of what we take from and discharge to the environment.

TG 28   Interpersonal Relationship

Your professor is teaching a class on Interpersonal Relationship. Write a post responding to the professor's question. In your response, you should:

• express and support your opinion

• make a contribution to the discussion

An effective response will contain at least 100 words. You will have 10 minutes to write it.

Dr. Backman:

As I mentioned, the relationship between people is important but not easy to maintain, so let's go and discuss if people should keep their distance between them in order to sustain a good relationship. Some believe that one should spend more time being far away from the people they care about because it helps them understand the importance of their relationship, while others think being away from people whom they care about damage their relationship. Do you think staying away from people you care about strengthens or weakens your relationship? Why?

Diana:

It is not uncommon to see disagreement surfacing among friends, relatives, classmates, colleagues, or family members, and sometimes disagreement even turns into conflict, so distance seems to be important for improving relationships between people. In addition, when people regulate the distance with the people they care about, they may see the value of their relationships clearer.

Fredric:

I don't agree with Diana since when people stay away from each other, they don't get a connection, so their common interests and beliefs may reduce. Consequently, they do not share a few topics of conversation, which causes them to drift apart. Besides, when people remain distant from each other, they don't accompany each other, so they don't have common memories and experiences. In this case, it is impossible for them to maintain a tight relationship.

© Sample Response

Diana argues that distance can improve relationships by providing individuals with a chance to reflect on the importance of their loved ones. When we are in close proximity to someone, we may take them for granted or overlook their positive qualities. However, when we are far away, we may be more likely to appreciate the role that person plays in our lives. In contrast, Fredric believes that distance weakens relationships by reducing common interests, knowledge, and memories. When individuals are far away from one another, they may not have as much to talk about or share with one another, leading to a decline in closeness. Moreover, when individuals are not able to be present for important moments in each other's lives, they may miss out on creating shared memories. In my opinion, both Diana and Fredric have valid points. While distance can provide opportunities for reflection and independence, it can also create challenges in maintaining contact and shared experiences. However, I believe that the impact of distance on relationships ultimately depends on the nature of the relationship itself. For example, living away from parents can help an individual realize the care and sacrifice of a mother or father, thus helping one appreciate the relationship more. Overall, it is important for individuals to communicate with their loved ones about their needs and to find a balance that works for their particular relationship.

TG 29 Volunteer and Student Club

Your professor is teaching a class on Volunteer and Student Club. Write a post responding to the professor's question. In your response, you should:

- express and support your opinion
- make a contribution to the discussion

An effective response will contain at least 100 words. You will have 10 minutes to write it.

Dr. Chopin:

As I mentioned, when university students have spare time, they can do something useful for society. There are many associations, clubs, or organizations in universities for students to join if they want to enrich their school life and make a contribution to their community. Apart from studies, university students may spend some time taking part in activities or projects. What activity or project do you think is the best choice for university students to help others? Why?

Joyce:

I think that helping students in a nearby primary school with reading and mathematics is a good choice. It is constructive for university students to sometimes be useful to the community, and at the same time develop their practical ability. What's more, teachers in primary schools are always too busy to help all the students to keep up with their studies. With the help of university students, primary school students with difficulty in their studies may learn more efficiently.

James:

Volunteering to visit the elders in the elderly nursing home is a better choice for university students. It is easy to do since it doesn't require any skills or knowledge. The only things to do are just to have a conversation with the elders or help them do household chores. Additionally, visiting nursing homes aids residents to kill time and have a pleasant day.

© Sample Response

There are many different activities and projects that university students can choose to help others. In my opinion, volunteering at a local community center or charity organization is the best choice for university students to make a positive impact on their community. They offer a wide range of benefits for university students. Firstly, it allows them to help a broader spectrum of people in their community, not just primary school students. They can work with people of all ages and backgrounds, and make a difference in multiple ways. Secondly, it provides opportunities for students to learn new skills and develop their leadership abilities. For example, they may be able to organize events or coordinate with volunteers, which can help them gain valuable experience in project management and leadership. Finally, it helps to build a sense of community and social responsibility among university students. While Joyce suggests that assisting primary school students with reading and mathematics is a good choice, there are drawbacks to this approach. University students may not be qualified or experienced enough to provide effective tutoring or teaching. Moreover, by focusing only on primary school students, university students may miss out on opportunities to help a wider range of people in their community. Furthermore, there is a risk that university students may become overburdened with this specific project, leading to burnout or a lack of engagement.

TG 30　Internet

Your professor is teaching a class on Internet. Write a post responding to the professor's question. In your response, you should:

- express and support your opinion

- make a contribution to the discussion

An effective response will contain at least 100 words. You will have 10 minutes to write it.

Dr. Murphy:

Last class, we talked about the welfare of the citizens provided by the government without cost, such as infrastructure, public services, and public education. Today let's talk about the Internet. As a basic tool, the Internet is now almost used in every corner of the country. Do you think that the Internet should be free like the mentioned services, such as roads, and the government should provide it to the public at no cost? Why?

Louise:

The government needs income to make up all the expenses in a year, especially governments with a tight budget, which is common at present. If the government offers Internet for free, the income of the whole industry will be cut from the nation's revenue. This will make the financial situation of the government worse. Besides, the industry needs to profit to uphold maintenance and development. If the bottom line is compromised, the future of the industry can not be secured.

Neily:

I disagree with Louise. When society develops to a certain stage, the government should offer more free services to the citizens to reduce their economic pressure. The Internet is one of the tools that people use almost every day. It is now just like public services, roads, parks, or other amenities, provided to the public. So the government should add Internet service to the list of social welfare.

◎ Sample Response

In response to Neily's view, while it is true that the government has a role to play in providing public services to citizens, it is not clear whether the Internet should be provided in the same manner as physical infrastructure such as roads or parks. The Internet is a constantly evolving and complex system, and it is not clear that the government would be the best equipped to manage and regulate it. Moreover, while access to the Internet is certainly important, other public services may be more pressing priorities for government investment, such as healthcare or education. Also, there are some drawbacks to this approach. Firstly, it is not clear how the government would fund the provision of free Internet services, and whether this would require significant investment of taxpayer money. Secondly, there is a risk that providing free Internet access could lead to a reduction in the quality of services, as private companies may have less incentive to invest in improving their infrastructure and technology. Finally, there is a danger that treating the Internet as a public service could lead to government censorship and control over online content, which could have negative implications for freedom of speech and expression.

TG 31 Education

Your professor is teaching a class on Education. Write a post responding to the professor's question. In your response you should:

• express and support your opinion

• make a contribution to the discussion

An effective response will contain at least 100 words. You will have 10 minutes to write it.

Dr. Graves:

Last week, we talked about how students can make full use of their time during school, and we have formulated several schedules for them to achieve this goal. This week, we're going to extend this topic and discuss time spent at home. So here's a question for the class discussion board: Do you think that students should spend more time doing homework or participating in organized activities related to school or sports, or they should be given more time to do whatever they want?

Samantha:

I think students are supposed to take advantage of the time at home to apply the knowledge they learn from school because, during school time, students are engaged in absorbing new knowledge, yet they don't have time to practice it. For example, mastering a new language requires time-consuming practices, which they can't find the time to do at school. Moreover, students can freely experiment and make mistakes with their newfound knowledge at home without worrying about criticism from teachers or peers.

Serge:

Home is where we enjoy life, even for students, so I think they should be given enough free time to do what they want. Not all school work and activities interest their participants, so even when they are doing them, they can't find enjoyment and thus can't learn well. On the contrary, if parents permit more time for their children to explore their interests, they gain experiences different from during school and a more memorable childhood in a larger sense.

◎ Sample Response

Surely, there is something to be said for Serge's view, but with some confines. Students do need their own time to do something that can shift them away from their school assignments, but there should be a line drawn by their parents on how their kids should do those things. The first rule should be time: it is necessary for parents to train their kids into punctual terminators, especially in the activities they tend to get addicted to; also should it be on space: kids are supposed to keep perfectly noticed about the places that can not guarantee enough security. As long as students can perform their parents' warns and orders, they should be rewarded with the time that belongs to their very own. For example, if a student is passionate about music and decides to join a band, he will not only learn about music theory and performance but also collaboration, communication, and teamwork. Similarly, if a student is interested in volunteer work, he may develop empathy, compassion, and leadership skills. After all, there must be more to childhood than school. Apart from being a student, myriads of roles can be played by kids.

TG 33 Economics

Your professor is teaching a class on Economics. Write a post responding to the professor's question. In your response you should:

• express and support your opinion

• make a contribution to the discussion

An effective response will contain at least 100 words. You will have 10 minutes to write it.

Dr. Smith:

Better living standards have provided us with more opportunities for traveling abroad, but in a more intensified international tourism market, it is crucial to attract more tourists by making the destinations more appealing. Now I propose two approaches for the government to achieve this goal, and I'd like you to give your view about them:

The government could either improve the safety of a site by hiring more security personnel or improve its appearance by repairing old buildings and streets. Which way do you think is more effective?

Jane:

Between the two, I'd like to choose the first one. Security is more important than having fun and thus can attract more tourists. I have read news reports that tourists are often the target of local criminals when they are sight-seeing, and it makes me cross those places off my list. I'm not saying being safe can make a tourist hot-spot more successful, but it can really improve its image.

Marion:

I think the budget spent on repairing old buildings and streets is quite worthwhile. The environment where tourists are going to experience their journey serves as a key factor in how they would feel. Imagine walking down broken streets or living in a shabby hotel. This can hardly compel a vacationer to write a positive review of the destination. It is reasonable to say with improved appearance comes better feedback.

◎ Sample Response

The government should prioritize spending its budget on repairing old buildings and streets in order to make the tourism destinations more attractive. What makes a tourist destination successful is its sceneries, landscapes, culture, architecture, and traditions instead of its safety in the first place. If people want to live in a safety bubble, traveling to an unfamiliar city or country is not a smart choice for them; instead, they should stay in their community without ever thinking about leaving. In fact, the standard security measures and police power provided by the local government in tourist destinations are sufficient. There is no need to sacrifice a tight budget and increase police employment just for a pickpocket or two. However, if the buildings and streets lack repair or maintenance, the shabby walls and cracked pavement would arouse contempt and discomfort among tourists, leading to the decline of a once-favored destination, fading from the tourists' view. Moreover, the reality is that most scenic spot authorities invest heavily in repairing buildings and improving infrastructure each year to attract more tourists.

TG 34   Education

Your professor is teaching a class on Education. Write a post responding to the professor's question. In your response you should:

- express and support your opinion
- make a contribution to the discussion

An effective response will contain at least 100 words. You will have 10 minutes to write it.

Dr. Graham:

In class tomorrow, we are going to talk about the roles that are supposed to be played by teachers in high school, but before you come to class, I want you to think about this question: Which is the most important ability for a high school teacher? The ability to help students plan for their future, the ability to find the student who needs the most help and to give that help, or the ability to encourage students to learn on their own outside of the classroom?

Ross:

I think giving up no one should be a principal to an educator. It is easier to teach a good student than a problematic one, and the significance of a teacher lies in his or her resourceful ways to cope with those less favorable students. Not all kids sail smoothly throughout their childhood, and those who can don't need much help, but for those who can't, someone has to offer support and guidance for them.

Cousins:

The day will come sooner or later when students finally leave their teachers, so teachers need to leave a long-standing, positive mark on their students, especially regarding plans for the future. Cultivating a good student should not be the ultimate goal of education, but a prosperous life is, which requires a lingering influence of a teacher. In this case, helping students make plans that suit their future will be the best gift that students can receive.

◎ Sample Response

I agree with Cousins that teachers should help students make their plans, which they can follow accordingly, so as to achieve their life goals punctually. Even though giving a helping hand to a troubled student is warm-hearted and practical for them temporarily, support and guidance are not infinitely available; students eventually must face the world independently. Therefore, they need to be independent so that they can live their lives better. In fact, helping students to equip themselves with the ability to make suitable plans will influence their whole life positively. That's the reason why most educators put a top priority on making plans for their students, and they even require students to make plans for themselves too. A long-term plan guarantees students to fight through the adversities and obstacles they will face in their studies, cultivating diligence, which lowers the possibility of them giving up their dreams. Besides, a good and efficient plan gives them a detailed guide that prevents them from messing up their tasks during the course of their endeavor. Teachers can lead students to learn how to make detailed plans, according to which they realize future goals and finally fulfill their expectations, resulting in a successful life.

TG 37 Computer Science

Your professor is teaching a class on Computer Science. Write a post responding to the professor's question. In your response you should:

• express and support your opinion

• make a contribution to the discussion

An effective response will contain at least 100 words. You will have 10 minutes to write it.

Dr. Kerr:

Today, we're discussing the way children play. Among the factors that contribute to the changes in how children play, technology may be the most prominent one. Born in the age of electronic devices, children rely too much on technology at home, like computers, smartphones, and video games for fun and entertainment. However, there is also a view that playing with simpler toys or playing outside with friends would be better for children's development. What do you think about the two views I mentioned above?

Dennis:

I would say that everything in our age may exert a huge impact on the way we behave, and naturally, how our kids entertain themselves is also subject to the prevailing elements of their generation. Even when old people can't accept their children playing on computers of sorts, it has become an irreversible trend that the new ways of play are replacing the old ones, and everyone has to follow them.

Bass:

I agree with the second view that traditional ways for children to play are better for their development in the future, especially playing outside with their friends. On the one hand, playing outside can give children more opportunities to practice, which will be a valuable skill when they start working. On the other hand, it is also constructive when children communicate with others, and this is a key factor in a rewarding social life.

◎ Sample Response

Playing simple toys with friends outdoors is a better choice for enhancing children's development. Even though it is irreversible for human beings to enter the electronic era and it is also inevitable for people to come into contact with electronic devices and computers, playing games on computers or swiping through videos on cell phones are detrimental for children in the process of their physical and mental development. By contrast, participating in outdoor activities, such as a friendly game of soccer, allows children to take a break from burdensome studies and stimulates their physical growth. More importantly, playing frequently outdoors offers children opportunities to develop their interpersonal skills like communicative or expressive skills because when children play games together they make conversations, tell jokes, or get on each other's nerves. What's more, playing with others enables children to cooperate with each other when they have to team up for a task in games, benefiting every participant. Cooperative will and ability are essential characteristics to a successful career in the modern world since it is common to encounter teamwork situations in professional settings.

TG 38　Sociology

Your professor is teaching a class on **Sociology**. Write a post responding to the professor's question. In your response you should:

• express and support your opinion

• make a contribution to the discussion

An effective response will contain at least 100 words. You will have 10 minutes to write it.

Dr. Rivers:

In modern human history, we have been receiving news from different platforms. Currently, with the emergence of private media, the objectiveness of the news is being distorted by mounting pieces of news reports with hidden agendas and personal rhetoric. Now, I'd like to ask you this question: Should people read or watch the news presented by people whose views are different from your own or presented by people whose views are similar to yours?

Derrick:

I would choose to read or watch the news from those who share similar views with me. By reading news from reporters with opinions similar to mine, I find strong support for my ideas and become more encouraged while discussing with my friends. The citation from an authoritative source lends credibility to my argument, so I will gain more confidence in my own thoughts.

Susan:

From my perspective, it is advisable to be a good listener to different viewpoints. Receiving news presented by people with dissenting perspectives can help people access comprehensive information and get closer to the truth of events. As is common sense, an event or piece of news is not as simple as we expect. So it is an indisputable fact that nobody has a panoramic view of the truth due to their limited experience and knowledge span.

◉ Sample Response

Reading or watching the news presented by those whose views are different is a better choice since they broaden people's horizon and prevent them from making mistakes because of their knowledge limitations. Even though reading and watching the news that is similar to one's view is easy for him to accept and reinforces his beliefs, it also limits the development of his understanding of the world. However, if people watch the news comprised of alternative perspectives, they can avoid misconceptions and misinformation since they can examine their ideas through a bigger lens. That's the reason why many educators encourage students to read a vast range of information, such as current news from multiple countries. In this case, the students are able to make comparisons with reports that consist of different angles and details, giving them a better picture of the context. What's more, as Susan mentioned, nobody has a panoramic view of the truth or knows everything; so, while reading and watching the news from a different perspective expands a person's knowledge base, it also invokes thought processes for more integral beliefs. In addition, ideas from different viewpoints inspire people to think more so that they may come up with new and creative ideas. It is common to see innovated individuals read and watch books or information that offer diversity.

TG 39　Economics

Your professor is teaching a class on **Economics**. Write a post responding to the professor's question. In your response you should:

• express and support your opinion

• make a contribution to the discussion

An effective response will contain at least 100 words. You will have 10 minutes to write it.

Dr. Shelly:

When people are asked about the things they can do to improve their health, they usually mention something whose effects are immediate and obvious, such as changing the kinds of food they eat. Here comes the same question for you to answer on the discussion board, and your task is to come up with your own thing to do for better health and explain your reason.

Anthony:

I think I would try to get rid of the pressure in my life. To start with, I would go for a walk after class every day in the evening, which I think will help me recuperate from a hard day's work. Then I would take a long bath since a long time in hot water can relax my muscles and joints, making me feel revitalized and refreshed. Finally, I would keep myself from using my cell phone before hitting the sack because it can help me fall asleep easier.

Grace:

I think I'm not in a healthy condition for the lack of exercise. So, I'm going to spend more time exercising than before. Exercise can prevent obesity or help control or lose weight. Plus, daily exercise increases muscle strength and endurance, which I need the most. It can even give me the benefits mentioned by Anthony, making the body relaxed and falling asleep easier.

© **Sample Response**

Doing physical exercises is a better way to improve one's health because it strengthens the muscle and the body so that people can recover from high pressure and intense work more efficiently. Even though relaxation activities have effects to a certain degree when it comes to relieving stress, their impact on one's health is limited. In fact, indulging in pleasures for too long may idle away one's time and even waste their life. For example, playing games or watching videos on a cell phone for a long time is neither healthy nor meaningful. By contrast, it would be a different story if people choose to do physical exercises. It is, first of all, beneficial for people to build a physique healthy enough to endure the arduous labors of work and studies. Nowadays, there are more and more people going to the gym to build a vigorous and healthy body. Besides, physical exercise helps people avoid sedentary lifestyles that lead to unhealthy conditions such as obesity or coronary diseases. Moreover, when people exercise, the brain secretes chemicals that put people in a better mood, which is why exercise also helps relieve stress.

TG 40 Sociology

Your professor is teaching a class on **Sociology**. Write a post responding to the professor's question. In your response you should:

• express and support your opinion

• make a contribution to the discussion

An effective response will contain at least 100 words. You will have 10 minutes to write it.

Dr. Francis:

Apart from each other's personalities, distance is another important factor that influences people's relationships, but it can be a mixed blessing. Some people think we should keep away from others to improve our relationships because being away from people reminds us of how important they are. Others think we should always stay with others to have good relationships because we can communicate with them more often. What do you think?

Kevin:

I think I like it when there is a relatively long physical distance between me and my friends. In the process of maintaining the relationship, we can also keep our independence and get to know ourselves better. If I am always with my friends, our hobbies and habits tend to be identical, and we will lose our individualism, which is not good for developing my own personality.

Grate:

For me, staying close to each other can be a better approach to maintaining a better relationship. The reason is simple: people need frequent meetings and interactions to develop synergy and harmony between them. Living far from each other, on the contrary, deprives such an advantage. Furthermore, having friends close by can allow you to receive help when emergencies arise, which is something a friend staying far away can't provide.

© Sample Response

It is beneficial for people to maintain an intimate relationship if they stay close to each other. Even though they may seem to have identical personalities because they share the same interests and hobbies as they grow closer, people sharing the same memories and experiences can really enhance their relationship. Positive emotions such as compassion and affection for each other come from the reinforced companionship through various situations. In addition, when people become accustomed to one another, they know more about the other's merits and shortcomings. When they pick up their friends' strengths, they naturally emulate these qualities. Learning from friends is an efficient way to improve oneself, which elevates the relationship since all parties become better individuals. It is not uncommon to see friendship become stronger among the members of a sports team or a group of colleagues since they cooperate with and help each other consistently. By contrast, the distance between people may weaken the relationship since they will lose physical interaction and opportunities to forge valuable memories. Their previously shared memories may fade away with the passage of time and the decline of communication, ultimately leading to the disintegration of their relationship.

TG 42   Education

Your professor is teaching a class on Education. Write a post responding to the professor's question. In your response you should:

• express and support your opinion

• make a contribution to the discussion

An effective response will contain at least 100 words. You will have 10 minutes to write it.

Dr. Harry:

When people are asked about their favorite pastimes, they often mention something typical, such as reading or watching movies. And of course, these two are very popular forms of entertainment for many. However, nowadays there are more and more movies made by adapting books, which poses the choice between reading the book before watching the movie or vice versa. I'd like you to think about this topic. So here's the question: If you were facing such a choice, which option would you choose? Why?

Alison:

I'm a little on the fence with this one, but I'm leaning toward reading the book first. I think, in general, movies can't fully interpret the details within a book, like a character's range or the ins and outs of a plot. So compared to the quality of the original writing, movies are somewhat inferior. And I wouldn't want to miss out on a good book just because I found the movie disappointing.

Brad:

I'm going with movies all the way. Thinking of movies as a preview of the book is a quick way to see whether a book is worth reading. Instead of spending a long time reading a book only to find out you've wasted time on a mediocre piece of work, you only need to spend an hour or two to get a sense of the quality of the writing. In this way, I can fully exploit my leisure hours.

◎ Sample Response

As technology advances, movies have become increasingly popular, and have given rise to a new phenomenon where movies are based on books. Different from Brad, I believe pursuing efficiency doesn't apply to the appreciation of the subtlety, beauty, and glamour of a story, which can only be felt by close reading, so it's better to read the book first. Firstly, reading the book allows us to have a better understanding of the story. Books provide more detailed descriptions of the characters, settings, and events that are sometimes left out in movies due to time constraints. For example, in "The Lord of the Rings", the book provides a lot of detail about the backstory and world-building that is not included in the movies. Secondly, reading the book before watching the movie enables us to form our own opinions about the story and the characters. This is because books are often open to interpretation, and we can imagine the characters and their actions in our own unique way. When we watch the movie first, our imagination is limited by what we see on screen, and we may not be able to fully appreciate the depth of the characters and their motivations.

TG 43　Public Administration

> Your professor is teaching a class on **Public Administration**. Write a post responding to the professor's question. In your response you should:
>
> • express and support your opinion
>
> • make a contribution to the discussion
>
> An effective response will contain at least 100 words. You will have 10 minutes to write it.

Dr. Jack:

When people are asked what makes a qualified leader, they may have different answers, such as inclusiveness, openness, or integrity, but today we will talk about another quality: decisiveness. Do you think a successful leader must make decisions quickly? When a leader takes too much time to make decisions, will he be seen as inefficient by the people he leads?

Joanna:

A quick decision means a quick mind. If a leader can make swift and accurate decisions, he or she would be regarded as a nimble thinker, which would be an ability admired by others. In contrast, if a leader always hesitates to determine what to do next, he is no different from ordinary followers and thus incapable of leading others.

Paul:

I don't think making quick decisions equals being efficient, even for the one who leads a group. Making decisions, especially critical ones, is about considering all the odds, the interests of those affected, potential consequences, etc. So the time spent on contemplation before reaching a conclusion is worthwhile instead of a waste of time. Better decisions can be more productive and efficient, which more than compensate for the time spent on thinking.

◎ Sample Response

It is important to note that quick decision-making is not always synonymous with quick thinking. A leader who is able to make quick decisions is not necessarily a better or more effective leader than one who takes more time to consider all available options. In fact, a hasty decision can often be the result of inadequate information, insufficient analysis, or an over-reliance on intuition. On the other hand, a leader who takes the time to gather all relevant information, consult with others, and carefully evaluate all options before making a decision is more likely to make the right choice. This type of leader is also more likely to have the support of their team, as they have taken the time to consider all perspectives and are more likely to have a well-thought-out plan. It is important to recognize that there are situations where quick decisions are necessary. In times of crisis, for example, a leader may need to make quick decisions to ensure the safety and well-being of his/her team. However, this is not always the case, and taking the time to consider all options and gather information is often a more effective approach to decision-making.

TG 44   Education

Your professor is teaching a class on Education. Write a post responding to the professor's question. In your response you should:

• express and support your opinion

• make a contribution to the discussion

An effective response will contain at least 100 words. You will have 10 minutes to write it.

Dr. Polly:

Many of you have siblings, and you and your siblings often support each other while growing up. Despite varying age differences, the older ones are usually those who take up more responsibilities in the absence of parents. Some people think that older children should be required to help take care of the younger children. Others believe that this should be done by parents or guardians only. Which idea do you agree with?

Rita:

In most cases, even the older children are not mature enough to make the right decisions and guide their little brothers and sisters in place of their parents until they become adults. For instance, cooking a meal requires to use cutlery and fire, which are dangerous for a child to handle. Can the older child consider every safety hazard when caring for their younger siblings? I don't think so.

Richards:

It is necessary for parents to prep their first kid into a "small parent" of their younger kids. An advantage of doing this is it can cultivate a sense of responsibility their oldest kid has for his family and compassion for those who are weaker. Also, it can cultivate a strong sense of kinship between the siblings, which not only makes their childhood more harmonious but also facilitates their interpersonal skills in the future.

© Sample Response

In my opinion, the best approach is for parents and older children to work together to care for younger children. There are several benefits to this approach. Firstly, it allows parents to share the responsibility of caring for their children with their older ones, which can be especially helpful in large families. This can also help foster a sense of teamwork and cooperation among siblings and provide opportunities for older siblings to develop vital life skills such as responsibility and leadership. Secondly, the contribution made by older children when they care for their younger siblings reduces the pressure on parents in many less affluent families since, in many cases, both parents are obligated to work excessive hours to provide for the family, depriving them the time to care for the young ones. However, it's necessary to recognize that caring for younger siblings can be a significant burden for older siblings, especially if they are expected to do so alone. So, by working together with parents or other adults, older siblings can receive support and guidance in caring for their younger siblings, which can help mitigate the stress and burden of this responsibility.

TG 45 Education

Your professor is teaching a class on Education. Write a post responding to the professor's question. In your response you should:

• express and support your opinion

• make a contribution to the discussion

An effective response will contain at least 100 words. You will have 10 minutes to write it.

Dr. Sabrina:

People have been trying to make improvements in the quality of education, and with more advanced technologies and methods being employed, they have obtained some marvelous achievements. In today's class, we are going to talk about the best way to improve education, but before that, I want you to think about this question: What kind of measures would you apply to improve the level of education if you were a policymaker in the government?

Ruth:

I think organizing smaller classes than before would be an effective change we can make if we want to improve our teaching outcomes. A critical problem in class is that there are so many students having class at the same time that the teacher couldn't impartially give his attention to all of his students. So a smaller class, which consists of fewer students, will provide an effective solution to this problem.

Helping kids get well-prepared before they go to primary school would be a key method to improve education levels. On the one hand, it can make preschool kids accustomed to the upcoming study from an earlier age rather than after they have already become pupils. On the other hand, they will have stronger memories about what they learn and thus lay a better foundation for knowledge in high school and even college.

◎ Sample Response

One of the key measures that I would consider implementing is reducing class sizes. As Ruth has suggested, smaller classes can be an effective way to improve teaching outcomes. By reducing class sizes, teachers are able to give more individual attention to each student, which can help ensure that each student receives the support they need to succeed. However, reducing class sizes is not a simple task. It requires a significant investment in education infrastructure, including constructing new schools and hiring additional teachers. It is crucial to recognize that reducing class sizes will also demand a long-term commitment from the government, as smaller class sizes will require ongoing investment to maintain. In addition to reducing class sizes, providing teachers with better training courses would be an effective method. Ultimately, the quality of education is closely linked to the ability of the individual teacher, since they are the ones conveying knowledge to students and overseeing their performance. If teachers' professional capability can be enhanced, they will be able to conduct more insightful lectures, resolve students' issues more productively, and command the classroom more assertively. Nevertheless, it is important to also recognize that improving the level of education requires a multi-faceted approach and that there is no one solution that can solve all of the problems facing our education system.

TG 47　Social Studies

Your professor is teaching a class on Social Studies. Write a post responding to the professor's question. In your response you should:

• express and support your opinion

• make a contribution to the discussion

An effective response will contain at least 100 words. You will have 10 minutes to write it.

Despite the multitude of government agencies dedicated to civil services, people still find that they don't have to rely on the government to solve the problems they meet in their lives, instead, they can ask their families or friends for help. Here is a question for you: Do you think people who meet problems in their daily lives can solve them by themselves or with the help of their families or friends without any assistance from the government?

Mamie:

I think people depend more on the government than we realize in daily life. When we are victims of crime, we may need to rely on the justice system. In emergency situations, we look to government dispatch for immediate aid. These services are so common in our society that sometimes we tend to forget their existence and take them for granted.

Mabel:

The government's role is outstanding according to Mamie, but I would ask how often those things happen. What makes up our ordinary days is one trivia after another, such as forgetting your keys at home, a malfunctioning car, or just suffering from the flu. Can the government help you with these small things? In these cases, the help from a friend or family would be much more effective.

© Sample Response

While it is true that many trivial problems can be resolved through personal or familial efforts just like what Mabel has said, there are some situations where government aid may be necessary. Some problems are beyond our individual control, such as natural disasters or large-scale economic crises. In these situations, the government can play a crucial role in providing resources and support to individuals and communities in need. Additionally, some issues require collective action and government intervention to be effectively addressed. For example, issues such as environmental degradation, public health crises, and systemic inequality cannot be solved through personal or familial efforts alone. These issues require coordinated efforts at the local, national, and global levels, and require the participation and support of government institutions. However, it is important to recognize that government intervention is not always the best solution. In some cases, government programs and policies can be ineffective, bureaucratic, or even harmful. It is necessary to contemplate the potential benefits and drawbacks of government intervention in each situation and to seek the most effective and efficient solutions. Overall, I would insist that citizens cannot overcome every challenge in life solely with their own efforts and social relationships.

TG 49 Social Studies

Your professor is teaching a class on Social Studies. Write a post responding to the professor's question. In your response you should:

• express and support your opinion

• make a contribution to the discussion

An effective response will contain at least 100 words. You will have 10 minutes to write it.

Dr. Dave:

Throughout life, we are likely to form friendships with the ones close to us, but we may also part with for various factors, such as moving to new cities or having a serious dispute. Terminating a relationship is a decision most of us must face in life. Now, I would like to ask you this question: Imagine having an extended friendship with someone. If they do something that you don't like, should you still be friends with them?

Cindy:

Differences exist in every one of us, so it is perfectly reasonable for a friend to do something I don't like. It is important to have shared interests and similar preferences to maintain a healthy relationship, but it doesn't mean there's no room for individuality and privacy. I have a friend who has a hobby of smoking, which I don't appreciate, but he never smokes in front of me. I never felt that our relationship was compromised by our different preferences.

Michael:

Friends are about caring for each other's feelings and thoughts. If a friend keeps doing something that crosses me, especially after having clearly expressed my feelings, I would regard it as an act of disrespect or contempt. Since I always treat my friends wholeheartedly and consider whether my actions would offend them, I'd expect them to reciprocate the deed.

◎ Sample Response

Contrary to Michael's view, it is not always a sign of disrespect or contempt when a friend does something that crosses you. People are unique individuals with different values, beliefs, and personalities, and it is natural that conflicts may arise from time to time. Furthermore, it is important to remember that no one is perfect, and everyone makes mistakes. It is possible that your friend may have acted without fully considering the impact on you, or may not have realized that their actions were causing you discomfort or displeasure. In deciding whether to maintain the friendship, it is important to consider the nature and severity of the action, as well as the overall quality and history of the friendship. If the action was minor or unintentional, it may be worth discussing the issue with your friend and working together to find a resolution. However, if the action was a serious breach of trust or values, it may be necessary to reevaluate the friendship and see whether it is still healthy and beneficial for both parties. All balanced, it is important to recognize that friendship is not just about having someone who shares the same attitudes or behaviors as you. Rather, it is about accepting and supporting each other through both the good times and the bad. It is possible to maintain a strong friendship even if you don't always agree with each other's actions or choices.

TG 50 Social Studies

Your professor is teaching a class on Social Studies. Write a post responding to the professor's question. In your response you should:

- express and support your opinion
- make a contribution to the discussion

An effective response will contain at least 100 words. You will have 10 minutes to write it.

Dr. Cherry:

Character and personality are two main factors we consider when we make new friends, and people are attracted to those who have appealing qualities. So to some extent, friendships are formed based on personal traits. I'd like to ask you a question about making friends: Do you think it is better to make friends with intelligent people or people with a good sense of humor?

Cora:

I would like to make friends with those who can make me laugh. Making friends with humorous people can improve my sense of happiness in every single aspect of life, making me see the positive sides of life. In addition, humorous people are usually popular, which can also help me make new friends by hanging out with them.

Todd:

Intelligence is more valuable than humor. Instead of making me laugh, I prefer the ones who can give me more insights and more inspiration. In daily life, I can learn from the way they think and study and ask them the tricky questions I have encountered. I think such a friend can help me make progress and succeed in the future.

◎ Sample Response

In my opinion, I would prioritize making friends with intelligent people. While a good sense of humor can certainly make life more enjoyable and help alleviate stress and tension, intelligence can provide a wealth of other benefits. Intelligent friends can provide stimulating conversation and new perspectives on various topics, as well as inspire personal growth and intellectual curiosity. In addition, intelligent friends may also be able to offer valuable advice and guidance in various areas of life, such as career or personal relationships. However, it is important to recognize that intelligence and humor are not mutually exclusive qualities. It is certainly possible to have friends who possess both intelligence and a good sense of humor, and it is this combination that can truly make for a dynamic and enjoyable friendship. In fact, many intelligent individuals are also known for their wit and sense of humor. Being intelligent can involve having a deep understanding of human nature, recognizing irony, and having a broad range of interests and experiences that can lead to comedic insights.

Furthermore, being able to make others laugh often requires a certain degree of intelligence, as it involves the ability to read social cues, think on one's feet, and use language creatively.

综合写作例文

1 EX 08 综合写作例文

阅读与听力录音参考 EX 08。【见配套音频】

Introduction	The reading passage states that the fuel-cell engines could be a substitution of internal-combustion engines due to three advantages, while the speaker in the listening holds a complete opposite view that none of them is convincing.
Notes:	
燃料电池发动机（fuel-cell engines）是内燃机（internal-combustion engines）的替代品，这个信息要有。另外 substitution 是关键点。	
Body Ⅰ	Firstly, the reading conceives that the internal-combustion engines depend on a finite resource, petroleum, while the resource of the fuel-cell engines would hardly be consumed out. However, the professor in the listening disagrees with it because the hydrogen is not easily available as the reading material indicates. Although the hydrogen is present in common substance, such as water, this form of substance is not useful. In fact, the hydrogen must be converted to the pure liquid state, which is difficult to produce and store. Specifically, the cool process needs to keep minus 253℃ degree to store it. Thus, the perspective in the reading has been challenged heavily.
Notes:	
阅读部分要体现 internal-combustion engines 所依赖的资源有限，而 fuel-cell engines 所依赖的资源无限。听力部分，要根据 hydrogen、easily available 等重点信息进行细节还原，即氢（hydrogen）无法以水的状态使用，它需要被制作并储存为纯液态，这一点非常难，需要将温度降到零下253 摄氏度才能完成。	
Body Ⅱ	Secondly, in the reading passage, hydrogen-based fuel cells have been considered owning the ability to relieve the pollution situations in the world. Nevertheless, the speaker in the listening passage debates it by saying that the fuel cells will not solve pollution problems. In order to obtain pure hydrogen from water or natural gas, the purification process will be required, costing lots of energy. Since the energy is provided by burning coal or oil, which could cause the pollution, providing the source of fuel cells will create environmental pollution, even though driving cars equipped with fuel-cells engines do not pollute. Hence the statement in the reading is not convincing.
Notes:	
阅读中的 hydrogen-based fuel cells 和 reduce pollution situation 要在文章中有所体现。听力中重要信息"提纯（purification）的过程会大量燃烧煤或石油（burn coal or oil），从而造成污染（pollution）"要清晰还原，另外让步表达"尽管驾驶配备燃料电池发动机的汽车（drive cars with fuel-cell engines）不会污染环境（pollute the environment）"最好也在文章中体现出来。	

Body Ⅲ	Finally, the author claims that the price of the fuel-cell engines holds a higher competition than internal-combustion engines because of its higher efficiency to power cars. While in the listening, the indicator debates that the process of manufacturing fuel-cell engines is expensive, because the components in the fuel-cell engines require platinum, which is a kind of rare and expensive metal. Without the platinum, the hydrogen could not undergo chemical reactions to produce electricity to power the automobiles. Besides, the attempts for cheap replacement of platinum are unsuccessful. Therefore, the economical merits of fuel-cell engines mentioned in the reading have been contradicted.
Notes:	
阅读部分指出燃料电池发动机的价格更优惠，因为效率（efficiency）更高。听力部分则指出其制作过程很贵，因为需要一种稀有、昂贵的金属铂（rare and expensive metal platinum），没有它就无法进行化学反应，进而得到驱动汽车的电力（electricity）。另外其他尝试替代它的实验都没有成功。	

2 EX 09 综合写作例文

阅读与听力录音参考 EX 09。【见配套音频】

Introduction	The author of text claims that the decline of the sea otters along the Alaskan coast is better explained by the pollution theory than by the predation theory. On the contrary, the professor argues that predation is actually the likely cause of this decline.
Notes:	
体现海獭数量减少（sea otter population decline）是由于污染（pollution）而非捕食（predation）这一信息。	
Body Ⅰ	First of all, the reading material suggests that the scientists have already found water samples that could reveal the pollution problem, such as the increased levels of chemicals that are lethal to sea otters of the Alaskan coast. However, the speaker of the lecture opposes against this opinion by saying that the pollution theory is weakened by the fact that no one could find dead sea otters washed up on the sea shore, which would not be expected if the decline is caused by the infection due to the pollution. But this fact is consistent with the predation theory. Since sea otters were eaten immediately after being captured (killed 也可以) by predators, they would not be washed up on the coast.
Notes:	
阅读部分要体现科学家发现水样本（water sample）中化学物质含量高，更符合 pollution 的特点。听力部分要体现出来海獭如果是因为污染而死，应该有被冲上海岸的尸体（dead body washed up the shore），但是并没有人发现海獭的尸体（dead body）；如果它们是被捕食者捕食，则马上会被吃掉，因此自然没有尸体。	

Body Ⅱ Notes: 这段是比较有难度的，如果要得到高分甚至满分，要将听力内容理清，得出以下信息：尽管虎鲸（orcas）更喜欢捕杀鲸，但是由于鲸被人类猎杀到数量很少，所以虎鲸改变了食物，开始捕食包括海獭在内的小型海洋哺乳动物（small sea mammals），所以捕食更有可能是导致海獭数量减少的原因。	Furthermore, the writing indicates that other small animals such as seals and sea lions have declined too, but the only predator orcas that could hunt them prefers to hunt much larger prey (whales 也可以). By contrast, the listening material rebuts that even if orcas prefer to hunt the whale as food source, the population of whales has declined because of human hunters. Thus, the orcas might have changed their diet, and due to the fact that the small sea mammals are available food sources, they could have started hunting these animals such as seals, sea lions and sea otters. Therefore, the predation of orcas is very likely to account for the decline of small sea animals.
Body Ⅲ Notes: 这段听力部分要重点理清海獭数量下降的特点跟虎鲸是否能轻易到达的关系更能证明是捕食导致海獭数量减少，即虎鲸能轻易到达的地方海獭数量下降最厉害，而不能到达的地方像多岩石的地方和水位浅的地方（rocky and shallow locations），海獭数量下降得少。同学们要特别注意例文细节的详细度和准确度。	Moreover, the author of the passage mentions that the uneven distribution (pattern 也可以) of the decline might be better explained by the pollution theory, since current or other environmental factors might contribute to it. However, the lecturer in the speech refutes that the predation theory is a more reasonable explanation for this. Facts have shown that the decline is consistent with the accessibility of the regions to orcas. At places where it is easily reachable for orcas, there was a significant decline in the number of sea otters. However, since orcas are huge in size, they could not reach rocky and shallow locations, and the population of sea otters at such locations did not decline dramatically.

3 EX 10 综合写作例文

阅读与听力录音参考 EX 10。【见配套音频】

Introduction Notes: 首段主要把阅读中"人类不可在金星上生存，因为环境很不友好，压强过大"这一信息写清楚。听力部分可以点明让太空站（space station）建在 50 千米高空能解决该问题。	In the reading passage, the author claims that it is unlikely to maintain human presence on Venus, where the environment is extreme and inhospitable. However, the professor in the lecture holds a totally different view, suggesting that permanent station on Venus is possible, although with challenges, by building a balloon-like station fifty kilometers above the surface in the floating atmosphere.

Body Ⅰ Notes: 阅读部分要体现出由于压强过大，人类登陆金星会被挤压变形。听力部分要还原细节信息，体现出将太空站建在 50 千米高空可以解决压强的问题；另外还要体现出在这个高度，压强跟地球相似，航天飞船可安全停靠。	First of all, the reading material points out that almost anything that we might land on Venus would be crushed due to the great atmospheric pressure. However, the speaker of the lecture rebuts that the well-known problem of Venus's surface pressure could be solved by using the floating station, since the atmosphere pressure at areas far above the surface is similar to that of the earth at the height of fifty kilometers. As a result, the spacecraft and other things that we try to land on Venus would not be crushed.
Body Ⅱ Notes: 阅读部分要体现出金星上缺水，所以需要运送，但这是不切实际也不可能的。听力中要指明金星上其实有化学元素（chemical compounds）可用于制造水和氧气。应注意尽量不漏掉二氧化碳（carbon dioxide）、氧（oxygen）等细节信息。	Furthermore, the writing claims that the lack of reservoirs of water on Venus's surface and water vapor in the planet's atmosphere requires us to transport water and oxygen supply, which is in fact impractical and impossible. On the contrary, the listening material refutes that chemical compounds in the atmosphere, such as carbon dioxide, could be refined to produce water and oxygen. Since these compositions are easy to obtain, it is not necessary for us to import the oxygen and water.
Body Ⅲ Notes: 阅读部分要体现出由于云反射、遮挡阳光（clouds reflect and block sunlight），所以太空站得不到电力（station could not get electricity）。听力中要指明在距离金星表面 50 千米的地方，阳光可透过较薄的云层，而且厚云层还可以反射阳光，因此太空站有足够的阳光可利用来制造电。细节上多对比与摸仿例文，取长补缺，尽可能还原精准。	Moreover, the author of the passage indicates that humans in the station could not get enough electricity, due to the fact that the clouds reflect and block a lot of sunlight. By contrast, the lecturer in the speech holds a different opinion and says that since the station could be built to float far above the surface of Venus, the sunlight it receives would not be blocked, since the sunlight could pass through the clouds more than 50 kilometers above the surface, which are not thick at all. In addition, the station could also utilize the sunlight reflected by the cloud. As a result, the station could receive enough sunlight to generate all the electricity humans need.

4 EX 11 综合写作例文

阅读与听力录音参考 EX 11。【见配套音频】

Introduction Notes: 这篇文章将阅读中的背景问题写得比较清楚，值得学生完成练习后与例文进行对照，取长补短，精益求精。	In the reading passage, three ways are suggested to solve the problem that birds always mistakenly fly into the glass windows, which is very dangerous for wild birds. However, the professor holds a totally opposite view. He believes that the proposed three solutions cannot effectively stop the birds from getting injured.

Body Ⅰ	First of all, the writer suggests that the problem can be solved by **replacing regular clear glass with one-way glass** which is transparent in only one direction. The speaker, on the other hand, refutes that there are problems with that solution. Although **birds cannot see through the glass from the outside**, one-way glass whose surface can reflect any light is just as bad as a mirror. In reality, **when birds see the reflection in the windows, such as the image of sky and trees, they assume that the sky and trees are real**, hence **flying right into the windows**. Therefore, the idea to replace windows is not practical.
Notes: 阅读部分要把用单向玻璃(one-way glass)替换常规玻璃(regular glass)这一方案写清楚。听力部分要将"鸟从外往里看，会将玻璃反射出的树木、天空等镜像误认为是真实的，从而往里飞而撞伤"的细节写清楚。听力部分要特别注意还原的细节性和精准度。同时不能自己臆造内容，信息必须来自听力部分。	
Body Ⅱ	Secondly, the writing material mentions that another solution is to **paint colorful lines or designs such as thin stripes** on the windows. But the lecturer strongly disagrees with that idea by stating that **colorful patterns are also problematic**. Actually, while some openings are designed in the patterns for people to see out, **birds perceive them as several opening holes**. And as to **prevent birds from flying right through them**, the **unpainted spaces should be extremely small**. But this time, it will be **too dark for people inside the building**.
Notes: 阅读部分要把画彩色线条或装饰性图案(paint colorful lines or designs such as thin stripes)这一方案体现出来。听力部分要体现对此的反驳，即鸟会将亮光看成孔洞(opening holes)，为避免鸟往里飞，就要画得特别密，但这样会影响建筑物里面的光线。	
Body Ⅲ	Last but not least, according to the article, the third solution is to **create a magnetic field to guide birds away from the buildings**. To argue against it, the listening says that **magnetic field does not work either**. **It is true that birds use magnetic field to navigate**, however, this happens only when birds are **travelling very long distances**. For example, **their magnetic sense** figures out which way to take when they are **migrating from a cold country to a warmer one in the winter**. Nevertheless, **they use eyes and brightness to determine the routes when taking short trips** such a flight from one side of a city to the other side. Thus, the artificial magnetic field doesn't have much effect.
Notes: 听力部分要将长途飞行(long term travelling)和短途飞行(short distance travel)的区别，并将下述细节信息写清楚：use their eyes and brightness to determine the routes when they take short-distance trips。	

5 EX 12 综合写作例文

阅读与听力录音参考 EX 12【见配套音频】

Introduction	In the reading passage, the author believes that the nest structures were not built by bees 200 million years ago. However, the professor in the lecture holds a totally opposite viewpoint. She suggests that it is quite possible that bees made those nests, and the reasons provided in the passage are not convincing.
Notes: 开头段体现阅读部分的主题 "nest structures were not built by bees 200 millions years ago"，听力部分则对比进行反驳。本段写短一点也没关系。	
Body I	First of all, the writing indicates that no fossils of actual bees have been discovered. However, the lecturer refutes that a lack of bee fossils is due to the absence of preservation of fossil bees. She mentions that a kind of rare sticky liquid produced by trees is necessary in preserving bee fossils. But the tree species that produce such kind of liquid commonly existed much later. Therefore, even though bees existed 200 million years ago, their remains could not be preserved for the absence of the trees to produce the right kind of liquid. In this way, bees might have constructed those nests.
Notes: 阅读部分提出了 "没有化石可以证明" 的观点，听力部分则从当时缺少保存蜜蜂化石 (preservation of fossil bees) 的材料入手对此进行反驳，指出能产生一种稀有黏液 (a kind of rare sticky liquid) 的树出现得比蜜蜂晚，这才导致早期的蜜蜂无法变成化石。写完作文后可对照例文，取长补短，完善细节。	
Body II	Secondly, according to the writer, the absence of flowering plants shows that bees could not live at that time. But the speaker strongly disagrees with this idea by stating that it is possible that bees appeared before the flowers. In reality, bees might feed on non-flowering plants which preceded flowering plants during the evolutionary history. For example, firs and pine trees also serve as food resources for bees. Later, after the flowering plants appeared, bees may have adapted on them for food and established a new relationship with them and the relationship remains stable.
Notes: 对于阅读中当时并没有开花植物的说法，听力给出的理由与支撑论点是虽然开花植物出现得晚，但是早期的蜜蜂是以无花植物 (如 firs and pine trees) 为食的，后来植物进化，有了开花植物，蜜蜂才改变食物并跟开花植物建立了稳定关系。	
Body III	Last but not the least, the article makes the assertion that a lack of finer details of bees' nests also indicates that the bee theory is false. Nevertheless, the listening selection refutes that lack of spiral caps in the fossilized chambers does not necessarily indicate the absence of bees. Modern bees use a kind of chemical composition that prevents the nests against water. Moreover, chemical analysis reveals that the waterproofing material also exists in the nest structures of modern bees. Thus, bees must have made up those nests.
Notes: 对于阅读中由于缺少有关巢穴的细节，所以不能确定上文所述结构是蜜蜂所造的说法，听力认为就算缺少螺旋帽 (spiral caps) 的结构，由当时使用的防水化学成分 (chemical composition) 跟现代蜂使用的防水成分一致也能看出它们有共性，从而得出结论：该结构是蜜蜂建造的。	

6 EX 13 综合写作例文

阅读与听力录音参考 EX 13。【见配套音频】

Introduction Notes: 前面其他例文更多以细节还原为重点，本文除了这点，还讲解框架，以作补充。	The author of the text indicates that adopting electronic medical record system might be a wise choice and points out several advantages of it. On the contrary, the professor argues that these benefits are all uncertain and not as significant as mentioned by the passage.
Body Ⅰ Notes: 文章会四次引用阅读内容，最好每次的说法都要有变化，所以第一段用 the author of the text，后面各段分别用 the reading material、the writing、the author of the passage 替换。	First of all, the reading material claims that using electronic record system could help save money in the storing and transferring process. By contrast, the speaker of the lecture rebuts that this could not reduce the cost, since the doctors could not throw out or discontinue the paper records stored in the database. Instead, they have to keep the paper records as emergency backup or for legal reasons. Hence, hospitals still need to pay for the storing of the paper records.
Body Ⅱ Notes: 文章引用听力部分时用了 the professor、the speaker of the lecture、the listening material、the lecturer 四个不同的表达，这是为了让表达更具多样性。另外机改作文评分时也会看文章的用词是否具有多样性，实义词的替换是增强词汇多样性的一种方式。	Furthermore, the writing suggests that this system could also reduce the chance of medical errors. However, the listening material refutes that even though the doctors use the electronic records, they would not be able to eliminate errors caused by poor handwriting or mistakes in transcription of data. The doctors would still use pens and paper when examining patients, and the electronic records are just typed into the system by the staff at a later time so that mistakes would still exist due to poor handwriting. From this perspective, errors would still not be avoidable since the staff might misinterpret the information left by the doctors.
Body Ⅲ Notes: 阅读的"说"与听力的"驳"也都要尽可能换不同的词汇，例如文中"说"用 indicate、claim、suggest 和 point out 等不同的表达；"驳"用 argue、rebut、refute 和 hold a totally different view 等常用表达。总之，不求复杂，只求多样。 可先写作文，再一一对照例文细节进行参考，取长补短，精益求精。	In addition, the author of the passage points out that all the research locations would be capable of viewing the medical records. Nevertheless, the lecturer in the speech holds a totally different opinion and says that the research centers are unlikely to benefit from this system. They would not be able to get access to all the information in the database, since their access would be subject to the privacy law in America, which allows the patients to keep their medical records private. Thus, researchers must follow strict and complicated procedures and get many permissions, which are often not granted. For instance, the privacy law enables the patients to block the use of their medical records for any other purposes other than their own medical cure.

7 EX 14 综合写作例文

阅读与听力录音参考 EX 14。【见配套音频】

Introduction Notes: 阅读指出三个问题；听力指出三个相应的解决方案。	The author of the text indicates three problems of the round-trip to Mars, while the professor argues that although the trip would be challenging, there are still solutions to each of these problems.
Body Ⅰ Notes: 阅读重点指出飞船容积不足；听力对此进行反驳，指出可利用技术在太空实现自给自足，彩色标记的是相关的细节，尽量还原全面。相对较难的有以下细节信息：hydroponics, cultivate their food, nurturing the plants in water, recycle water, release oxygen、photosynthesis。	First of all, the reading material suggests that the cargo capacity would not be enough to bring supply for a few years. On the contrary, the speaker of the lecture rebuts that using hydroponics would be a practical method to cultivate their food, namely nurturing the plants in water rather than soil. This technology only requires little space to grow plants, so the astronauts could be able to crop food that is enough to supply them. Additionally, this could also help to recycle water, and therefore the astronauts could collect drinkable water. Growing plants could also release oxygen because of photosynthesis, thus fresh air could also be provided.
Body Ⅱ Notes: 阅读部分的因果关系即肌肉量和骨密度（muscle mass and bone density）下降跟零重力状态（zero gravity condition）之间的关系要表达清楚。听力部分指出有解决方案，例如定期锻炼（regular exercise）和补充矿物质（如钙），这些细节信息要还原全面。	Furthermore, the writing points out that astronauts travelling to Mars would face problems of the decrease of their muscle mass and bone density, due to the zero gravity condition. By contrast, the listening material refutes that there are several solutions that astronauts who were sent to stay for long time in zero gravity condition had already tried, such as taking regular exercise or taking specific minerals such as calcium so that they can remain their muscle's health and the bones mass.
Body Ⅲ Notes: 这段阅读内容重点较多，可概括为辐射问题（radiation problems），并且将后面的因果逻辑表达清楚。听力部分对高分有贡献的原因之一是逻辑清晰，对原文意思还原度高。听力部分指出就算有辐射也不一定带来危险，因为辐射只是偶尔才有，宇航员可以用设备监测辐射，并且建造小型庇护所解决强辐射的问题。	In addition, the author of the passage claims that astronauts would be exposed to serious radiation problems, since the earth magnetic field won't be able to protect them and creating a shield to protect the whole ship is impossible and would add too much weight. However, the lecturer in the speech holds a totally different opinion and says that even if there would be some radiation, it would not always be dangerous, due to the fact that the sun only emit radiation occasionally. Hence, astronauts could avoid the radiation by using a special instrument that serves as a monitor and building a small shelter that won't add much weight. They could work normally when there is no radiation, but they could hide in the shelter when the monitor indicates high radiation.

8 EX 15 综合写作例文

阅读与听力录音参考 EX 15。【见配套音频】

Introduction Notes: 这段开头虽然简短，但十分清楚完整地表达了背景信息，即 Salton Sea 中的盐浓度上升，阅读提供了降低盐浓度的方法，而听力对此进行了反驳。	Regarding the rising salinity of the Salton Sea in California, the reading passage provides a few solutions, all of which the professor refutes.
Body Ⅰ Notes: 阅读部分把通过蒸发淡化，使水和盐分离的逻辑关系讲清楚。听力部分指出问题所在，即蒸发方式留下的化学物质可能被人吸入进而危害健康。中间的细节还原看右边的彩色字体标记。	First of all, the passage proposes desalinating the salty water by means of evaporation, allowing the water steam to return to the lake while leaving the salt behind. The professor rebuts this by saying that this would effectively reduce salinity but at the same time would also create other problems, especially health ones. She states that although most of the material left behind would be salt, there are a number of chemicals, including selenium, that can be very detrimental to people's health if people breathe it in as a result of the wind spreading it. Therefore, she believes that although this solution could work, it is not without very serious drawbacks.
Body Ⅱ Notes: 这部分阅读较简洁，指出用海水稀释湖水（diluting the lake by ocean water）的方法，听力则指出这个方式需要建造一个管道，但太贵了，当地政府承担不了这么高的费用。特别注意在还原这一基础信息时的细节还原度和精准度。	Secondly, the article also provides the idea of diluting the lake with less salty water from the ocean. However, the professor debates it because this would require the construction of pipelines and canals which she views as impractical. She points out that the local government might not have the required resources for building a pipeline from the nearest coastal line, nearly one hundred kilometers away, to the lake. Thus, the professor thinks that building pipelines or canals would be highly unrealistic.
Body Ⅲ Notes: 这部分阅读内容较多，提出了把湖分为几部分并建隔离墙（divide the lake into sections and building walls），从而分离湖水，降低盐度的方案。听力部分指出从长远来看该方案不行，因为地处地震带，隔离墙容易因地震受破坏，湖水容易重新混在一起，再一次形成盐湖。细节还原上同样关注右边彩色字体，尽可能全面还原信息。	Finally, the passage brings up the solution of dividing the lake into sections and building walls in between these sections. This would separate the lake into main sections, which would be controlled and reduced, and smaller ones that would be allowed to remain the same. The professor views this solution as a possible short-term one but definitely not a good long-term solution. She believes the frequent and often intense geological activity in the area, specifically earthquakes, would break down the walls very soon, possibly as soon as the first major earthquake hits. Then, the water that was controlled would mix back with the water, leading to a very salty lake once again.

9 EX 16 综合写作例文

阅读与听力录音参考 EX 16。【见配套音频】

From the reading passage, the writer claims that building high-speed rail system to connect San Francisco and Los Angeles in California has many benefits. However, the lecturer in the listening material holds a completely different point of view and claims that the benefits are not as ideal as claimed by the writer.

Firstly, the reading material puts forward that the construction of the railway system can lower the maintenance costs on road. On the other hand, the professor in the speech argues that, although it can save some money on road maintenance, this saved money is only a little compared to the cost for building the system. The state government has to borrow one billion dollars to build the railway system, which is 70% of the state tax income for one year. Hence, even if the government borrows the money and builds the railway system, it will be hard for the government to pay back, which triggers financial issues.

Secondly, the writer of the text suggests that the railway system can lower traffic congestion in the region. Nonetheless, the speaker refutes this by saying that people will only use this system if they find it more convenient, which depends on how easily they can access to the railway routes. On the East Coast, convenient public transportation makes the access to their high-speed railway system easy, which is why it is popular there. However, the public transportation in the urban areas of the West Coast is less convenient, which makes it harder for people to reach the railway system, making them unwilling to use it and the traffic congestion problem remains unsolved.

Lastly, the reading text proposes that high-speed trains are one of the most environmentally friendly transportations, because they are fuel-efficient. On the contrary, the listening material rebuts this by pointing out that the high-speed railway system will not be constructed in the whole region. Thus, the high-speed trains still have to travel on the regular routes that do not allow high speeds for trains, which means that these trains have to slow down, leading to them being less fuel-efficient. The fuel emission, consequently, cannot be reduced as much as the writer in the reading text claims.

10 EX 17 综合写作例文

阅读与听力录音参考 EX 17。【见配套音频】

The reading suggests that the 200 plate-sized ceramic disks found in Greek may be used as pans for cooking food, drums or mirrors. However, the listening holds a totally different opinion and believes that none of the statements in the reading is actually convincing.

First, the author of the reading claims that they were used as pans for cooking food since the designs, such as the edge and the handle, are suitable for placing food. However, the listening material refutes it. If people use something to cook at home for a while, it will be blackened or become discolored due to the common contact with high heat. But there wasn't any similar marks of discoloration found from the disks, indicating that they were not used as pans for cooking.

Second, the passage says that the disks are used as drums since stretching animal skins over the raised edge can create an air chamber, which can make sound when being stuck. However, the professor in the listening disagrees with this because ceramic disks of such a size and shape cannot produce pleasant sound even when they were covered with animal skin stretched over them. The ceramic disks are heavy and hard to play, while drums made of wood material with animal skins are easier to play and sound better. It is hard to understand why people use ceramic disks while there are better materials available.

Third, the reading believes that they are used as mirrors by adding liquid into the shallow basin to create a reflection. However, the listening holds the opposite side. To make a mirror by those disks, people have to fill the basin with liquid, place it on a horizontal surface and bend over to look down. This would hide the decorations behind the disks since they are placed downward. It is unlikely that people design the decorations that no one can see. The metal mirrors with similar decorations are used vertically, making the decorations visible for everyone.

11 EX 18 综合写作例文

阅读与听力录音参考 EX 18。【见配套音频】

In the reading passage, the writer puts forward three theories that explain the missing sailors who had been aboard the Mary Celeste, which was discovered floating in the Atlantic Ocean. However, the speaker rebuts that none of these theories is convincing.

First of all, the writer of the text indicates that the crew might be captured by pirates for money. By contrast, the lecture refutes that if the pirates captured the sailors, they would later ask for money in exchange for the crew's freedom. However, the pirates didn't contact the ship company in request of money. What's more, nothing precious in the ship was found missing. It's unlikely for pirates to capture those sailors without asking for money as well as leaving valuable items behind.

In addition, the author suggests that the ship crew used the lifeboat to escape from the danger of explosion of leaking flammable liquid but got lost in the ocean. Nonetheless, the lecture argues that there is no evidence that records the leaking liquid. The flammable liquid has a strong smell that could linger for a long time once leaking. If the liquid had leaked, there must be strong smell staying around. The sailors who discovered the ship would have noticed the smell and carefully recorded it. However, the report didn't mention anything about the smell.

Lastly, the writer of the passage mentions that the crew found that the ship was sinking and they got into the lifeboat to reach the nearby island. However, the professor also contends this point. Although the water had leaked into the ship's bottom, the ship could maintain floating for a few days since it was still floating when it was discovered. Since the crew on board was experienced sailors, they must notice that the Mary Celeste was still good enough to reach the nearby Island of Santa Maria. Therefore, instead of abandoning the ship and taking the lifeboat that was more risky, they would sail to nearby island, which was a better way.

12 EX 19 综合写作例文

阅读与听力录音参考 EX 19。【见配套音频】

The writing lists three possible ways to reduce the number of snakeheads, which is now causing severe damage to the ecosystem in America, while the professor argues that none of these three approaches are able to protect the ecosystem.

First of all, the author of the text indicates that the government could develop certain laws that prohibit people to transport or release snakeheads. On the contrary, the lecturer in the speech rebuts that this solution would be practical only if the snakeheads have not yet entered America, while the fact is that the snakeheads are already part of the ecosystem. Additionally, the snakeheads have a special feature that enables them to spread by themselves, which is the ability of living and moving on land as long as they remain moist. The snakeheads could move by wriggling, and also remain wet, so they are able to cross the lands and find new water habitats even though people do not transport them.

Furthermore, the reading material suggests that the government could educate the fishers about the virtues of the snakeheads, since this kind of fish is not a common part of the North American diet now. By contrast, the listening material refutes that educating the fishers would bring another serious problem. If the fishers do catch the fish and make the snakeheads a common part of the local diet, then they would soon figure out ways to increase the number of this kind of fish in order to make more money. It is very likely that they would intentionally introduce the snakeheads to other fishing spots, which ends up spreading the fish. Hence, this method could not reduce the number of the snakeheads.

Moreover, the author of the passage points out that scientists could treat the body of water with toxic chemicals, and therefore eliminate all the snakeheads. On the other hand, the speaker of the lecture claims that besides wiping out the native fish, the poison developed by the scientists would also have negative impacts on small organism in water, which could not be restored later on. However, the small organism plays as an important part in the ecosystem, since it is food sources for lots of fish. Therefore, it would be not an easy thing to restore the ecosystem.

13 EX 20 综合写作例文

阅读与听力录音参考 EX 20。【见配套音频】

In the reading passage, the author states three theories about what the extinct short-faced bear in North America ate to sustain its massive body size. However, the lecturer in the listening material holds a totally different view and claims that all of the statements given in the text are wrong.

First of all, the author of the text suggests that the short-faced bear ate extremely large mammals that used to live in North America since they had massive front legs and feet that allowed them to attack giant mammals. But it is refuted by the professor because their front legs seemed big enough to pull the giant mammals down to the ground, but their skeleton showed that they had unusually thin bone, so their front legs and paws were weak despite their giant body. Therefore, without the strong bone, the short-faced bears were not strong enough to pull the giant mammals to the ground.

Secondly, the passage indicates that the short-faced bear ate fast-running animals considering the fact that they had long legs that would have allowed them to chase down these fast-moving prey animals. However, the speaker debates it due to the reason that the fast-running animals such as deer and antelope were not running straight lines. They took sharp turns when running and changed direction quickly, so it was hard for the bears to follow them because the bears were very heavy. Therefore, it was impossible for the short-faced bear to catch the deer and the antelope.

Finally, the writer also suggests that the short-faced bear was a scavenger because they can frighten or fight off predators and eat the prey that those animals had killed. But the professor opposes against this opinion because the bear's teeth didn't show that it was a scavenger. When the scavenger was eating the partial died prey, it had to chew the bone of the partial prey. Since the bone was very hard, it would leave marks on the scavenger's teeth. However, on the short-faced bear's teeth, there were no characteristic marks. Therefore, the short-faced bear was not a scavenger.

14 EX 21 综合写作例文

阅读与听力录音参考 EX 21。【见配套音频】

In the reading passage, the author wrote about reasons why the U.S. law restricting the importing, buying, and selling of nonnative species of animals should be opposed. Meanwhile, in the lecture, the professor said that the reasons were unconvincing, and she thought that the protocols made sense.

To begin with, the reading passage worried that the law would force owners to return their pets back to authorities, because many pet species are not native. However, the lecture said that the law won't affect pet owners, as the law only banned the importation and sales of nonnative animals, so it won't affect the pets that people already own. If a tropical fish is banned from importation and sale, then current owners of the fish won't be affected, but they can't buy more that came from the same species.

Furthermore, the reading passage claimed that too much money would be spent to conduct all the studies on every nonnative animal that has ever entered the border, yet the lecture stated that the money spent for doing so is worthy. If the law was not executed, then more money might need to be spent consequently. For example, when a nonnative snake from Asia was imported to Florida, the population grew large. The snakes can grow up to 5 meters long, and they damaged plenty of native species, and some of them were rare. The removal of pythons took a lot of money, while the damage of native species was unacceptable at any cost.

Finally, the reading passage argued that the law was unreasonable because it applied a single standard for all regions of the U.S. while some species don't pose a threat to the environment when they are in a different region. However, the lecture argued that the escape of nonnative animals can still be dangerous even if they can't survive for a long time in another region. For example, the Brazilian rabbit carries a type of virus, and even if it can't survive in the cold climate, the virus can still be transmitted. In fact, the virus is known to have killed 99% of native rabbits. In this way, it is reasonable that the law has no exceptions.

尊敬的读者，衷心感谢您选择阅读这本关于托福考试写作的书。撰写这本书是一个充满挑战的学习过程，同时也是一段有趣而丰富的经历。

作为一个团队，我们共同努力，撰写了这些例文。在此要特别感谢所有参与的成员：Ken, Echo, Hunter, Felix, Henri。他们的智慧和贡献使得这本书的内容更加充实和精彩。没有他们的支持，这本书将无法如此成功地呈现在您面前。在编写过程中，我们始终本着严谨的学术态度，反复校对每一句话，以确保书中内容的准确性和可靠性。我们希望这本书为您提供最优质的学术资源，帮助您在托福考试中获得优异的成绩。我们的团队对托福考试教学有着深深的热爱，理解作为考生的您所面临的压力和困惑，因此我们努力将实战经验注入书中的例文，让您更好地了解应对考试的技巧和策略。

在这本书的创作过程中，我们团队经历了一些困难和挑战。初稿完成后，我们遇到了关于学术讨论方面的改革。这个出乎意料的变化要求我们重新评估和调整创作中的一些内容，确保内容能够与最新的学术要求保持一致。这对我们来说是一项巨大的挑战，但我们全力以赴，对内容进行了充分的修改和更新，以确保您获得最新和最准确的知识。除此之外，我们的团队成员在创作过程中还要忙于其他教学事务，每个人都有自己的工作和责任，这使得我们的时间非常紧张。这种多重任务的负担给我们带来了许多压力和困难，但团队的每个人都展现了出色的组织能力和团队合作精神，确保完成了这本书的全部内容。我们为能够克服这些困难而感到骄傲，并希望这本书能够满足您的期望和需求。当然，我们也深知这本书可能存在不够完善的地方，因此，我们希望能够得到您的指点和建议。您的反馈对于我们的改进至关重要，我们将会在接下来的工作中精益求精，不断完善和提升这本书的质量。

再次感谢您选择阅读这本书。我们希望这本书能够满足您对于托福写作的需求，并为您取得优秀的成绩提供帮助。如果您在阅读过程中有任何问题或反馈，请随时与我们联系。我们欢迎您提供任何意见和建议，让我们能够改进和完善我们的工作。

祝愿您在托福考试中取得成功！

谨致问候

万塾团队

图书在版编目（CIP）数据

新版托福写作手册/姚钦等编著.--北京：中国
人民大学出版社，2024.7
ISBN 978-7-300-32891-1

Ⅰ.①新… Ⅱ.①姚… Ⅲ.①TOEFL-写作-自学参
考资料　Ⅳ.H315

中国国家版本馆CIP数据核字（2024）第108790号

新版托福写作手册

姚钦　丁洁　[加]胡杨　罗健　吴国彬　编著

Xinban Tuofu Xiezuo Shouce

出版发行	中国人民大学出版社			
社　　址	北京中关村大街31号		**邮政编码**	100080
电　　话	010-62511242（总编室）			010-62511770（质管部）
	010-82501766（邮购部）			010-62514148（门市部）
	010-62515195（发行公司）			010-62515275（盗版举报）
网　　址	http://www.crup.com.cn			
经　　销	新华书店			
印　　刷	唐山玺诚印务有限公司			
开　　本	787mm×1092mm　1/16		**版　　次**	2024年7月第1版
印　　张	13.75		**印　　次**	2024年7月第1次印刷
字　　数	299 000		**定　　价**	48.00元（全2册）